THE JEWS OF OTTOMAN IZMIR

Stanford Studies in Jewish History and Culture

THE JEWS OF OTTOMAN IZMIR

A Modern History

DINA DANON

Stanford University Press
Stanford, California

STANFORD UNIVERSITY PRESS
Stanford, California

© 2020 by the Board of Trustees of the Leland Stanford Junior University. All rights reserved.

No part of this book may be reproduced or transmitted in any form or by any means, electronic or mechanical, including photocopying and recording, or in any information storage or retrieval system without the prior written permission of Stanford University Press.

Printed in the United States of America on acid-free, archival-quality paper

Library of Congress Cataloging-in-Publication Data

Names: Danon, Dina, author.

Title: The Jews of Ottoman Izmir : a modern history / Dina Danon.

Description: Stanford, California : Stanford University Press, 2019. | Series: Stanford studies in Jewish history and culture | Includes bibliographical references and index.

Identifiers: LCCN 2019012452 (print) | LCCN 2019013728 (ebook) | ISBN 9781503608283 (cloth : alk. paper) | ISBN 9781503610910 (pbk. : alk. paper) | ISBN 9781503610927 (ebook)

Subjects: LCSH: Sephardim—Turkey—İzmir—History. | Sephardim—Turkey—İzmir—Social conditions. | Sephardim—Turkey—İzmir—Economic conditions. | Jews—Turkey—İzmir—History—19th century. | Jews—Turkey—İzmir—History—20th century. | Turkey—History—Ottoman Empire, 1288-1918.

Classification: LCC DS135.T82 (ebook) | LCC DS135.T82 1963 2019 (print) | DDC 956.2/5—dc23

LC record available at https://lccn.loc.gov/2019012452

Cover photograph: Chief Rabbi Abraham Palacci with members of the Jewish community, Izmir 1896.

Cover design: Rob Ehle

Typeset by Kevin Barrett Kane in 10.25/15 Adobe Caslon Pro

*Dedicated to the memory of
my paternal grandmother,
Dona Sazbon Danon*

CONTENTS

A Note on Language, Transliteration, and Systems   ix

Acknowledgments   xi

INTRODUCTION   3

1 The *Djudería* and Public Space   35

2 *Kualo es la Vera Karidad?* What Is True Charity?   61

3 "Make a *Monsieur* Out of Him!"   91

4 Sustaining the Kehillah: Taxing *el Puevlo*   123

5 Authority and Leadership: Representing *el Puevlo*   151

CONCLUSION   177

Notes   183

Bibliography   225

Index   243

A NOTE ON LANGUAGE, TRANSLITERATION, AND SYSTEMS

The primary language spoken by the Jews of Izmir has been called Ladino, Judeo-Spanish, and Judezmo, among other names. Although in the strictest sense "Ladino" signifies the calque form of the language and not a spoken vernacular, the term has become commonplace in denoting the vernacular of the eastern Sephardi diaspora, and I employ it to facilitate broad comprehension. In transliterating Ladino sources, I have followed the system set forth in *Aki Yerushalayim* with some modifications to better represent the pronunciation specific to the Sephardi diaspora (for instance "Sedaka" and not "Tzedakah," "Agada" and not "Haggadah"). In all other cases, I have used standard English spellings such as "matza" and "mitzvah." Where Ladino sources provide their own transliteration of names or titles in Roman characters, I have preserved the orthography of the original (for instance "El Comercial" and not "El Komersial"). Otherwise, I have used the established English spellings for personal names. In transliterating Hebrew, I have followed the Encyclopaedia Judaica system, without diacritics.

Like most locales in the Ottoman Empire, the city discussed in this book had multiple names—"Izmir," "Smyrne," and "Smyrna," among multiple others. The Jews of the city typically used "Izmir," as well as variations including "Izmirna" and "Izmirne." Following the spelling prevalent in most English language literature, I have opted for "Izmir" rather than "İzmir." For Turkish place names and terms that do not have standard English spellings, I have retained Turkish orthography.

For biblical references, I have used the translations in the *JPS Hebrew-English Tanakh: The Traditional Hebrew Text and the New JPS Translation* (Philadelphia: The Jewish Publication Society, 2003). For references to Mishnaic sources, I have used Jacob Neusner, *The Mishnah: A New Translation* (New Haven: Yale University Press, 1988). As for calendrical systems, where the Jewish or Hicri calendar is used for published sources, I have provided the Gregorian date in parentheses.

Weights and Measures

1 *okka* = 1282 grams

1 *metelik* = 10 *paras*

1 *kuruş* = 40 *paras*

1 *mecidiye* (silver) = 20 *kuruş*

1 *lira* (gold) = 100 *kuruş*

ACKNOWLEDGMENTS

In writing this book I have benefited from the help of many teachers, colleagues, and friends. First and foremost I thank my primary advisor, Aron Rodrigue, who has served as an intellectual role model since my undergraduate days, when, in the course of writing my senior honors thesis in history at the University of Pennsylvania, my long-standing interest in Sephardi Jewry evolved into a professional aspiration. My exploration of the Sephardi past has been enriched by Aron's mentorship in innumerable ways. The depth of his knowledge of the Sephardi and Ottoman worlds is matched by his constant accessibility, guidance, and support. I feel truly privileged to have worked under his direction and can only hope to build upon his enormous contributions to the field. Steven Zipperstein has been an inspiring teacher and devoted mentor throughout my graduate school career and beyond, and has had a profound influence upon my conceptualization of Jewish history as well as the art of history as a discipline. I am deeply grateful for his steadfast support and wisdom.

I am also indebted to my undergraduate advisors in history, David Ruderman and Benjamin Nathans of the University of Pennsylvania. They both supported my early study of Ottoman Jewry and nurtured my emerging interest in the academic pursuit of Jewish history. They encouraged me to continue my studies in the field and still serve as important scholarly role models today.

It is hard to imagine a more supportive and collegial professional environment than the Judaic Studies Department at Binghamton University. In particular, I thank my department chair, Randy Friedman, for his support of my research and commitment to fostering an enriching intellectual environment. I have benefited from the guidance and advice of Allan Arkush, Jonathan Karp, Bat-Ami Bar-On, and Beth Burch, and from discussions with Assaf Harel and Bryan Kirschen. Lior Libman has been a treasured colleague, conversation partner, and friend. I thank Maja Dragojlović for her superb administration of the department and facilitation of my research endeavors.

It has been an immense privilege to work at an institution with such a long-standing commitment to Ottoman Studies. I thank Kent Schull not only for his support of my work and his expertise, but for fostering ongoing opportunities for collaboration. I am grateful to Gregory Key of the Classical and Near Eastern Studies Department for sharing his encyclopedic knowledge of both Ottoman and modern Turkish language with me, which has facilitated my research in important and lasting ways.

I have been fortunate to receive multiple grants that enabled me to pursue this project. I thank the Taube Center for Jewish Studies and the History department of Stanford University, which provided funding in the book's early stages for archival research and language study at Boğaziçi University. The Department of Judaic Studies, Harpur College of Arts and Sciences, and the Institute for Advanced Study at Binghamton University have facilitated my search for sources across the globe and allowed me to immerse myself in their study. I completed this book as a fellow at the Herbert D. Katz Center for Advanced Judaic Studies at the University of Pennsylvania. I am deeply grateful to the Katz Center and its wonderful staff for fostering a stimulating and rigorous intellectual environment in which to pursue my own work on Ottoman Sephardi Jewry. I am also deeply grateful to the larger group of Katz fellows studying "Jews in Modern Islamic Contexts" for sharing their research and insights.

Midway through this project, I was privileged to participate in the Paula Hyman Mentorship Program for Emerging Scholars through the Women's Caucus of the Association for Jewish Studies. The guidance and inspiration I received through the program, especially from Rebecca Kobrin, remain vital to me.

This book draws on an array of primary sources in multiple languages. The year I spent conducting research at the Central Archives for the History of the Jewish People in Jerusalem was greatly facilitated by Hadassah Assouline, who made access to the vast communal archive of Izmir as well as to the voluminous letters to the *haham bashı* possible. I am grateful to the entire staff of the Central Archives, who day after day faithfully searched for each box, file, and *pinkas* that I ordered. It was at the Central Archives that I experienced the thrill of quite literally blowing dust off of old manuscripts and received my first exposure to the paleographic challenges and rewards of reading *soletreo*. Dov Hacohen provided valuable guidance as I explored Ladino materials at the Ben Zvi Institute in Jerusalem. I also thank Jean-Claude Kuperminc for facilitating my exploration of the archives of the *Alliance Israélite Universelle*.

Ufuk Adak and Nürçin İleri provided crucial assistance in locating and deciphering documents from the *Başbakanlık Osmanlı Arşivi* in Istanbul, as well as other Ottoman language sources. I am grateful for their willingness to share their expertise and look forward to continued conversations and shared discoveries of urban life in the eastern Mediterranean. Annie Greene offered important help in deciphering Ottoman sources. I thank Shiran Shevah and Derek Vladescu for gathering various sources, as well as Mark Davidson, whose incomparable skills in the digital humanities were enormously helpful as I tabulated and studied voluminous census material. I appreciate the assistance of Rachel Amado Bortnick in identifying illustrative material for the book. I thank Daisy Sadaka Braverman for her language help over the years and for her ongoing interest in my work.

I have benefited from crucial feedback in presenting portions of this work in multiple venues. Along with conferences at the Association for Jewish Studies and the Middle East Studies Association, I am especially grateful for having participated in a panel on urban life in the Ottoman Mediterranean at the Annual Meeting of the American Historical Association in 2015. It was there that Sarah Shields, who served as respondent, casually posed a question that ultimately catalyzed a comprehensive reframing of the book and its interpretive lens. I am grateful for the opportunity to present my work at the Scholars Working Group on Gender and Jewish History at the Center for Jewish History, which helped me develop exciting new points of entry into the social history of the eastern Sephardi diaspora.

Conversations with colleagues, especially Paris Papamichos Chronakis, Julia Phillips Cohen, Sidney Dement, Devin Naar, and Ronit Stahl, have provided important insights. I am grateful for the support and guidance of Nancy Berg. I owe a tremendous debt of gratitude to Hartley Lachter and Jessica Cooperman, who have been not only steadfast mentors but dear friends, as we toiled together in the most unlikely of places.

At Stanford University Press, I am indebted to series editors David Biale and Sarah Abrevaya Stein. I thank Sarah especially not only for serving as a personal role model and intellectual mentor but for offering incisive suggestions on the manuscript and advice on the complexities of writing a history that stands at the intersection of multiple fields. I thank the anonymous reviewers, who provided crucial feedback that improved the final product in numerous ways, as well as Margo Irvin, Nora Spiegel, Anne Fuzellier Jain, and my copy editor, Marie Deer, for their attentiveness and careful stewardship of the manuscript through the production process.

My deepest debt of gratitude goes to my family. I extend my most sincere appreciation to my parents, Arleen and Benzion Danon, my earliest and most important teachers. They have been an unwavering source of love, support, and encouragement, having patiently listened, offered suggestions, and read numerous drafts. Their confidence in my abilities has had an immeasurable impact on this book as well as upon my growth as a scholar. My brother, Eitan Danon, shared not only his impressive command of history with me, but, along with Emily Danon, has also been a source of indispensable comic relief. My aunt, Perla (Penina) Katan, eagerly helped me decipher Ladino texts and search for long-lost professions seemingly present only in the nineteenth century. I thank Geoffrey and Aviva Bock and the extended Bock clan of Washington, D.C., for their support and encouragement. Lastly, I am deeply grateful to my husband, Eliav, who has been there from the very inception of this project and watched it evolve with patience, humor, and self-sacrifice. Eliav has not only explored the remnants of Jewish life on the streets of Izmir with me. He has allowed the Jews of Izmir to monopolize countless conversations over the course of multiple years, and now knows more about Ottoman Sephardi Jewry than I think he ever thought possible. His love, companionship, and encouragement have sustained me. Our children have been a source of incomparable joy and much-needed reminders that the present is just as important as the past, if not more so.

I dedicate this work to the memory of my grandmother, Dona Danon, née Sazbon, for whom I am named. It was she who first exposed me to the sounds of Ladino and the lost world of Ottoman Izmir, the city of her birth. I treasured the special connection we shared and hope that the echoes of her wisdom and profound gift for storytelling can be heard on every page.

THE JEWS OF OTTOMAN IZMIR

INTRODUCTION

In 1899, the Jewish community of Ottoman Izmir came to a near standstill. The death of Chief Rabbi Abraham Palacci in January led to the first transfer of rabbinic power in over thirty years, and the ensuing turmoil over the appointment of a successor as well as a range of problems that had long plagued the communal administration now polarized the community. The most contentious issue was management of the local kosher meat industry, which, through its levy of a sales tax known as the *gabela*, generated the vast majority of the community's revenue. Warring factions advanced competing visions of how a new chief rabbi might improve the system, lessening its inefficiencies and distributing its burden more equitably.

In the spring, *La Buena Esperanza*, then Izmir's longest-running Ladino newspaper, published a fictional, quasi-Talmudic dialogue between "Simon" and "Reuben" distilling the arguments circulating in the community regarding payment of *shohatim*, or ritual slaughterers. While Simon remained skeptical about changing the traditional system, Reuben insisted that slaughterers had monopolized communal coffers for too long. The two engaged in a protracted debate:

    S: But that goes against the [religious] rulings.
    R: I beg you, enough! The rulings were made in other times. Now our public is poor. If it cannot support itself, should it die to help others?

S: Is this something new? There have always been *shohatim* and we never complained. What has now changed that we should pick a fight with these good people?

R: It is true that this evil is quite old. If we pick a fight with them now, it is because of how [the situation] has spun out of control! What would you prefer? That they exploit the people, cost us more than one hundred thousand *kuruş* a year, cause conflicts and, as they say, ignite the community? Until now we tolerated it, but we no longer want anything to do with them![1]

Reuben's position pivots on a keen awareness of a changed socioeconomic reality. Indeed, while the Jews of Ottoman Izmir had greatly prospered during the city's early modern period, playing an essential role in its emergence as a major port in the seventeenth century, by the nineteenth century a constellation of global and local factors had combined to dramatically destabilize their position. By the time *La Buena Esperanza* published the above-cited dialogue in 1899, the Jews of Izmir were no longer the customs agents, tax farmers, and translators they had once been but rather greengrocers, tailors, peddlers, and beggars. So dramatic had been their downfall that in the late nineteenth century, it is reported that nearly one-third of the Jewish community in Izmir subsisted solely on charity.[2]

Yet as this book demonstrates, most significant about Reuben's reading of Jewish poverty was not its prevalence, nor its exacerbation in the nineteenth century, but rather its position in a larger rupture between *agora*, or "now," and *otros tiempos*, or "other times." Reuben's understanding of the fundamental difference of *agora* and its ability to necessitate new solutions to age-old problems such as that of Izmir's *shohatim* was framed by numerous assumptions. For Reuben, Izmir's Jewish poor constituted a collectivity that might intervene in communal affairs and advocate for itself. This collectivity represented its interests through the vehicle of *el puvliko*, a new entity that might not only check abuses but also mount a lasting challenge to traditional religious authority. Moreover, Reuben's palpable indignation suggests that the *agora* of 1899 had ultimately compelled a reconsideration of poverty itself, betraying a sense that its unchecked persistence and expansion was not only undesirable but fundamentally unacceptable.

It is Reuben's understanding of how the modern age had reordered such social hierarchies and relationships that animates the central interpretive claim of this book. By 1899, the marked impoverishment of Izmir's Jewish community had come to stand painfully at odds with modern attitudes that recategorized poverty as a social ill, as well as with the local triumph of middle-class values. I argue that it is this disjuncture, this rupture with a centuries-old worldview that cast poverty as a natural, acceptable, and even stabilizing force in society, that propelled Izmir's Jews to engage in a series of modern reforms. Jewish leaders rallied to remove beggars from the streets and reorganized their collection and distribution of charity. They experimented with a range of anti-poverty initiatives such as vocational training, apprenticeship programs, and rudimentary education in commerce and began to adopt decidedly bourgeois patterns of associational life, residence, leisure, and philanthropy.

Communal leaders typically denounced the community's socioeconomic decline as a source of weakness and decay. Yet this book demonstrates the reverse, capturing how the growing empowerment and self-awareness of Izmir's poor and lower classes catalyzed a dynamic reimagining of Izmir's *kehillah*, or semi-autonomous Jewish community structure, which was often referred to as the *kolelut*. Through the lens of two crucial elements of Jewish self-government, namely its financial and leadership structures, I explore how "progress" demanded the reordering of social hierarchies along modern lines. This book traces ongoing efforts to rid the community of its most critical yet increasingly controversial source of revenue, the regressive *gabela* sales tax on kosher meat, which disproportionately burdened the poor. It tracks the elaboration of rationalized statutes and representative assemblies that would better address the needs of the poor and working classes and reconstructs the reversal of the long-standing rabbinic alliance with the wealthy. Undergirding all of these initiatives, as the book demonstrates, is the evolution of a vibrant and robust Ladino public sphere where the needs of *el puevlo* or "the people" were constantly debated with recourse to an expanding modern vocabulary of "rights."

This case study's emphasis on socioeconomic factors as primary agents of change invites a reconsideration of assumptions that have long governed the study of modern Jewish history. Prevailing conceptual paradigms such as assimilation, acculturation, integration, and secularization, among many others, are largely the intellectual legacy of extensive reflection on the Jewish experience in numerous modern European contexts. While European communities differed in many respects, across nation-states and empires alike Jews in Europe were often confronted with the notion that their religious and cultural distinctiveness was somehow incompatible with the modern age. From the absolutist Russian Empire, to the nascent German nation-state, to the secular French republic, among other polities, European Jews had to contend in some way with a homogenizing pressure resulting from a relentless tension between the "universal" and the "particular"—a tension they negotiated in countless ways.

The view from Ottoman Izmir reveals these categories to be of little interpretive value. While never static, the prevailing social hierarchy as refracted through the Ottoman interpretation of *sharia* law, coupled with the profound ethnic and religious diversity characterizing the empire itself, cultivated a social fabric that was not only tolerant of difference but predicated upon it.[3] The legitimation of religious and ethnic distinctiveness persisted in the nineteenth century despite and even in concert with efforts to promote other forms of shared belonging, such as the Ottomanism of the *Tanzimat* era and the constitutional fervor of the Young Turks.[4] Notably, this continued affirmation was especially the case for Ottoman Jews as opposed to their Greek and Armenian neighbors, as their position in the Ottoman landscape was not complicated by the rising tide of various nationalisms sweeping Europe. While the emergence of Zionism in the years after 1908 did spark controversy, for the Ottoman Sephardi community Jewish nationalism functioned largely as a vehicle for cultural and religious revival and was frequently cast by its proponents as beneficial to the empire's interests.[5] For the long arc of Ottoman history, the legitimacy of Jewish difference was simply not in question.

As this book demonstrates, this context requires a different set of questions: What happens when Jewish distinctiveness is wholly unremarkable? What happens when Jewish communal autonomy is not only tolerated, but affirmed, amplified, and even cast as a necessary precondition for the modern age? What types of change might we anticipate when there is no "Jewish question"? Following Izmir's Jews on the street and in the marketplace, in the home and in the synagogue, from the mid-nineteenth century to the end of empire, the view from Ottoman Izmir suggests that it was new attitudes to poverty and class, not Judaism, that most significantly influenced this Sephardi community's encounter with the modern age.

Origins

Although formally incorporated into the Ottoman Empire in 1424, the port of Izmir did not rise to prominence until more than a full century later, when a confluence of local and international circumstances led to its emergence as a major entrepôt. By the early seventeenth century, European traders had succeeded in circumventing long-standing spice and silk trade routes operating through Bursa, Aleppo, and Alexandria. Regrouping after the resulting decline of their local markets, Ottoman merchants found attractive alternatives in the agricultural products of the rich Anatolian hinterland of Izmir. Although Istanbul had traditionally regarded Izmir not as a center for international commerce but largely as a center for provisioning the capital, a series of countryside rebellions, known as the *celali* revolts, had dramatically weakened the authority of the imperial center and enabled provincial notables to shirk its directives. Thus the state did very little to intervene when the agents of Dutch, English, French, and Venetian merchants began to arrive in the area in the early seventeenth century. By 1640, the port of Izmir, which had the advantage of a well-protected harbor, had become the main hub for all European trade in the region.[6]

Although Jews had been scattered across western Anatolia since antiquity, there is no solid evidence of a formal Jewish community in Izmir prior to 1605.[7] Like European merchants as well as Ottoman Greeks and Armenians, Jews then began to flock to the port in order to participate in its economic boom. The first Jewish migrants arrived in Izmir from surrounding areas in western Anatolia, and they were soon followed by significant numbers of Jews from Salonica, where the local textile industry had collapsed in the late sixteenth century, propelling many of its Jewish workers to search for opportunities elsewhere.[8] The brisk activities of the European Levant trading companies also facilitated the migration to the city of Portuguese Jews, who were valued for their mercantile connections and often benefited from consular protection. While late-sixteenth-century Ottoman records make no mention of Jewish taxpayers in Izmir, a 1661 survey found that the city was home to 271 Jewish households.[9]

Izmir's Jews played a crucial role in the port's robust activity during the early modern period, as representatives of the European Levant companies relied on them extensively in making their way through the world of Ottoman commerce. Serving largely as intermediaries, Jews were heavily represented among the city's brokers, translators, agents, and moneylenders. As the state began to take more of an interest in the port's boom and sought to regulate its trade, Jews also became involved in the collection of customs. As Daniel Goffman has shown, between 1610 and 1650 nearly all customs collectors in Izmir were Jewish.[10]

The economic prosperity of the community during the port's early boom enabled it to sustain a robust cultural and intellectual life. While in the early years of the seventeenth century Izmir had only one synagogue, by the 1630s it had five, and by the end of the century it was home to nine, with each congregation likely reflecting a different wave of migration to the port.[11] Unlike other Ottoman Sephardi communities, Izmir developed from the outset a centralized leadership structure. The chief rabbinate was initially split between two rabbis, Rabbi Azariah Yehoshua and Rabbi Joseph Eskapa, both of Salonica. Naturally enough in a newly established community, the two differed on matters of Jewish law, each favoring legal precedents from different Ottoman Jewish communities in establishing local custom.[12] They were constantly at odds, but after Yehoshua's death, authority was consolidated in Joseph Eskapa, who set forth numerous financial and administrative codes for the new community that remained authoritative in Izmir through the modern period.[13] So robust was the religious and cultural life of Izmir's Jewish community that we find it categorized in the Ladino responsa literature as *ir va-em be-Yisrael*, or a "mother-city in Israel."[14]

A Parting of the Ways

The port of Izmir continued to prosper, as it ably supplied increasingly productive European industries with crucial goods. By the close of the eighteenth century, Izmir by itself managed thirty-four percent of the Empire's total exports and thirty percent of its imports.[15] Reaching "unprecedented levels" by the second half of the nineteenth century, the port's total volume of trade increased fourfold between the 1840s and 1870s, making it unrivaled across the empire in exports and second only to Istanbul in imports.[16] Undergirding this economic prowess was a highly developed commercial grid, with markedly refined services in insurance, brokerage, and customs[17] as well as bold new infrastructure projects such as expanded quays, a customhouse, and rail lines. Scholars have found in this dramatic growth evidence that the port of Izmir itself served as "a principal vehicle for the integration of the Ottoman Empire into the world economy."[18]

The contrast between the port's continued economic prosperity and the position of its Jewish community could not be starker. As Izmir's commerce began to expand in the early seventeenth century, Jews were prized for their ability to interface with the state and adeptly navigate the world of its customs and taxes. Yet over the course of the next century, the state would see its traditional authority challenged by powerful local clans, such as the Karaosmanoğlu family, which wrested away local and regional tax collection.[19] Additionally, European merchants were increasingly emboldened to circumvent the official apparatus in Istanbul altogether, making the intimate knowledge Jewish factors possessed of these systems much less valuable.

Further hastening the eclipse of Izmir's Jewish mercantile class was a shift in the nature of the port's activity, as it became less of a transit point for goods produced further east and increasingly oriented towards meeting European demand for raw materials from its hinterland.[20] It was Izmir's Greeks who were most notably well-positioned in this new economy, operating ably on both the production and export sides of the market. The predominance of Greek merchants in Izmir represented a larger trend emerging across the eastern Mediterranean region, perhaps best encapsulated by the image of the "conquering Balkan Orthodox merchant."[21] The economic and political capital of these merchants was further bolstered by the ongoing renegotiation of capitulations and associated treaties that privileged European states and their Christian coreligionists at the expense of Ottoman Muslims and Jews.[22]

The retreat of Izmir's Jewish merchant class continued during the port's rapid development over the eighteenth and nineteenth centuries. Starting in 1840, Izmir's population increased by more than two percent a year, and by the 1880s the city was home to more than two hundred thousand people.[23] Driving this population growth was the immigration of a variety of groups, most notably foreign merchants, who, numbering approximately fifty thousand in the 1880s, comprised one quarter of the city's total population.[24] In 1890, Izmir was home to twenty-five thousand Hellenic Greeks and fifty-two thousand Ottoman Greeks,[25] and whether they were Ottomans, Hellenes, or beneficiaries of European protection, it was the Greeks who predominated across all segments of Izmir's trade, as they continued to benefit from their extensive knowledge of the Anatolian market, robust kinship networks across the empire and beyond, and ease in securing European protection and privileges. Comprising between forty and fifty percent of all of the city's merchants by the early twentieth century, Izmir's Greeks were heavily represented in trade on the international, regional, and local levels. They were also active in coastal shipping, banking, and tax farming, as well as speculative ventures such as arbitrage and money changing.[26] Joining the city's Greeks in propelling Izmir's commerce were powerful and long-standing colonies of Levantine merchants as well as a small but prosperous Armenian community involved in banking and finance.

Thus by the nineteenth century, the early nexus between the port's economic prowess and Jewish settlement there had been almost fully dismantled. Outpaced by Izmir's Greeks, Levantines, and Armenians, Izmir's Jews, now numbering approximately twenty-five thousand,[27] had undergone a complete socioeconomic reconfiguration. An internal census of approximately eight hundred individuals conducted in the mid-1840s reflects this trend. The census employs the traditional Ottoman division of *cizye* (poll tax) taxpayers, *ala*, or "high," *evsat*, or "middle," and *edna*, or "low." The census also employs the category of *muaf*, or "exempt," as well as *fakir*, or "pauper."[28] Setting aside approximately eighty individuals recorded without tax brackets, largely due to their young age or special circumstances, more than half of all taxpayers assessed were categorized, as Table 1 demonstrates, as *edna*, or "low." Approximately one fifth were categorized as *muaf* and were exempted due to old age, unemployment, or indigence.

The census also allows us to paint a detailed portrait of the occupations in which Izmir's working Jews were concentrated. As Table 2 makes clear, the Jewish workforce of Izmir was overwhelmingly concentrated in small-scale artisanship, petty trade, and unskilled labor. The situation seems to have

TABLE 1

Tax Brackets Recorded in 1845–1850 Communal Census*

TAX BRACKET	PERCENTAGE
ala (high)	5.4%
evsat (middle)	15.1%
edna (low)	54.4%
muaf (exempt)	20.8%
fakir or *dilenci* (pauper)	4.3%

* Data based on CAHJP Tr/Iz. 713 (*soletreo*).

TABLE 2

Occupations Recorded in 1845–1850 Communal Census*

FIELD	PERCENTAGE	TYPICAL OCCUPATIONS
Petty tradesmen	30%	greengrocers; peddlers; sellers of coffee, fabrics, fezzes, remedies, spices, sweets, woolens, tobacco
Unskilled laborers	14%	porters, servants
Crafts	14%	cobblers, tailors, tinsmiths, stonecutters
Commerce	16%	agents, brokers, middlemen
Community	8%	butchers, rabbis, town criers
Unemployed	16%	

* Data based on CAHJP Tr/Iz. 713 (*soletreo*). The difference between petty trade and artisanship is difficult to discern with absolute clarity in Ladino sources, as the Turkish suffix *-ci* is used to denote both makers and sellers of goods.

worsened in the following years, as in 1858, sixty-eight percent of taxpayers were recorded as *edna*, twenty-seven percent as *evsat*, and six percent as *ala*.[29]

The overall socioeconomic profile of the community does not seem to have changed dramatically throughout the late Ottoman period. Yet by the 1880s, some notable internal reconfigurations are in evidence. The number of workers in both unskilled labor and commerce each decreased by half from the 1840s, with the fields of petty trade and craftsmanship absorbing the difference, growing by fifteen percent and eight percent respectively.[30] Additionally, while some new professions—such as censors, musicians, restaurant workers, and *enpiegados* or "employees"—begin to make an appearance by the 1880s, they remain markedly limited in number, totaling just four percent of working adults.[31]

The growth of white-collar professions across the community seems to have continued in the following years, albeit very incrementally. A tax assessment done in 1910 shows that alongside heavy representation in petty trade and crafts, approximately eight percent of Jewish Izmirlis were categorized as professionals and employees, some of whom worked at places such as the *Poste Française* and *Crédit Lyonnais* as well as commercial establishments such as *Bon Marché*, *Athanasoula*, and *Singer*. Yet again, the significance of this trend in sketching the general socioeconomic position of the larger Jewish community should not be overstated. There were four income brackets newly delineated for the internal *derito komunal* tax, and approximately fifty-five percent of all taxpayers assessed were categorized in the lowest bracket, at 25 *kuruş*. Thirty percent were assessed at 50 *kuruş*, while eleven percent were assessed at 100 *kuruş*. With numbers that were similar to those in the 1840s census undertaken for Ottoman tax purposes, the 1910 assessment shows only four percent in the top bracket, at 200 *kuruş*.[32] It is no wonder, then, that Izmir's Jews became accustomed to watching their city's bustling port activity from the sidelines. As one Ladino newspaper would lament in 1907, "it is an incontestable truth that we Jews are entirely foreign to the commercial, financial, and industrial worlds."[33]

The clustering of Izmir's Jews in small-scale professions made them more vulnerable to the hardships faced by all Ottoman Jews. Taxes imposed by the state as well as internal communal levies were a near-constant burden. The *bedel-i askeri*, or military exemption tax paid by non-Muslim groups, caused

FIGURE 1. Jewish Basket Dealer of Smyrna, Jewish Missionary Intelligence, December 1892, 199.

significant financial strain, as the community frequently struggled to pay the full amount assessed by the authorities. By 1885, for example, after managing to pay only a fraction of the *bedel* for three consecutive years, the community had incurred a nearly insurmountable debt to the authorities of 664,042 *kuruş*.[34] While communal assessors experimented with different strategies in levying the *bedel* on individuals,[35] it was sometimes assessed as a flat tax regardless of income, making it regressive and thus particularly burdensome for those hovering just above a state of poverty.[36] Similarly, the community continued to rely almost exclusively on regressive *gabela* sales taxes on kosher goods to finance its institutions and charities. *Gabela* taxes on kosher meat in particular were a perennial source of bitter strife long associated with *sa'akat ani'im*, or "the cry of the poor."[37]

Intermittent anti-Jewish violence exacerbated the poverty in the community. Described by an observer as "a Greek city in Turkish hands,"[38] Izmir witnessed numerous blood libels over the course of the nineteenth century. Blood libels also plagued neighboring areas, erupting in Milas in 1875,[39] Çeşme in 1877,[40] and Corfu in 1891.[41] Compounding the physical violence accompanying such accusations were economic repercussions, such as destabilizing boycotts of Jewish businesses.[42] The heightened political tensions of the late Ottoman period often intensified such antagonisms, as Jewish loyalty to the state was seen as hostile to the growing irredentist aspirations of local Greeks. Against the backdrop of the Ottoman war with Greece over Crete in 1897, for example, the ardent Jewish support for the Ottoman military provoked deep resentment.[43] What began as the banishment of Jewish peddlers from Greek neighborhoods evolved into a full boycott of all Jewish businesses, affecting not only peddlers but tailors, carpenters, cobblers, capmakers, milliners, and coal workers.[44]

Izmir's Jews were also vulnerable to the same hazards of Ottoman urban life that all of the city's residents faced, among them earthquakes, fires, and epidemics. Their impoverishment made it difficult to rebound from such crises, which were not infrequent. Multiple outbreaks of cholera afflicted the community, as the highly communicable disease tore through the densely populated Jewish quarter with ease.[45] In 1889 there was an eruption of dengue fever,[46] while a year later, a severe outbreak of the plague devastated the Jewish community and in particular its *Lazareto*, a shelter housing nearly three hundred impoverished families.⁴⁷ Although the plague had dire consequences for the entire province, in the Jewish quarter in particular business came to a virtual standstill when people reportedly halted all interaction with Jews for fear of contagion.⁴⁸

As a result both of shifts in the world economy and of local circumstance, the majority of Izmir's Jews encountered the modern age in a socioeconomic position radically inferior to that of their seventeenth-century predecessors. As Reuben reminded his interlocutor Simon in the dialogue regarding *shohatim*, "one can say, without exaggeration, that nine out of ten Jews in this city are poor. It is only with great effort that they manage to feed their children a crust of bread."⁴⁹

Ruptures

Before the nineteenth century, Jews understood poverty to be a divinely ordained and permanent social phenomenon. While a range of both positive and negative characteristics were associated with the poor, in the Ottoman Sephardi world, Ladino *musar*, or ethical, literature typically represented poverty not only as acceptable but as essential to the functioning of Jewish society, since its persistence made possible the fulfillment of the mitzvah of giving charity.⁵⁰ Poverty was also associated with a certain righteousness and piety, as the *Me'il Sedaka*, written by Rabbi Elijah Hakohen in Izmir in the eighteenth century, describes the poor as "beloved" by God.⁵¹ Ottoman Jewish views on poverty were reinforced in the Islamic tradition of their Muslim governors and neighbors, who shared the notion that poverty ultimately had divine origins and enabled the faithful to meet the obligation of almsgiving, or *zakat/sadaqa*.⁵² By no means inherently shameful, poverty in the Islamic world was a visible and public phenomenon, amply displayed by beggars and members of Sufi orders who were common sights on the streets of Ottoman cities well into the nineteenth century.⁵³ Aleppo, for example, was home to a guild of professional beggars, who had a sheikh at their head and a code of conduct.⁵⁴

A variety of factors would combine to disrupt this view of poverty in the modern Ottoman Sephardi world. By the sixteenth century, breaking with medieval attitudes, European states had begun to rethink the place of poverty in their midst. Economic crisis, food shortages, and a pronounced increase in the number of the poor combined with the emergence of capitalism to put poverty in a different light, shifting it from an unremarkable fixture of the social landscape to an urgent social ill that had to be addressed.[55] Increasingly associating poverty with idleness, deviance, and sin, European states implemented a range of strategies to control the problem, among them identifying badges, beggars' prisons, houses of correction, and expulsion.[56] Such attitudes only intensified with the emphasis that Enlightenment thinkers placed on utility and productivity.[57] The large-scale economic and social dislocations of the modern period provoked a further reconsideration of poverty in Western Europe, as the focus shifted from policing deviant behavior to identifying its roots as a "mass phenomenon."[58]

Scholarship on poverty in the Ottoman Empire—on how people both experienced it and represented it—is in its very infancy. Yet both the new discourses and the state initiatives that emerged in the nineteenth-century *Tanzimat* reform era (1839–1876) and beyond suggest that views on poverty shifted there as well. Recent research has shown how the concept of *medeniyet*, or "civilization," that Ottoman intellectuals debated was profoundly shaped by engagement with theories of capitalism, which emphasized the importance of efficiency, productivity, and industriousness.[59] Among the many reforms instituted during the *Tanzimat* period was a transformation of urban space, as cities became laboratories for the implementation of a Western approach prizing order, rationality, and the safeguarding of the "public good."[60] A corollary of this preoccupation with the "public good" was an increasing anxiety regarding vagrancy, which was seen as not only a threat to the flow of commerce but a threat to new norms pertaining to shared public space as well.[61] Vagrants, defined as those lacking a specific occupation or residence, were regarded as potential criminals, and were subjected in 1890 to formal categorization.[62] Against the backdrop of strong population growth and its attendant uneven distribution of wealth, Ottoman observers focused more and more on the presumed nexus between vagrancy and crime, as elites became increasing fearful of *muzhir eshas*, or "dangerous classes."[63] In Ottoman Izmir, for example, the city's poorer and working-class neighborhoods were disdained as sites of disorder and "closely linked with the manifold threats of the streets."[64] By 1909, the Young Turks had revisited the 1890 regulation, ultimately replacing it with the "Law on Vagabonds and

Suspected Persons," which fully criminalized vagrancy and allowed for increased police surveillance of the poor.[65]

While such broader cultural shifts undoubtedly had an impact on Izmir's Jews, their most intimate engagement with these new attitudes regarding poverty and its vices may have been through the curriculum of the *Alliance Israélite Universelle*. Opening its first local school in Izmir in 1873, the *Alliance* brought with it a discourse of regeneration based on the Enlightenment-era critique of Jewish society advocated by *philosophes* and *maskilim* (proponents of the *Haskalah*, or Jewish Enlightenment) alike. In the eyes of *Alliance* teachers, among the most urgent problems to be addressed was the unbalanced economic profile of "eastern" Jewry and the absence of "productive" trades.[66] The matter seemed particularly acute in Izmir, where the poverty of the community made "the Jewish quarter one of the saddest and most unpleasant."[67] Through their curriculum, vocational training programs, and social clubs, *Alliance* teachers relentlessly impressed upon their students the evils of poverty and the virtues of hard work. In tandem with these efforts, both through the curriculum they implemented and the personal example they themselves set, *Alliance* teachers constantly communicated the "regenerating" potential of European middle-class values, reinforcing the importance for both men and women not only of economic self-sufficiency but of cultivating sobriety, discipline, and self-restraint.[68]

The *Alliance*'s *maskilic* emphasis on "productivization" found particularly fertile ground in the Ottoman Empire, where poverty was denigrated not only because it limited Jewish utility to the state, but because it was read as proof of the moral deficiency of the "Orient." Reporting back to his superiors in Paris after arriving in town to begin setting up Izmir's first *Alliance* school in 1873, David Cazès remarked "Why is the Jewish community of Izmir so backward, so poor, so despised? The answer, in my view, is fairly obvious. It is backward because its members are egotistical; it is poor because they are lazy; [and] it is despised not only because they are poor and ignorant, but because they are very fanatical."[69] Additionally, some *Alliance* administrators seemed to harbor the suspicion that there were certain characteristics particular to the Jews of Izmir and not shared by any of their Sephardi coreligionists that predisposed them to a life of poverty. Gabriel Arié, for example, a native of Samakov, outside of Sofia, routinely denigrated the Jews of Izmir as more "backwards" than others. Shortly after arriving in town, Arié noted that "one tames parrots with sugar and Orientals with sweet words. In this regard, Smyrniots seem a little more Oriental to me than others."[70] A year later, Arié made the following observation:

> It is known that the Jewish community of Izmir is one of the poorest in the Orient. The causes of this social inferiority of our coreligionists of this city are very diverse. The most important, in my opinion, are the absence of a spirit of enterprise—which I will freely call laziness, disorder in spending, and above all, an excessive love of *kief*, that *gemütlichkeit* of Orientals that costs them dearly at times. The Jews of Izmir enjoy themselves very much, [even] enormously, they adore good wine, good food, their women know how to belly dance perfectly, but are they poor! My God, are they poor![71]

Arié's colleague, David Angel, shared his sentiments, remarking in 1900 that Izmir's Jews had unfortunately "borrowed very little" from their Greek neighbors. Angel described the Jewish "Smyrniot" as "[the bearer] of a superficial intelligence," "lacking in insight," a "friend of pleasure," and "sometimes incapable of a long effort and sustained perseverance," all of which distinguished him from the "habits of economy and sobriety" that supposedly characterized the Jews of Salonica.[72]

Crucially, Izmir's Jews engaged with these new attitudes concerning poverty and class in a dynamic and changing urban landscape. The marked economic growth of eastern Mediterranean ports spurred the formation in many locales of a bourgeoisie that was typically, but by no means exclusively, dominated by non-Muslim merchants and professionals, many of whom took cultural cues from the West.[73] Regarding the activities of such groups as crucial to the economic vitality of port cities, scholars have posited a mutually reinforcing dynamic between the two, arguing that "port-city prosperity was an indication of the momentum of bourgeois development."[74] Though the bourgeoisie has remained crucial in the study of the modern eastern Mediterranean, recent scholarship has destabilized the assumptions undergirding the study of their nature and function, particularly with respect to their ethnic fragmentation, political preoccupations, and economic interests.[75] As Edhem Eldem has recently observed, even the very application of the term "bourgeois" to the Ottoman context is problematic. Not only does the term presuppose an essentially Western model of capitalist economic development, but it is typically employed in discussions emphasizing the non-Muslim nature of such groups and their supposed protection of European economic interests as compradors, thus divorcing them from the local Ottoman social fabric.[76]

When considering the impact of this "bourgeoisie" on Izmir's Jews and the transformation of their society, most consequential was not the economic role such groups played in the commerce of the city but the constellation of discourses, practices, and attitudes they mobilized in their self-fashioning as middle class. Recent scholarship instructively emphasizes the interpretive gains to be made by conceiving of social class not as a strictly economic position but as a cultural practice that can be exercised in a broad array of settings and situations.[77] Such an approach reveals the emergence of a middle class in the Ottoman Mediterranean to be not a predetermined by-product of the incorporation of the Ottoman Empire into the world economy, but the result of the deliberate cultivation of discourses and practices meant to reinforce such an identity.[78] Consumption patterns, for example, have been studied as a revealing mechanism of social differentiation among Izmir's upwardly mobile Greeks, as the strategies they employed in negotiating "luxury" and the penetration of Western goods into the local market "re-drew social boundaries on the basis of the model of the self-sustained and prudent middle-class individual."[79] Tracking responses to the Young Turk Revolution of 1908, it has been argued that the striving for "civilization and order" among Izmir's Greeks evidences a "middle-class morality."[80] In mapping Ottoman history along spatial lines, Cem Emrence has outlined a particular "coastal" path to modernity in the eastern Mediterranean characterized most notably by its "middle class hegemony."[81]

The "hegemony" of middle-class culture in port cities like Izmir found ample expression in manifold aspects of daily life and, in turn, provided constant reinforcement of a new social ideal towards which its Jews might strive. The city's Greek community in particular was home to a robust network of clubs and associations that afforded participants numerous opportunities to express their bourgeois identity. In 1819, Greek merchants founded the "Merchant Club" (which was subsequently renamed the "Greek Club" in 1841 and the "Hellenic Club" in 1898) as an association open to "all who maintain[ed] an independent and free social position."[82] Both the Panionios and the Apollon sporting clubs gave Greeks the opportunity for physical exercise, sponsoring regional competitions that attracted thousands of spectators.[83] The city's Levantines socialized at the *Cercle Européen*, while Izmir's Armenian community was home to its own reading club, theater, and numerous active publishing houses.[84] Further suggesting a broader, citywide middle-class culture, while many associations and clubs emerged within the boundaries of ethnic groups, there is ample evidence that the upwardly mobile also began to pursue such activities together. In addition to its numerous Masonic lodges,[85] by the late nineteenth century Izmir saw the emergence of clubs with mixed membership, such as the *Cercle de Smyrne*, the prestigious Sporting Club, and the *Club des Chasseurs*.[86]

The expansion of such middle-class pursuits was facilitated in part by a dynamic and evolving urban canvas. By the mid-nineteenth century, Izmir had become home to numerous establishments catering to bourgeois patterns of consumption and leisure, such as clubs, theaters, and department stores, in and around Frank Street. The profound physical transformations of the city in the 1870s further expanded the number of such spaces, most notably with the construction of the *Kordon*. A granite quay stretching for two miles along Izmir's shoreline, boasting an underground sewer system, a pedestrian promenade, and tramway lines, the *Kordon* dramatically changed both the physical appearance of the port and the experience of its residents. Home to maritime agencies, insurance companies, and warehouses, the quay and its surrounding area saw the emergence of a dense assortment of hotels, brasseries, beer gardens, and cafés.[87] Those seeking to socialize in cafés could choose from the *Alexandria*, the *Monaco*, the *Ionia*, and the *Stella d'Italia*, among numerous others, while theatergoers attended live performances at *Le Théâtre des Quais* and the Sporting Club's theater. The Kraemer Hotel and Palace offered its patrons Viennese delicacies and European newspapers in grand dining rooms and an adjacent glass brasserie, while the new pedestrian promenade of the *Kordon* offered upwardly mobile Izmirlis a much-needed venue for *flânerie*.[88] And though spaces such as the *Kordon* were theoretically shared public spaces, they often heightened awareness of class-based differences. As one scholar has pointed out, while the *Kordon* may have been able to be "borrowed" by anyone, only the elite could truly "access" it, leaving others to covet it from the sidelines.[89]

No less important than its argument regarding socioeconomic class as a primary agent of change in modern Jewish history is this book's attempt to remedy a long-standing historiographical silence. In a particularly revealing example of how ideological preoccupations shape historical narratives, the modern history of Izmir's Jewish community has received scant attention. For the scholars who originated the study of the eastern Sephardi diaspora, the Jews of Izmir were worthy of attention largely in the context of their early modern origins, with respect either to their heavy involvement in the commercial activity of the port or to their distinctive patterns of communal organization.[90] Perhaps most notably, it was Izmir's role as the birthplace of Sabbatianism that has monopolized the study of its Jewish community, making it more a dubious setting for an infamous episode than anything else.

This focus on the early modern period has persisted in more recent work on the community, even as the literature on the rest of the eastern Sephardi diaspora has considerably expanded in its chronological reach. Boasting neither the storied demographic majority of Salonica nor Istanbul's links to the imperial center, Izmir's Jews have merited little study on their own terms as a collectivity, as opposed to as the home of isolated figures or the setting for one crisis or another.[91] To the extent that any synthetic narrative exists, the resulting portrait of Izmir in the arc of modern Jewish history is one of a marginal community of little consequence to either the Sephardi diaspora or the wider Jewish world.

Similarly, Izmir's Jews have largely eluded the attention of scholars studying late Ottoman port cities. As has been the case for many ex-Ottoman sites, the profound social dislocations wrought by the dissolution of the empire have framed the questions posed in the study of their past. Such dislocations were of particular consequence in Izmir, which was irrevocably changed by a devastating fire in 1922 and the population exchanges of 1923, which "unmixed" and "repatriated" its residents along religious lines to the new nation-states of Greece and Turkey. The violent and dramatic culmination of the Ottoman era has made Izmir—already treated as a mythical homeland in Greek historiography—into a revealing site for interrogating the evolution of competing political loyalties and nationalist aspirations, questions that by default render the city's Jews somewhat of an afterthought. Similarly, the homogenizing framework of the nation-states that replaced the empire across the Mediterranean has in turn been contrasted with a presumed "cosmopolitan" past, a trope that has found fertile ground in the linguistically, culturally, and ethnically diverse setting of Ottoman Izmir.[92] Yet scholars have shown that the emphasis on Mediterranean cosmopolitanism captures little beyond the experience of the upper-class, Westernized strata of such port cities, leaving much of the urban fabric out of the picture.[93] Much like their often-overlooked Muslim neighbors, Izmir's Jews typically fall through the cracks in studies on the "cosmopolitan" nature of the port, as they were neither particularly affluent nor particularly influential. Perhaps the most striking example of this phenomenon can be seen in the recent documentary *Smyrna: The Destruction of a Cosmopolitan Port, 1900–1922*, in which the city's Jewish community, dating to the early 1600s, is mentioned but once in passing.[94]

An Ottoman Sephardi Modernity

I narrate the history of Izmir's Jewish community in the late Ottoman period as a "modern" story for multiple reasons. First, as stated above, on the level of mere chronology a confluence of historiographical preoccupations in both Jewish and Ottoman histories has ultimately relegated the community's experience during the nineteenth and early twentieth centuries to the margins, depriving it of a synthetic and robust modern history of its own. Yet far more important than remedying a certain chronological gap are the ways in which the history of this largely impoverished community can invite a reconsideration of how modernity has been treated so far in Jewish and Ottoman histories, as well as in the subfield of Sephardic studies.

Since the birth of Jewish Studies as an academic discipline in the mid-nineteenth century, itself a product of the "modern" age, scholars have defined modernity in the Jewish world according to various characteristics, metrics, and periodizations.[95] For many years, a disproportionate amount of scholarly attention remained focused on the Jews of central Europe, where the emergence of the *Haskalah* and the subsequent protracted battle for political emancipation irrevocably altered Jewish life. Predicated upon both ending Jewish marginality and the possibility of Jewish "regeneration," these events catalyzed many of the larger processes that have come to be regarded as classic markers of Jewish modernity, among them the splintering of Jewish tradition; varying degrees of integration, acculturation, and assimilation; and the retreat and even dismantling of the *kehillah*.⁹⁶ As one scholar more recently observed in the case of revolutionary-era France, the marked alterity of the Jews served as a broader symbolic test for the Enlightenment and the radical political, social, economic, and religious reordering it was meant to have introduced.⁹⁷

Work on the Russian Empire, which was home to a majority of the world's Jews in the nineteenth century, has productively complicated the picture of Jewish modernity. While the *Haskalah* made significant inroads among Russian Jewry and *maskilim* frequently found state support for their drive for Jewish reform, crucial structural differences yielded divergent patterns in Russia from those associated with the Jews of central and western Europe. Because Russian Jews were not citizens of emerging nation-states but imperial subjects of an autocratic regime, scholars of Russian Jewish modernity have pointed not to emancipation, which would only be partially granted to the Jews in 1905, but rather to the new and robust patterns of politicization that emerged in its absence. These new patterns were catalyzed not only by an unremitting "Judeophobia," which became brutally violent in the 1880s, but by structural changes in the *kehillah* that empowered new interest groups of intellectuals to speak on behalf of the people.⁹⁸ More recent work has insisted upon the applicability of the Western model to at least segments of the Russian case, finding evidence of a state-driven experiment of "selective integration" that "produced effects remarkably similar to those of European-style emancipation" such as upward social mobility, the emergence of a voluntary Jewish community, and marked acculturation.⁹⁹

Similarly, the view from the western Sephardi diaspora has destabilized the earlier preoccupation with the *Haskalah* and emancipation. Pointing to Jewish communities in cities such as Amsterdam, Trieste, Bordeaux, and London, among others, scholars have found that many of the patterns typically associated with Jewish modernity were in fact present as early as the 1600s. Descended from *conversos*, or Jews who had converted to Catholicism over the course of the preceding two centuries, these "port Jews" were valued by mercantilist states for their economic utility and enjoyed extensive privileges on this basis. Highly acculturated, "port Jews" exhibited an openness to secular knowledge well before the age of *maskilic* critique, thus making a radical program of regeneration unnecessary.[100] Scholars had already found the same to be true, though in different contexts, in places such as early-nineteenth-century Odessa and Georgian England.[101]

In addition to their acculturation and elite economic position, scholars have found equally compelling proof of modernity in the religious life of western Sephardim. With their access to normative Judaism effectively severed due to the legacy of conversions to Catholicism, Iberian *conversos* exhibited new formulations of Jewishness upon their return to the faith in places such as Amsterdam. Their prolonged exposure to Christian doctrine as well as a legacy of crypto-Judaism gave rise to their conceptualization of Judaism not as a comprehensive and wide-ranging lifestyle but as a religion confined to the private realm.[102] In addition, their return to rabbinic Judaism also coexisted with the emergence of a new ethnic identity based not on religion but on shared Iberian lineage, known as the *nação*.[103] One scholar has recently argued that the experience of marranism anticipated not only Jewish modernity, but Western modernity more broadly, most notably with the rise of individual subjectivity and the fractured identities that attended it.[104]

While diverse not only in their geographies but also in their mechanics, catalysts, and periodizations, these approaches still conceive of Jewish modernity according to similar metrics. Whether tracking various historical moments of either de facto toleration or state-driven emancipation; Jewish acculturation and integration with or without ideological underpinnings; the emergence of various formulations of religious identity; or a broadening range of political options available to Jews in debating their future, ultimately, all presuppose that modernity necessitated the negotiation of Jewish difference. While such negotiation was mediated by different political arrangements, economic conditions, and local circumstances, the arc of modern Jewish history as it has been narrated is a shared script—one that finds Jews balancing varying degrees of inclusion and exclusion and cultivating new relationships to the very meaning of Jewishness. As Tony Michels and Mitchell Hart have recently posited in surveying modern Jewish history, "the individual Jew was increasingly free to choose what it meant to be a Jew. Jewish identity, then, becomes a question, a challenge, or problem, a matter of individual decision over the course of a lifetime."[105]

Yet, when mapped onto the Jewish community of Ottoman Izmir, this interpretive paradigm of modernity falls flat. Against the backdrop of an empire that was predicated on religious difference and remained so even through the homogenizing ideologies and political movements that emerged in its final decades, the view from the Jews of Ottoman Izmir offers a study in contrasts. There were no protracted struggles for tolerance or emancipation, no implicit or explicit demands on Jewish particularism, no calls to dismantle the semi-autonomous *kehillah* or even criticism of it as reflective of dual Jewish loyalties. Ottoman Sephardi Jews did not experience an ideologically driven push towards secularization, nor radical challenges to religion in general. Even the categories of "acculturation" and "integration" are an uneasy fit for the Ottoman setting, suggestive as they are of minority-majority culture relationships in a nation-state.[106] All of this is certainly not to suggest that Ottoman Jewish communities were static or unchanging, but rather to underscore that searching for "multiple modernities" based on European patterns merely pluralizes a construct undergirded by categories of change that are ill-suited to the Ottoman Sephardi world.

More instructive in situating the experience of the Jewish community of Ottoman Izmir is the robust body of literature exploring modernity outside of the West. Work on diverse locales has destabilized the once regnant notion that modernity was a script of European provenance that was exported through colonialism and merely rehearsed in other settings.[107] In Ottoman history, scholars have challenged this in numerous ways. Adherents of world-systems theory have situated the role of the Ottoman Empire in an expanding global capitalist economy, thereby questioning categories such as "developed" and "underdeveloped," while others have found that some processes long assumed to have derived from the encounter with the West were actually present centuries before.[108] A renewed focus on the dynamism of the local landscape has also informed approaches to "Westernization," a process that, while unquestionably significant, had long served as the primary prism for conceptualizing the numerous administrative, economic, social, and legal transformations seen by the empire in the nineteenth century. Far from simple imitation, scholars have found such changes to be active, dynamic, and complex and often characterized by the coexistence of supposedly dichotomous "traditional" and "modern" elements.[109] Crucially, the interpretive gains of postcolonial theory have called the very notion of the "West," as both a conceptual category and an agent of change, into question, as so many of the forces frequently associated with European "modernity," such as nationalism, were heavily influenced by, if not predicated upon, constructions of the "East" and the broader context of colonialism. As Timothy Mitchell has argued, "if modernity had its origins in reticulations of exchange and production encircling the world, then it was a creation not of the West but of an interaction between West and non-West."[110]

These correctives have facilitated an understanding of modernity as a shared, global phenomenon bearing no unique point of origin and no "authentic" versions. Indeed, studying modernity outside of Europe reveals the very limitations of construing it as any singular package of political, cultural, economic, or social phenomena.[111] At the same time, as Keith Watenpaugh has observed, the various contingencies shaping modernity across the globe must not cloud the universalizing nature of the discourse associated with it, arguing that "it is precisely the unity and coherence of modernity in the imagination and consciousness of those seeking to be modern that marks its overarching historical significance."[112] The shared nature of this discourse suggests that modernity, and the broader conceptualization of "new times" on which it was based, might be best construed as a mindset, or "a mental temper distinguished by perpetual self-consciousness and critique."[113]

Seen from the perspective of Izmir's Jews, the late Ottoman period was nothing if not a "new time" that demanded constant self-consciousness and critique. Yet, as this book demonstrates, modernity as Izmir's Jews understood it necessitated a protracted reckoning not with Jewishness but rather with poverty and social stratification. While many of their European coreligionists grappled with poverty during the modern age as well, for the Jews of Izmir this criticism emerged not as a by-product of a "Jewish question" nor as a preoccupation with any supposed deficiencies specific to Jews. Rather, Izmir's Jews grappled with poverty not because it reflected something specific about their Jewishness but because their socioeconomic position, which was shared by Ottomans of many faiths, was increasingly at odds with new attitudes towards social stratification. These attitudes were disseminated by both the *kehillah* and the Ottoman state and reinforced by the changing canvas of the eastern Mediterranean port city itself. Jews negotiated these shifts as students in the local *Talmud Tora* and as the elderly subsisting on the communal dole; as stevedores, fishmongers, and greengrocers; as both givers and receivers of charity. New constructions of class affected their relationship to space, reconfiguring their attitudes towards home, street, and neighborhood, and reordered their priorities as consumers, from the purchase of kosher meat in the local marketplace to theater tickets on the *Kordon*. It is thus in the mundane, the routine, and the ordinary that the ways in which Izmir's Jews grappled with this "new age" become most visible. As Harry Harootunian has argued in studying modernity outside of Europe, which he regards as exposure to global capitalism, the category of "everydayness" reveals the perpetual tension between the modern, or the new, and the "durational present."[114] As scholars of China remind us, "the everyday reminds us that modernity never exists outside particular material conditions."[115]

The experience of Izmir's Jews also has implications for the study of some processes regarded as crucial to the Ottoman Empire's broader modern transformations. Paramount among them is the *Tanzimat*, a sweeping program of "reorganization" initiated under the rule of Sultan Abdülmecid I (r. 1839–1861) and formalized through the 1839 Hatt-ı Şerif of Gülhane, or "Rose Chamber Edict," and the subsequent 1856 Hatt-ı Hümayun. Following a series of military reforms implemented in the late eighteenth century, nineteenth-century Ottoman bureaucrats embarked on a project of Western-style reform that they regarded as both a bulwark against European encroachment and a metric of their own "progress." Undergirding these reforms was a universalizing spirit that sought to foster unity amongst all Ottoman subjects regardless of religion, a sentiment that was concretized by the empire's 1856 declaration formally granting "equality" to all non-Muslims. Existing taxation and conscription systems were rationalized, while the legal landscape was reconfigured by the introduction of both the *mecelle*, a codification of Hanafi Islamic law, and new commercial and penal codes based on French models. New educational institutions, such as the *rüşdiye* (primary) and *idadi* (secondary) schools, emerged, while new structures of provincial and municipal government dramatically reshaped Ottoman cities according to emerging principles of order, safety, and hygiene.[116]

Recently, the study of the *Tanzimat* has expanded beyond the world of elite bureaucrats to those whose lives were dramatically altered by its new institutions, such as impoverished children placed in new state-run orphanages, those incarcerated in Ottoman prisons, and officers in the newly centralized police force.[117] Similarly, scholars have also explored the purchase of the *Tanzimat* among the empire's non-Muslims. Challenging assumptions that the state's efforts were met with skepticism and suspicion in these communities, new work has demonstrated the opposite, from Christian peasants of various ethnicities who mobilized the language of the *Tanzimat* against both Christian and Muslim landlords, Armenians in the empire's eastern regions who found strategies to combat discrimination in the period's promise of equality, and Bulgarian Christians who successfully navigated the conventions of the new *nizamiye* courts.[118] This book, with its focus on a non-Muslim community in the provinces, adds a new perspective to this literature by showing how the discourse and principles of Ottoman reform had a far-reaching impact on Jewish self-governance. Efforts to rationalize taxes, ensure broader representation, and administer the community more efficiently were undoubtedly informed by a doctrine of "order *cum* prosperity," a principle that was "at the heart of the *Tanzimat* political idiom."[119] Through their reorganization of Izmir's *kehillah*, communal leaders were engaging in the "new sciences" discussed and advocated by Ottoman intellectuals of their day, which referred not just to certain facts and skills but to a broad array of personal characteristics to be cultivated by rulers and subjects alike, such as virtue, morality, industriousness, and loyalty.[120] Just as Ottoman statesmen brought this philosophy to bear on state practices, so too did the Jews of Izmir implement it on a smaller but still symbolic scale.

With its focus on socioeconomic issues, this book underscores another area of mutuality between broader Ottoman society and Izmir's Jewish *kehillah*. During the Hamidian era, an increased engagement with economic thought on the part of reformist intellectuals led to the promotion of a "soft social engineering project" that would transform Ottoman society from the bottom up.[121] By cultivating "the formation of human capital" among Ottoman Muslims, who were vastly outnumbered by Christians in the empire's commercial and industrial spheres, intellectuals hoped to reinvigorate the empire and better equip it for the modern age, a philosophy that was later ardently promoted by Young Turks.[122] Additionally, while the Unionists did not seek to broaden participation in their decision-making,[123] their drive to reorder Ottoman society nonetheless catalyzed marked social mobilization and the empowerment of the lower classes across the empire.[124] Almost immediately after the Young Turk Revolution in 1908, labor unrest manifested itself in a wave of strikes, as Izmir saw the workers of its port, railway, and tramways demand improved working conditions and fairer compensation.[125] The revolutionary press capitalized on this mobilization by frequently depicting the Ottoman public as a destitute individual or beggar. Its cartoons also made ample use of the *hamal*, or stevedore, as the "quintessential image of the worker, impoverished and downtrodden," to symbolize a fight against tyranny.[126] The changes that emerged in Izmir's *kehillah* must be read against this wider backdrop, as its members increasingly shared the conviction that the modern age necessitated socioeconomic transformation. Scrutiny of the communal old guard intensified, as the long-standing authority of the rabbinic establishment, the lay oligarchy, and powerful interest groups such as the *shohatim*, or ritual slaughterers of animals for the kosher marketplace, became increasingly suspect in the eyes of the far more numerous petty tradesmen and craftsmen. When the Young Turks began to speak on behalf of "the people," the debates that raged within the *kehillah* about *el puevlo* found reinforcement and justification.[127]

Moreover, by tracking change through a socioeconomic prism, this book contributes to the literature on non-Muslim communities in the late Ottoman period while expanding it in new directions. A dominant trend has been an exploration of the varied political commitments of these groups, which has ultimately challenged assumptions about the successes of Ottomanism as well as the grip of competing nationalisms. Recent work on the Jewish community, for example, has instructively shown how Ottoman Sephardi elites undertook a larger project of fashioning their brethren into Ottoman patriots and cultivated new discourses and practices of imperial citizenship.[128] Works on specific communities, such as Ottoman Greeks, as well as specific locales, such as Palestine, have amply disproven the once regnant notion that non-Muslims as well as non-Turks were unquestionably drawn to irredentist nationalism.[129] At the same time, some have noted a persistence of "ethnic politics"[130] in the years after 1908 as competing visions of the new political system left some non-Muslim groups, such as Greeks and Armenians, anxious about the maintenance of their long-standing privileges as *millets* (ethnoreligious communities) and eager to advocate for them.[131] While Izmir's Sephardi Jews continued to function as an ethnoreligious *millet* in those years, this book captures how the "ethnic politics" that preoccupied and mobilized its members were not questions of belonging, protracted debates about the merits of Zionism, or any efforts to protect Jewish privileges from the encroachments of increased centralization.[132] For the vast majority of Jews in Izmir, the most pressing questions remained social ones—the management of poverty and ensuring the survival of schools, associations, and charities in the face of economic hardship. The revolution did not destabilize the *millet* but instead legitimized and reinforced the public sphere that had evolved within it by lending a new discourse to its efforts and setting a new agenda for its leadership structures. In this sense, Izmir's Jews understood their efforts to serve *el bien puvliko*, or the "public good," within their ethnoreligious community to be an extension of a broader imperial good in a world that they did not know would be short-lived.

Sources

To claim a voice for the community, this book draws on a large and diverse body of primary sources. Most importantly, it draws on the community's own vast archive, a body of Ladino material spanning several centuries, written in a cursive known as *soletreo* that has gone virtually untouched by historians. This rich repository of archival documentation, containing sources such as the records of the lay leadership, the community's numerous active charitable associations, and voluminous census and taxation records, allows an interpretation of the modern Sephardi past not solely through the eyes of Western observers or local elites but through the voices of those who actually lived it. Complementing the portrait emerging from this archival material is Izmir's thriving Ladino press, from long-running weekly periodicals such as *La Buena Esperanza* (1871–1917?), *El Novelista* (1891–1922), and *El Meseret* (1897–1922) to lesser-known high-brow newspapers such as *El Comercial* (1906–1909) and satirical journals such as *El Soytari* (1909–1914?). The frequent communications from Izmir's *Alliance Israélite Universelle* administrators, such as David Cazès, Semtob Pariente, and Gabriel Arié, to their supervisors in Paris provide keen, if deeply biased, observations pertaining to all aspects of communal life, while Ottoman records reflect the relatively infrequent gaze of government officials.

Proceeding thematically rather than chronologically through the late Ottoman era, this book tracks change on a progressively smaller scale. Taking the dynamic urban landscape of late Ottoman Izmir as its starting point, chapter 1 situates the Jews of Izmir in the *djudería*, or Jewish quarter. Accompanying the sweeping transformation of the city's old port into a modern waterfront was an emerging notion of a shared "public good" reinforced by improvements in sanitation, hygiene, and public safety. The young municipality's expectation that its residents promote this public good soon made the presence of Jewish beggars on the streets, long a fixture of daily life, a mounting source of anxiety for communal leaders. Chapter 1 tracks their efforts to cope with the poverty that plagued their community in a city no longer willing to tolerate its presence in public, from the formation of associations to stem begging, to the curbing of raucous Purim carnivals, to the creation of housing developments for Jewish refugees on the deserted outskirts of town. As the chapter demonstrates, all of these initiatives were motivated not by a discomfort with public displays of Jewishness but by an awareness that public poverty was antithetical to the port's emerging bourgeois culture. Once Izmir's Jews had managed to remove their poverty from the public eye, they completely refashioned their internal response to it, a process that chapter 2 reconstructs in detail. Through an analysis of claims received by Izmir's new *Gabbaé Sedaka* Society, this chapter demonstrates how efforts to rationalize the collection and subsequent distribution of charity ultimately redrew the boundaries around poverty itself, as charity administrators began to formally register the poor, examine their circumstances, and deploy varying taxonomies of "deservedness." Breaking with what they had inherited from both the Jewish and Islamic traditions, Izmir's Jews also began to appropriate post-Enlightenment Western attitudes categorizing poverty as a dangerous product of idleness that eroded society from within. Chapter 2 follows their attempts to eliminate it completely through a range of activities, such as vocational training, apprenticeship programs, agricultural endeavors, and rudimentary education in the fundamentals of commerce. Chapter 3 explores how the widespread denigration of poverty in Jewish Izmir was accompanied by the proliferation of a new social ideal: that of the European bourgeois.

Nourished by the Westernizing culture of the city as well as the discourse of regeneration employed by the *Alliance Israélite Universelle*, a growing segment of Izmir's Jews began to adopt new patterns of socialization, leisure, residence, and dress and to debate decidedly middle-class values such as the sins of luxury and the virtues of sobriety and self-sufficiency. Jewish women in particular saw their roles transformed, as expectations regarding motherhood, child-rearing, and family life were realigned.

Communal leaders typically deplored the community's diminished socioeconomic state, regarding it as a sign of decay and a source of weakness. Yet the book demonstrates that far from being a source of weakness, the growing empowerment and self-awareness of Izmir's poor and lower classes catalyzed a dynamic reimagining of Izmir's *kehillah* structure. Shifting the book's focus inward, chapter 4 explores the community's troubled communal finances, which were sustained almost exclusively through the *gabela*, the series of regressive sales taxes on kosher goods that heavily and disproportionately burdened the poor. While these *gabela* taxes had long been a source of turmoil, chapter 4 demonstrates that by the modern period, Izmir's Jews had begun to engage this traditional tool of Jewish self-governance using an expanding repertoire of discourses and practices. Increasingly empowered to criticize the conditions that contributed to their impoverishment, Izmir's Jews contested the *gabela* in new forums such as bulletins, pamphlets, and newspapers. They formed associations, publicizing their position on the tax and promoting their visions for reform, and even began to express themselves in the language of modern politics, signing petitions, organizing boycotts, and attending public demonstrations. As chapter 4 argues, tracking the *gabela* tax in late Ottoman Izmir illustrates nothing less than the evolution of a vibrant Ladino public sphere.

The fifth and final chapter tracks a parallel transformation in the community's leadership structures. Answering the state's mid-nineteenth-century demand that its religious groups implement reforms in line with "the age," both the rabbinate and the lay council, long the two main anchors of the traditional *kehillah* structure, were reenvisioned as vehicles for Jewish "progress." In Jewish Izmir, as the fifth chapter demonstrates, communal "progress" was shaped by heightened sensitivity to social inequity and increasingly pronounced class consciousness. New tools of modern self-governance, such as communal statutes and representative assemblies, invoked a discourse of rights and demanded fair representation for a collective *puevlo*, or "people." A similar process underlies the transformation of the rabbinate, which in the modern period had been stripped of its traditional juridical authority by the application of Western civil, penal, and commercial codes. With the new office of *haham bashı*, or "chief rabbi," serving as the personification of the community's broader commitment to progress, Izmir's rabbis abandoned their long-standing alliance with the wealthy, reconfiguring their role as protectors and advocates of Izmir's Jewish poor.

Through the voices of both beggars on the street and mercantile elites, shoe shiners and newspaper editors, rabbis and housewives, this book recovers a vibrant Ottoman Sephardi world that dissolved along with the empire it inhabited. Narrating the transformations of the modern age from the vantage point of a Jewish community in the Islamic world and highlighting the importance of its social dimensions, this book not only calls for a more expansive approach to Jewish history but invites a reappraisal of the very assumptions that have governed its study up until now.

(CHAPTER 1)

THE *DJUDERÍA* AND PUBLIC SPACE

"*Kualo es una munisipalidad?*" or "What is a municipality?" asked a 1910 pamphlet published in Turkish, Greek, Armenian, and Ladino. Written by the Municipal Council of Izmir, the pamphlet provided the following answer to the city's four largest communities:

> The municipality is the office that safeguards public health, the cleanliness of all streets, neighborhoods and bazaars, oversees the beautification of the city, alleviates the misery of the poor and the disabled, and ensures, in short, the peace and well-being of the entire honored public.[1]

The pamphlet further enumerated the many measures expected of the city's residents in protecting the public good. People were discouraged from throwing their garbage into the street or from letting their chickens, sheep, or other animals wander about. Butchers, bakers, and grocers were asked to keep their wares in glass display cases so as to protect them from dirt, while coffee sellers were required to wear clean white aprons and to wash their used utensils in fresh running water. Barbers were prohibited from dumping used water and soap into the street and were asked instead to dispose of them in special troughs. Coaches and carriages were to be parked only in designated areas. Additionally, people were asked to be mindful of the periodic inspections that the municipality's doctors would conduct for cases of infectious diseases such as smallpox, diphtheria, typhus, and tuberculosis.[2]

The adoption of these measures, among many others, would ensure that the people of Izmir would become partners with the municipality in protecting its shared spaces. In short, the people of Izmir were asked to treat the municipality as "the home of the public."[3]

For Izmir's Jews, meeting the demands of this new partnership required by the modern city was a fraught endeavor. Deeply informed by the Westernizing imprint of the *Tanzimat* on Ottoman urban life, the "public good" being constructed in late Ottoman Izmir cast open displays of poverty as threatening to the order, stability, and security that cities were meant to uphold.[4] Yet by the 1870s, nearly one-third of Izmir's Jews lived in a state of indigence, surviving exclusively on charity. The following chapter considers the range of strategies that communal leaders implemented in negotiating this disjuncture. With initiatives ranging from multifaceted efforts to police local Jewish beggars to plans to construct housing for newly arrived Jewish refugees, elites ardently sought to remove beggars from public view. They restructured traditional Jewish rituals that had long put the community's diminished socioeconomic status on display, urging the adoption of new ones that were more compatible with the port's emerging bourgeois culture. Undergirding all of these endeavors was the careful navigation of a mutually reinforcing relationship between a religious community and the shared city it inhabited. As this chapter will demonstrate, in the plural environment of late Ottoman Izmir, it was not open Jewishness but open poverty that most directly infringed upon the new "public good."

Izmir: A Shared City in the Making

Starting in the 1860s, Ottoman statesmen began to implement a series of laws aimed at rationalizing the Ottoman Empire's provincial administration. In 1864, they instituted a hierarchical system formally dividing the entire empire into a series of *vilayets*, or provinces, which were further divided into smaller units. The 1871 Law on the General Administration of Provinces further concretized the *vilayet* system, bolstering the powers of *valis*, or local governors, and mandating the creation of the municipality, an administrative unit that would see to the general welfare of its denizens.[5] After a brief experiment in 1868, the municipality of Izmir was formally instituted in 1874.[6] Alongside this new administrative apparatus was a series of infrastructural and technological innovations that transformed the texture of urban life. Already home to the first railroad in Anatolia, and with rail lines opened in 1866 connecting Izmir to both Kasaba and Aydın,[7] the city saw the advent of numerous additional public works projects by the late 1870s. Most notable among these were the enlargement of the port and the construction of an approximately two-mile-long continuous quay with a waterfront promenade called the *Kordon*, the culmination of a complicated project that had been debated and negotiated by numerous local actors since the 1840s.[8] By 1895, the city had gained a public water system, and by 1905, Izmir was home to three local horse-drawn tramway lines as well as a citywide electricity system. Further changing the urban landscape, by 1908, Izmir's streets had approximately three thousand gas-powered streetlamps.[9]

While Izmir had been home to significant colonies of European merchants, or "Levantines," for centuries, the dramatic physical transformation of the city's built environment in the nineteenth century lent it an even more pronounced Western appearance. Expecting an "Oriental" city, nineteenth-century European visitors to Ottoman Izmir were often surprised upon their arrival in the city's port. "Bathed by oriental seas, which promised us an Asian city, the first impression one has of Izmir's quays, with its European facades and tramways running along the length of the port, is of Genoa or Marseilles," noted one French traveler.[10] Counting more hats than turbans, another traveler remarked that Izmir had "the appearance of an Italian maritime city, one area of which is inhabited by Orientals."[11] Describing the activity that characterized the city's quays, a French guidebook emphasized how countless hotels, clubs, cafés, and theaters lent the city a "European physiognomy."[12]

As France's Consul General for Izmir reported in 1892:

> The quays are ... a magnificent promenade where the population gathers in crowds, especially on summer evenings so as to breathe in the pure sea air, which is cooled by the western breeze. ... [It is] a promenade that is even more pleasant given that the city is deprived of public squares, paths, and gardens. The city's wealthiest inhabitants have built superb homes on vast stretches of seafront land, of which quite a few are on par both architecturally and in terms of interior comforts with the most elegant European homes.

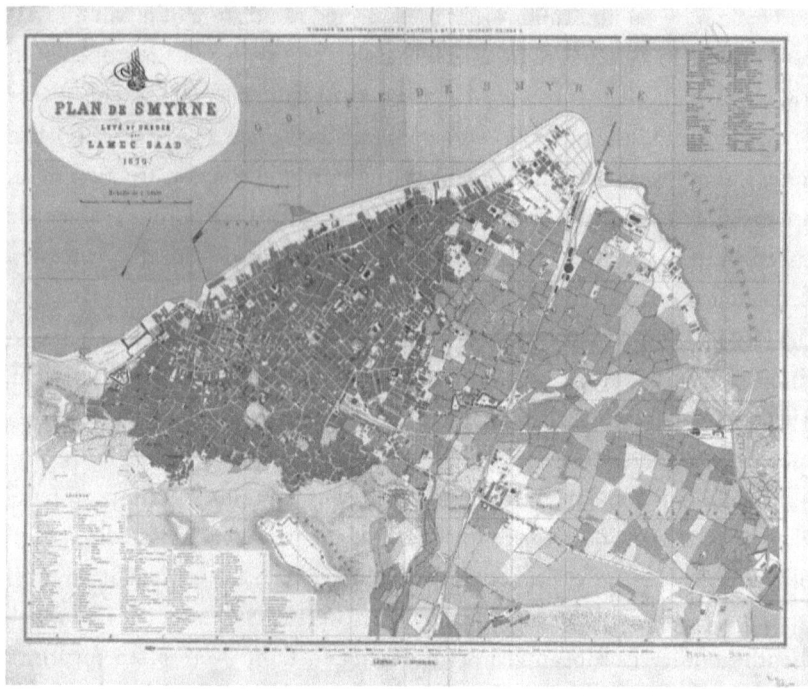

FIGURE 2. Map of Izmir by Lamec Saad, 1876.
Courtesy of the University of Chicago Library.

New parallel and perpendicular streets leading to the quays have been cleared and neighborhoods have been constructed in the most favorable of hygienic conditions. The rest of the city has equally benefited from these improvements as a result of the easier penetration of healthy sea air into older areas that are particularly overheated during the great summer heat.[13]

Further inland, southeast of the waterfront that captured the imagination of so many European visitors, was Izmir's Jewish quarter. Sharing a fluid border with the Muslim quarter, the Jewish quarter was in close proximity to the city's centuries-old *Kemeraltı* bazaar and was densely packed with tens of synagogues. Records point to the existence of numerous distinct neighborhoods within the quarter, including *Haham Bashı, Huruşdiye, Chaves, Sonsin, Bnai Yisrael, Yeni Mahalle,* and *Efrati*,[14] as well as particular streets, such as *Hacı Süleyman Sokağı, Yeheş Sokağı, Havra Sokağı, Eski Mahkeme,* and *Yazlı Sokağı*.[15]

The Jews of Izmir demonstrated a keen awareness of the rapid changes taking place around them. The Ladino press abounds with articles chronicling Izmir's transformation into a modern municipality, with reports regarding renewed efforts to attend to the well-being of the public and the "general improvement of the city."[16] In March of 1875, *La Esperanza* reported that the expulsion of "foreigners in our city with no profession" had yielded "great benefits," detailing how the "beneficial step taken by the *vali*" would protect the city's inhabitants from "these criminals."[17] Over the following decades, the newspaper (which changed its name from *La Esperanza* to *La Buena Esperanza* in February of 1880) frequently reported similar measures by the local police to ensure public safety. In 1893, the paper lauded the successes of Hefzi Pasha, head of the province's gendarmerie, in protecting "public peace" and announced the expansion of his duties to include the "cleanliness of the city."[18] *La Buena Esperanza* praised the "admirable" manner in which Hefzi Pasha assumed his new responsibilities, noting that he could be seen daily in the city's most densely populated areas "ordering [people] to see to the cleanliness of houses and neighborhoods."[19] In 1907, *El Novelista* celebrated the work of Izmir's "excellent chief of police," Mahzar Bey, whose "activity and zeal for the tranquility of the city are worthy of every praise."[20] Public safety was a priority not only for Izmir's local police but for the sultan as well. In 1907, responding to increasing crime on the part of "brigands," a phenomenon that had long characterized life in western Anatolia, notables from the city's various communities approached the governor general of the province to relay "complaints of the city's residents regarding public security."[21] The governor subsequently appealed to the sultan, who issued an imperial decree dispatching six hundred soldiers to the area to fortify local efforts against the threat.[22]

Both the new municipality and the imperial government went to great lengths to safeguard public health, employing a range of tactics in combating Izmir's frequent epidemics. In response to the cholera outbreak of 1893, Izmir imposed a quarantine mandated by the imperial health council.[23] In 1896, a variola epidemic lasting several months prompted the municipality to offer a free vaccination program, which Gabriel Arié used to vaccinate all students of the *Alliance* schools as well as the students of the *Talmud Tora*.[24] When news arrived of the appearance of diphtheria in nearby Foça, the municipality promptly sent serums to prevent its spread and took several more precautionary measures, such as mandatory medical checks, the disinfection of baggage at the "sanitary ports" of Jaffa and Rhodes, and the institution of quarantines.[25]

While local officials actively sought to stem the tide of epidemics, the responsibility was not theirs alone. In 1900, the city faced a particularly devastating outbreak of the plague. "In comparison to the plague, cholera seems like a mild illness," noted Gabriel Arié that year, observing that while cholera could eventually be "subdued," the plague proved resistant to even the most "vigorous of treatments."[26] While the governor and municipality had taken "serious and sound" measures in the crisis, *El Meseret* cautioned its readers "not to let all of the responsibility fall upon the municipality." Urging them to take action, the paper continued:

> Clean, sweep, and above all, whitewash—whitewash your homes a thousand times. Lime kills the germ. Pour disinfectant mixed with water in dirty places and in courtyards. Keep your bodies clean and wash your hands continuously. If you know of a person who has fallen ill being hidden at a neighbor's home, run to alert the doctor or the local police on the street. To do this would be an honor, not a sin. If you care about yourself and your family, do not cover this up. Do not delay in alerting the municipality.[27]

Here, *El Meseret* instructed its readers in their new duties as partners alongside the municipality in safeguarding the public good. Similarly, during a cholera outbreak ten years later, the Communal Council gathered in a special meeting to discuss strategies to keep the city's Jewish neighborhoods free of contagion.[28]

In 1898, *El Meseret* had already underscored the importance of this shared responsibility when it reported on the condition of the streets in Izmir's old *djudería*, or "Jewish quarter." While the city's main thoroughfares had been repaved with "great Maltese stone," which made cleaning easier and more efficient, the streets of the *djudería* had not. Given that the area was home to the busy bazaar, where all manner of fruits, vegetables, and fish were sold, its streets became easily littered and sometimes virtually impassable, especially during the busy periods before holidays. Compounding the problem was the location of the bazaar right at the entryway to the "street of the synagogues," which despite being swept and washed remained polluted and malodorous. *El Meseret* called

FIGURE 3. The Jewish Quarter, Smyrna, Greece [sic], 1900s.
M.E. Wright, Stereoscopic Slide.
Source: M.E. Wright/Hulton Archive/Getty Images. Reprinted with permission.

upon storeowners to renovate the quarter's streets and improve their paving: given that "this quarter is called the '*djudería*' and is the principal way to get to our synagogues, it is our duty as Jews not to create the impression that we do not value cleanliness and are indifferent to all laws of 'hygiene.'"[29]

Poverty and Begging

More pressing even than cleaning the physical streets of the *djudería* was the need to police the behaviors that took place on them. While both Ottoman Muslims and Jews had traditionally employed many strategies to alleviate the burden of poverty, the ultimate aim of these activities had never been to eradicate it or remove it from public view.[30] Public displays of poverty such as begging, while perhaps seen as noisome, were largely tolerated. Evidence of this in Izmir's Jewish community can be seen in census records from as late as the 1840s in which the terms *fakir*, or "pauper," and *dilenci*, or "beggar," are used as designations of professions.[31]

Yet, by the late nineteenth century, the previously tolerant attitude towards begging had begun to shift across the Ottoman Empire. Such attitudes had already taken shape in early modern Europe a few centuries earlier, where begging, especially on the part of the "able-bodied," came to be associated with disorder, laziness, and sin.[32] Early modern European states employed a range of tactics aimed at stigmatizing and marginalizing beggars, from badges, through confinement in specially designated "houses of correction," to actual expulsion.[33] By the early 1770s, for example, the French state had developed an elaborate "repressive machinery" in dealing with beggars that efficiently resulted in their arrest, incarceration, and sometimes even execution.[34] France also saw the emergence of *dépôts de mendicité*, or "beggars' prisons," institutions that sought to rehabilitate their inmates and restore their utility to the state.[35] Napoleonic France further rationalized such policies, criminalizing begging in its penal code and further requiring that each department across the French Empire establish such a prison.[36] The dramatic urbanization of the late nineteenth century heightened concerns over begging, as the modern city implemented strategies aimed at preserving order and stability in service of a greater "public good."

As the Ottomans reconfigured their urban spaces and structures according to Western standards, so too did the Western notion that cast begging as a pernicious threat to the public order become more prevalent.[37] Through the late nineteenth and early twentieth centuries, begging increasingly attracted the concern of the state, which fully criminalized it in 1909 with the "Law on Vagabonds and Suspected Persons." For Izmir's Jews, discomfort with public begging began as early as the 1870s, as what had once been an unremarkable aspect of daily life in the *djudería* emerged as a profound source of embarrassment. In 1874, an article entitled "*Los limozneros en Izmir*," or "Alms-givers in Izmir," appeared on the front page of *La Esperanza*, then Izmir's only Ladino periodical:

One of the biggest scandals in our community occurs on Wednesdays and Fridays, when the poor—[both] elderly and young, along with many children, go out to collect [charity] in bazaars and neighborhoods . . . It is also very sad to see old men and women, so sick that they cannot walk, forced to get out of their beds to go beg for *sedaka* [charity] so they will not die of hunger.[38]

A few months later, the paper identified begging as the primary source of the community's "backwardness," labeling it "a great dishonor."[39] This deprecating discourse would find echoes for years to come, as *La Buena Esperanza* consistently labeled begging a "scandal,"[40] "humiliation,"[41] and even a *hilul Hashem*,[42] or "desecration of God's name."

Convinced of the severity of the new problem, communal elites began to search for solutions. In 1878, they established a new association called the *Gabbaé Sedaka* Society. Announcing its establishment in *La Esperanza*, its founder declared its mission as "preventing the unfortunate poor from collecting [charity] on the streets, in homes, shops, and stores."[43] The association promised to implement a multifaceted approach to "remov[ing] this evil from our city" while "supporting the poor with honor."[44] The new association was met with adulation by *La Esperanza*, which celebrated the society for doing "holy" work and its "brave young men" for their initiative in "banish[ing] the disorder and '*hilul Hashem*' caused by begging for charity."[45] Years later, the communal notable and historian Abraham Galante would characterize the efforts of *Gabbaé Sedaka* to curb begging as having saved not only the poor from an "unhappy obligation," but the "prestige of the nation" from the "ridicule" of others.[46]

For the administrators of *Gabbaé Sedaka* and their supporters, begging in Izmir had evolved into an entrenched and sophisticated profession. The *Alliance* administrator Semtob Pariente disparaged begging in Izmir as "an object of trade and even brokerage," arguing that the city was home to "begging brokerages."[47] According to Pariente, after arriving in Izmir, foreign beggars availed themselves of an extensive network on the ground of locals who quickly schooled them in the "tricks of the trade," alerting them to which homes, establishments, and neighborhoods were the most lucrative. As for those native to Izmir, the situation was even more dire, as begging had evolved into a profession transmitted from parents to children. Mothers in particular were to blame, as they schooled their children in the trade from a very young age and took them on professional "excursions" once they were old enough.[48] Behor Yomtov Danon, the founder of *Gabbaé Sedaka*, shared these sentiments, calling begging an "evil profession"[49] and a lamentable scheme in which "capable" people turned it into "a business."[50]

To address the problem, *Gabbaé Sedaka* embarked on a comprehensive restructuring of the flow of charity, removing it from the streets and relocating it to the official registers and meetings of the association. After "repatriating" foreign beggars, *Gabbaé Sedaka* would investigate the "worthiness" of those who remained, determine their eligibility for charity, and officially register them with the association. Instead of giving charity to beggars on the street, *Gabbaé Sedaka* encouraged community members to redirect their funds to the association in the form of *mezadas*, or monthly subscriptions. Once the system had been centralized, the association would regulate an orderly distribution of charity to the poor on a weekly basis.[51] Initially, *Gabbaé Sedaka*'s comprehensive restructuring of charity met with success. It was reported in 1879, only a year after its founding, that "one does not see a single Jewish beggar in the neighborhoods of Izmir."[52]

Yet this success was short-lived. Although the association received a regular subsidy from the Jewish community's lay Communal Council, its heavy reliance on voluntary subscriptions left it vulnerable to the financial hardships endured by its supporters. By 1880, *Gabbaé Sedaka* faced a deficit of two thousand *kuruş*,[53] and in 1883, it found itself on the brink of collapse.[54] Although the organization quickly reemerged in 1883 as the *Ozer Dalim*, or "Aid to the Poor" Society,[55] by 1903 it had been dissolved and reestablished five additional times.

In contrast to the association's marked fiscal instability, the discourse it deployed remained steadfast. Notables consistently framed public Jewish begging in communal, and often "national," terms. Given the empire's ongoing legitimation of religious difference and communal autonomy in the modern period, the fact that the Jews of Izmir interpreted the problem of begging as a "national" concern is unremarkable. What is notable, however, is that "national" problems, as well as their solutions, were framed in terms of their implications for a new and urban shared collectivity. Against the background of late Ottoman Izmir's changing urban landscape, Jewish poverty was no longer strictly an internal matter, but now a public problem with dire consequences.

Even more significant than the citywide impact assigned to Jewish begging in Izmir was the manner in which efforts to protect a larger "public good" ultimately reinforced "national" belonging. While the presence of Jewish beggars on the streets was certainly detrimental to the city, it was consistently read by communal leaders as equally damaging to the Jewish community itself. In 1880, *La Buena Esperanza* warned of the "dishonor that will emerge for our community" if begging was not controlled, and in 1883 it labeled begging a "great scandal for our nation."[56] Likewise, in 1885 an open letter from the supporters of *Ozer Dalim* called the association a source of "honor for our community and in the interest of all Jewish Izmirlis."[57] In 1902, a new periodical on the scene, Alexander Benghiat's *El Meseret*, termed begging a "dishonor in the midst of our community" and urged *Ozer Dalim* to "rid the community of the eccentricity caused by beggars."[58] A few years later, *El Novelista* praised *Ozer Dalim* for "the honor it brings our nation" and the "humiliation that it spares us."[59]

This discourse emphasizing the "national" impact of concerns newly reconceptualized as "public" points to a distinguishing characteristic of the social fabric in a late Ottoman port city. Scholarship on the varied allegiances of Izmir's Greek urban elites has emphasized the coexistence of both communal and urban "public spheres" in the city, pointing to the fact that the strength of one did not necessitate the weakness of the other.[60] Study of similar phenomena during the Second Constitutional period has further shown how the municipality destabilized the robust local connection to the city exhibited by Izmir's Greeks, prioritizing instead the interests of the city's Muslim residents.[61] The experience of Izmir's Jews reinforces this dynamic interplay between city and community while adding a new dimension to the portrait. Seen from the perspective of Izmir's Jewish leaders, who were ultimately less embroiled in larger contestations regarding Izmir's ethnoreligious character than were their Greek and Muslim neighbors, the urban and communal spheres were not only contemporaneous, or even complementary, but in many ways fully dependent on each other. The anxiety expressed by communal leaders over Jewish begging and the strategies they implemented to curtail it reflect their deep investment in this mutuality of communal and urban interests and their ardent belief that removing Jewish beggars would safeguard the "modernity" of the city and their own community alike.

The Problem of Russian Refugees

The community's efforts to police its poor were further tested by an influx of Russian refugees during the early 1890s. In the summer of 1892, the settlement of forty Russian Jews in Izmir was noted by Ottoman authorities.[62] A year later, it was estimated that there were approximately seven hundred refugees in Izmir,[63] and by the winter of 1894, an additional hundred and fifty families had arrived seeking shelter.[64] Largely destitute families with many children, the refugees appealed to the Communal Council as well as to the *Alliance* for help. Izmir's Jewish institutions had successfully absorbed prior waves of refugees fleeing violence from both Alexandria[65] and Chios,[66] and in February of 1893, there had already emerged a special committee dedicated to helping ease the plight of the newly arrived Russian Jews across the province of Aydın.[67] For example, the committee secured five hundred *okkas*[68] of matza for the refugees, who had arrived very close to Passover.[69] However, their ongoing influx into a community already plagued by poverty ultimately proved to be a profound source of instability.

At the heart of the havoc wrought by these refugees was not only their taxing of already strained communal resources, but their public visibility. Their inability to speak local languages and therefore earn a living made them a conspicuous presence as beggars both in Izmir's Jewish neighborhoods and across the whole city. By the spring of 1893, *La Buena Esperanza* lamented that the refugees were "surrounding the bazaars and cafés, begging for charity," adding that "the most regrettable thing is that they teach their children the shameful profession of begging!"[70] Perhaps the most sensitive issue of all was the presence of these beggars in Izmir's most modern new spaces. As *La Buena Esperanza* again reported a month later: "in the cafés, in the bazaars, in the brasseries of the *Kordon*, one sees nothing but Russian Jewish beggars!"[71] To have beggars on the newly constructed waterfront promenade, the *Kordon*, one of Izmir's most prominent new venues of bourgeois respectability, seemed almost unbearable. "The arrival of these Russian émigrés in Izmir is, we must say with great regret, a calamity for our community."[72]

It was not only the refugees' begging, however, that threatened Izmir's public order. A year later, multiple local French papers reported on the preponderance of young Russian Jewish children, some as young as six years old, selling matchbooks on the city's docks. Of particular concern were the risks of this "industry" for young girls, as some had reportedly fallen prey to prostitution. *Le Journal de Smyrne* derided these descendants of "the tribes of Judah and Israel, Polish from Galicia or Russian from the swamps of Pultawa" for creating a threat to both "morality and public health," and feared that the matter might deteriorate into a "veritable disgrace for our city."[73] Similar sentiments were published in *Le Courrier de Smyrne*, which beseeched the municipality to "ensure that public morality does not have to suffer the unsavory spectacles taking place on our quays."[74] In an effort to rid Izmir of the problem, in early June the *Alliance* administrator Gabriel Arié asked local officials to intervene. The local *vali* reportedly ordered the chief of police, Niyazi Bey, to "'clean' the city of these merchants in short skirts."[75]

The potential for a "national" problem to yield wider, public implications is evidenced by the fear Jewish elites had of the threat that the refugees presented to public health. As many refugees found shelter in an old building belonging to the community, *La Buena Esperanza* argued that the safeguarding of public health required their relocation. "Given, God help us, their great numbers and the filth that exists among them in this place, they might cause an epidemic in the city."[76] Later coverage described their makeshift lodging as fit for "sardines."[77]

Just as the community attempted to police the behavior of local Jewish beggars, so too did it endeavor to remove the Russian refugees from public view and neutralize the broader threat they represented to the city. In a markedly unorthodox approach, a proposal surfaced arguing for the construction of *barakas* or "sheds" in the old Jewish cemetery to house the refugees. While quite notable in its focus on the cemetery, given Jewish traditions regarding the sacred nature of burial grounds, the plan to move an entire refugee population had local parallels carried out by the Ottoman state. For example, by the 1880s, Muslim refugees from the Balkans and Crete had been resettled in Değirmendağı, a planned housing district southwest of the city.[78]

Known as *Bahri Baba*, the "old" Jewish cemetery had been on the outskirts of town until the mid-nineteenth century, when it found itself next to the new, expanding neighborhood of Karataş. Because the Ottoman authorities, who wished to clear part of it for the construction of a new road, prohibited new burials there in 1885, the community purchased land for a new cemetery in Kan Çeşme and *Bahri Baba* fell slowly into a state of disrepair. *Bahri Baba* had also suffered vandalism, and by the 1880s had become a de facto home for small groups of poverty-stricken Muslims. While arguing that the *barakas* would provide the refugees with much-needed shelter, *La Buena Esperanza* also cast the building project as an effective way to ensure that the old cemetery remain the property of the community despite the designs of the Ottoman authorities.[79]

Remarkably, the plan received rabbinic approval, albeit with certain conditions. Chief Rabbi Abraham Palacci convened a special meeting of communal notables to discuss these conditions, among which were the requirement of absolute vigilance in assuring that no building take place on top of graves and the supervision of the construction by two rabbis and two notables at all times. It was also decided that the *barakas* would shelter not only Russian refugees but the local Jewish poor as well, and that the "settlement" would officially carry the name "for the Jewish Poor of our Community, Izmir."[80]

While the project ultimately failed due to financial and administrative setbacks, it stands as a moment of marked significance. The fear that the community might eventually lose official title to *Bahri Baba* was both well-founded and ultimately confirmed. In 1914, Ottoman authorities seized it to facilitate Izmir's urban expansion to the south and subsequently required the relocation of the cemetery's tombs.[81] Yet the larger context suggests that the proposal was motivated equally by the community's constant and varied efforts to police the poor and remove them from view. While the contrast between the crowded brasseries and cafés of the *Kordon* and an inaccessible part of a neglected communal cemetery on the edge of town is indeed striking, perhaps even more so was the plan to house the Sephardi poor there as well. Coinciding with a period during which *Ozer Dalim* had lapsed, the cemetery construction project was not meant to be a temporary solution geared towards one group of outsiders, but a longer-term strategy for controlling the injurious impact of begging on the community.

Purim Celebrations

Perhaps no moment reflects the deep anxiety catalyzed by shifting norms of public behavior better than the annual holiday of Purim, which commemorates the saving of the Jewish community of ancient Persia from annihilation, as recounted in the Book of Esther. The early spring festival was accompanied by celebratory meals, carnivals, the donning of costumes, and the distribution of charity, and in Izmir, these rituals were traditionally performed on the city's streets. As the *Alliance* teacher Abraham Benveniste remarked in 1891, "nowhere in Turkey or Bulgaria is the festival of Purim celebrated with as much noise, bustle, and animation as it is here."[82] Yet, in the late Ottoman period, the nature of Purim's annual "noise" emerged as a profound source of controversy. Shaping the urban life of port cities like Izmir was a "modernist and moralizing discourse" employed by an influential middle class.[83] Against this backdrop, Purim, with its boisterous dancing, music, costumes, revelry, raucousness, and carnivals, or *el karnavalik*, as the ritual was known in Ladino, soon came to preoccupy rabbinical authorities and lay leaders alike.

Benveniste's 1891 report on local Purim celebrations paints a vivid picture of the festivities on the streets of *Irgat Bazar*, the heart of Izmir's old Jewish quarter. Lit up through the night, the neighborhood's streets were adorned with "*arcs de triomphe*" of myrtle branches and signs declaring "*Vive le Sultan.*" The quarter's many cafés, which hosted brass bands that played through the night, were illuminated by lamps of multicolored Venetian glass and decorated with various national flags. The streets were filled with parades of musicians playing popular music, along with

> from the balconies above, women and men throw[ing] fistfuls of beans and candies on passers-by, a practice borrowed from the Greek carnival. Carriages filled with people disguised in masks stop every fifteen minutes and captivate spectators with their bizarre accoutrements. . . . Drunkards—and they are not as rare as you might think—walk unsteadily, repeating drinking songs to the roars of laughter of the masses. It is a constant whirlwind. The crowd is so compressed in certain areas that one only moves with great difficulty. Jewish families come from farther neighborhoods to take part in this spectacle, which happens but once a year. Greek and European notables do

not consider it beneath them to pay a visit to Argat [sic] Bazar to enjoy the animation and excitement that prevails there.[84]

Unsurprisingly, communal elites did not share Benveniste's sympathetic view. As early as 1880, *La Buena Esperanza* cautioned its readers to celebrate the upcoming holiday with "prudence," urging them to refrain from wasting money on frivolous things such as masks and carnivals, arguing that they were prohibited by Judaism.[85] In February of 1885, the Communal Council distributed an official announcement regarding upcoming Purim celebrations, to be read publicly in all local synagogues. Lamenting the increasing popularity of costumes and masks, the Council labeled such behavior as "contrary to our holy law" and criticized it for encouraging rampant "perversity" and "sin."[86] Not only was the practice in conflict with Jewish tradition, the Council argued, but it was wasteful "vanity," particularly on the part of the poor.[87]

While the Communal Council cautioned against the carnivals' "vanity" and inconsistency with Jewish tradition, it was the public nature of such celebrations that most disturbed them. Labeling the practice of wearing masks and costumes "an unfortunate custom," the Council condemned how revelers had taken to "walk[ing] along the plazas so much that we have arrived at a level where non-Jews look at them with astonishment."[88] Such a spectacle was their behavior, the Council lamented, that the local Ottoman authorities had apparently inquired whether such rituals were indeed mandated by Jewish law. The Council pleaded with the community to celebrate not on the streets, but in private, as "the true joy of Purim is eating and drinking at home with one's wife and family."[89]

The Ladino press typically supported the efforts of lay and rabbinic leaders to do away with carnivals. The reform-minded editor of *La Buena Esperanza*, Aaron Joseph Hazan, took an activist stance on the matter, appealing to the rabbinic establishment and the local police to restrict carnivals. In 1889, for example, his newspaper published a letter to the editor encouraging the chief rabbi to "seriously and categorically prohibit carnivals," adding that a "small request to the chief of police would suffice in ensuring that the rabbi's orders be respected."[90] *La Buena Esperanza* shared the hopes of the letter's anonymous author, arguing that such a measure would prevent "scandal" for the community.[91] The paper made many such appeals over its long history, and reported with satisfaction and relief in years when the carnival was officially prohibited.[92] However, it should be noted that even the outright ban of the carnival did not fully prevent inappropriate behavior on the streets. Again in 1889, borrowing a local Greek tradition, Jews unleashed a "rainfall of beans"[93] on passers-by from the balconies above *Irgat Bazar*.

Almost identically mirroring the discourse surrounding begging, the Ladino press continued to cast Purim carnivals as "scandalous," underscoring that it was their public nature that rendered them so threatening. When Purim was reportedly celebrated without the excesses of *el karnavalik*, as for instance in 1890, which was notably the same year the Ottomans had banned begging, *La Buena Esperanza* noted with pride how "our non-Jewish neighbors very much praised the good behavior of our coreligionists."[94] Yet the carnival of 1892, which lasted for three days, was reportedly particularly brazen, as revelers donned costumes mocking local personalities and engaged in improper behavior between the sexes. While this was a source of "great disgust," the paper asserted that recent festivities had "exceeded all limits" because revelers had been spotted on the streets of the upscale *kartier franko*, or European quarter. Lamenting that the festivities had provoked "much talk about our nation," the paper concluded that the "scandal" of costumed young women singing and riding in open carriages to the *kartier franko* should anger "any friend of the nation."[95] As with the embarrassment of Russian Jewish girls selling matchbooks on the *Kordon* or Jewish beggars pestering shopkeepers in the *kartier franko*, the "scandalous" nature of carnivals became only more amplified when they seeped into Izmir's most modern public spaces.

While the overall impoverishment of Izmir's Jewish community made the Purim carnival particularly fraught, the changing norms governing Izmir's streets provoked similar debates amongst the city's Greeks in advance of Easter.[96] In 1902, for example, *La Buena Esperanza* reported that the local Greek patriarch had sought to "prohibit the eccentricities that take place with the carnival."[97] A year later, the local police chief, Abdul Rahman Efendi, also attempted to curb the excesses of carnivals, imposing a fine of 1.25 *mecidiyes* (equal to 25 *kuruş*) on anyone who might throw beans in the face of passers-by. "Let us hope that the Jews do not partake of similar pastimes on Purim,"[98] warned *La Buena Esperanza*.

Jewish sensitivity regarding Purim carnivals must also be read within the wider context of the political, ideological, and religious statements encoded in such public celebrations. For example, the large-scale 1842 Corpus Christi procession orchestrated by Izmir's Latin Catholics was designed in large part to carve out a legitimate place for Ottoman Catholics among the city's Greek-Orthodox-dominated Christian population,[99] while Izmir's Greek Orthodox, in turn, who were divided between subjects of both Hellenic and Ottoman extraction, either participated in or refrained from annual public celebrations of the French Revolution as a way to broadcast their political loyalties.[100] In this context, calls to moderate public Purim festivities or even dispense with them altogether reflect a profound desire on the part of Jewish leaders to demonstrate the community's commitment to the order and stability of the larger city and, by extension, their own "progress."

Charity and *las Kojitas*

It was not only *el karnavalik* that threatened to disturb the public order during the Purim season. Celebration of the holiday also traditionally entailed the public distribution of charity to the needy, which, as we have seen, was an issue of enormous sensitivity. Abraham Benveniste described the annual distribution of charity this way:

> From the morning, one sees processions of beggars, lines of elderly women, blind, limping, ill—misery in all of its shapes and colors that continues uninterrupted and stops at each Jewish house. Both sides of the doors of prominent notables are opened, two people at the entrance, in between them a table on which are wooden "begging bowls" filled with small pieces of silver. Each poor person receives their portion and leaves, repeating, by way of thanks, the traditional "Happy Purim." The distribution continues like this uninterrupted until the late afternoon. One must give to all who extend their hand; if a person appears for the second or third time, one must pretend not to notice.[101]

Though seemingly orderly, this annual "procession" of beggars through the Jewish quarter stood as a marked disjuncture from the recent efforts of associations like the *Ozer Dalim* Society to both rationalize the giving of charity and remove it from the street. As Benveniste noted, "the rich person has direct contact with true misery—it is made tangible for him.[102]

Frustration with the beggars' procession emanated from multiple sources. Reflecting the increasingly prevalent notion that not all beggars were indeed worthy of charity, some came to see Purim's ritualized begging as a haven for imposters. In 1896, the local notable Alexander Benghiat published the following poem, entitled *"Buen Purim"*:

> Enough of the screams that we will hear tomorrow
> Screams that take away our desire to live
> You will see everyone will become handicapped and limping
> The only thing they are missing is to take out their own eyes
>
> All kinds of lazy poor people you will see
> From morning to night, this is how it will be
> And these miserable people pretend to be poor for small change
> We have already gotten to know such types over the years
>
> And the children of these poor debtors
> You will see them freezing and covered in rags
> And in this fancy clothing they show us their stature
> But you see that they are beggars to the core
>
> Firefighters, night watchmen, cart pushers and others
> You will see them fill your houses with mud
> It is as if you owed them something,
> And should give them all of your money.[103]

For Benghiat, Purim not only legitimized the disruptive screams of the poor in the streets but also indiscriminately enabled those who were fully capable of working, such as firefighters, metalworkers, and drivers, to receive handouts from the public. Paradoxically, even *pazvantes*, or "night watchmen," traditionally charged with keeping the peace, would participate in this disruptive procession. *La Buena Esperanza* revisited the matter again in 1902, when it complained that "Purim barely even starts, and one already sees children from the age of 5 up to the elderly, 80 years old, with handkerchiefs in their hands to go join the regiments of the beggars."[104] So numerous were the beggars, the paper lamented, that "foreigners who do not [already] understand this might say that it is an honor for us to become beggars on Purim."[105]

Yet again, the most troubling thing about the endless stream of beggars on the streets, both "worthy" and "alleged," was their occasional presence in Izmir's most respectable neighborhoods. Again in 1902, *La Buena Esperanza* railed against those "beggars of Purim morning," who by late afternoon could be seen celebrating raucously in the company of women. More scandalous than their squandering of charity was their visibility on the *Kordon*: "we do not even have to mention what foreigners say about such improper behavior and about our nation!" *La Buena Esperanza* demanded that "these people behave in a more noble way and stop making themselves and the nation look ridiculous."[106]

The frustration surrounding charity on Purim was in response not just to the preponderance of beggars but also to official collections, or *kojitas*, by charitable associations and institutions. Although executed in an orderly fashion, these collections came to represent a heavy burden for those already expected to give to any beggar who might arrive at their doorstep. In 1884, the lay Communal Council banned such collections due to "great fatigue" on the part of the community.[107] The Council instituted the same prohibition the following year, noting that in addition to the petitions of many beggars, collections by twenty local charitable associations and institutions had left many overburdened and subsequently more likely to "close their doors." Ruling that "no administration or association, whether large or small, may go out on Purim as is customary," the Communal Council hoped to prevent a situation in which the poor "would not find a [single] open door."[108] Similar prohibitions on official Purim collections became commonplace in the following years.[109]

Charity Events

The ability of such traditional rituals to publicly announce the socioeconomic status of the Jewish community becomes even more apparent when one considers the activities elites promoted to unseat them. They found an attractive alternative in charity "balls," "dancing soirées," and "evening parties." While such functions had become increasingly commonplace among Izmir's Jews by the 1870s, they soon came to be regarded as particularly well-suited to the Purim season, with its dual emphasis on merriment and caring for the needy. In their emulation of bourgeois respectability, these events provided a remarkably suitable framework for enacting the rituals of the holiday while honoring the integrity of public space.

During Purim of 1898, a "very brilliant soirée" held by a new association, *Agudat a-Perahim*, was highlighted by *El Meseret*. The event stood in marked contrast to the raucous excesses of Purim carnivals, and *El Meseret* lauded the "simplicity," "artfulness," and "grace" that characterized it.[110] Instead of crass customs such as the throwing of beans and riding in open carriages, the attendees enjoyed a leisurely evening of dance in a space that was "artistically decorated." Instead of outlandish costumes and masks, women arrived in "simple and elegant dress."[111] Dancing reportedly lasted until the early hours of the morning, and money was collected for *Ozer Dalim*.[112] In short, the author counted the soirée among "the most pleasant evenings and happiest times" of his life.[113]

In addition to formal dance events, many charitable associations also sponsored events featuring theater productions of Purim plays, the proceeds of which would benefit the association's initiatives. While the performance of comedic Purim plays had been customary for centuries, in late Ottoman Izmir they were recast as modern, "civilized" rituals. The respectability embedded in choosing such performances over street carnivals was only bolstered by their frequent location in opulent venues such as the Sporting Club or highly symbolic spaces such as the *Alliance* school building. In 1889, for example, a Purim play was staged in the grand entrance hall of the local *Alliance* school. Numbering approximately three hundred people, the crowd was comprised of "the finest families of our community."[114] Demand for tickets was so great that many people were turned away at the door, necessitating a second performance. Because the proceeds went toward the Jewish community's new *kabineto de lektura*, or reading room, the paper praised the audience for prioritizing the work of "a civilizing endeavor."[115] A similar Purim production in 1892 drew not only Izmir's prominent Jewish families, but also local Ottoman officials, including the chief of police and the inspector of public instruction.[116] Notably, at least one Turkish play was performed that evening, and the actors were lauded for their impressive mastery of the language.[117]

Elites promoted Purim productions not only because they offered revelers dignified alternatives to raucous carnivals but because the charity generated through ticket sales would unseat the holiday's legitimization of public begging. This is seen most vividly in the annual Purim show put on by the *Ozer Dalim* Society, which came to serve as a major source of revenue for the association, helping it to offset its frequent deficits.[118] In honor of Purim in 1906, for example, *Ozer Dalim* staged three plays at the Sporting Club. Clearly moved by the performances, *El Novelista* reported that the audience was "brought to tears during the drama and sidesplitting laughter during the comedies." Adding to the "moral success" of the event was the eighty *liras* (or eight thousand *kuruş*) of charity that it generated, all of it collected "without bothering the public" and with "no disorder, no chaos."[119]

The Rothschild Hospital

The establishment of the *Gabbaé Sedaka* Society, the *Bahri Baba* cemetery construction plan, and the restructuring of Purim rituals all point to an awareness on the part of Izmir's Jews that the modern city made certain demands of its inhabitants. Yet Jewish communal leaders not only implemented new strategies for managing communal poverty, but recast traditional ones as well. Such was the case with the Rothschild Hospital. The institution's genealogy dates back to the early nineteenth century, when it was established as a shelter for a few infirm foreigners in town.[120] In the wake of a fire that devastated Izmir's Jewish quarter in 1840, the Rothschilds of Vienna sponsored the construction of a new facility. Over the course of the nineteenth century, the hospital grew dramatically and, thanks to its location at the *hahamhane*, or rabbinical complex, came to occupy a central place in the physical landscape of the community. By 1896, the hospital had emerged as a venue of great symbolic importance as well and had come to be regarded as an "adornment" of the community.[121]

While they are few in number, the existence of hospitals is not without precedent either in the Jewish or the Islamic world. The small body of evidence points to the presence of hospitals in the Jewish communities of medieval Spain, as well as in the Ottoman Empire.[122] As most people typically found medical attention among family or kinship networks, these small institutions were dedicated to those destitute individuals, either local or foreign, with no other avenue of assistance. As has been documented, hospitals in the Ottoman Empire functioned to ensure not the health of a larger community but only that of individuals with no viable alternatives.[123]

A history of Izmir's Rothschild Hospital written in the 1870s clearly placed it within the longer trajectory of Jewish hospitals extending back to medieval Spain.[124] It always served as a "safe haven,"[125] and its shelter of the poor remained its most celebrated function:

> Thousands of ills, thousands of wounds torment the human body. The doctor runs to treat the rich. And the poor? What becomes of them? When healthy, they suffer from thirst, from the cold and the mud. When sick, what could be their lot? To counter this horrible lot, God created charity. And it is charity that raised up this glorious building, this shelter for the sick and poor, that we proudly call the "Rothschild Hospital."[126]

Because the hospital's traditional role in the community was closely aligned with *Gabbaé Sedaka*'s modern goal of removing poverty from public view, the two organizations maintained a close relationship. In fact, the founder of *Gabbaé Sedaka* was instrumental in securing funds for the construction of a new hospital complex in 1875.[127] As Semtob Pariente reported to the *Alliance* in 1878, "since the formation of *Gabbaé Sedaka*, this institution has served as a hospice for the elderly and the infirm. It is the only Jewish establishment of this type in Turkey."[128]

While the Rothschild Hospital maintained its long-established commitment to the poorest in the community, a new late-nineteenth-century discourse regarding the importance of its endeavors is evident in *Istoria del Ospital Rothschild de Izmir*, the above-mentioned history published by its administrators to celebrate its renovation and reopening in 1875 and later republished in serialized form in *El Novelista*.[129] Much as *Gabbaé Sedaka* had portrayed charity as both an internal communal affair and an instrument of the public good, the history casts the hospital as a boon not only to the Jewish community but to the whole of Izmir. For example, the work declares the identity of the hospital's pre-Rothschild founders immaterial, as "they worked for the good of the city and the love of [their] people."[130] Likewise, those who later solicited the help of the Rothschilds sought what would be "the most just for the city and for our people."[131] In this way, the hospital's traditional sheltering of the sick was reframed as benefiting the whole of Izmir. An even clearer expression of this modern discourse uniting communal and urban concerns is evident in the history's profile of Jacob Ben Gabai, who was among the hospital's most tireless supporters:

> Loving the city of one's birth is a natural sentiment, as the sages have said. Occasionally, there are people of high moral standing who exhibit this sentiment very deeply.... Mr. Jacob Ben Gabai lent both his moral and material support, and every time the hospital was threatened by some issue, he was its first and last defender.[132]

Other influential hospital administrators, such as Isaac Kuri, were labeled "dear friend[s] of the city."[133]

Similar to how Jewish communal leaders framed the activities of *Gabbaé Sedaka*, the Rothschild Hospital, which acquired a potent symbolism as a shelter for the poor, was consistently cast as a metric of the community's progress. Reporting on the positive reaction of a local Ottoman official when he visited the hospital, *La Buena Esperanza* declared that "our hospital greatly honors the Jews of Izmir, and can be considered among the best [institutions] of this kind in our city."[134] This discourse became particularly prominent after 1902, when the Rothschilds relinquished financial stewardship of the hospital to the community, with its very limited resources. Eager to prevent its collapse, *La Buena Esperanza* beseeched its readers to support "this institution that so deeply honors Smyrniot Jews and renders such immense services to the infirm poor."[135] After the community assumed official control of the hospital in 1903, the paper again urged its readers to "show [their] compassion for the poor infirm and [their] sympathy for the hospital,"[136] labeling it a "refuge for humanity."[137]

As the hospital fell victim to increasing financial instability due to the banning of the lottery that had helped sustain it, as well as irregularities in communal subventions,[138] the Ladino press amplified its call for help on behalf of Izmir's poor. In 1907, announcing the annual charity event held on the Jewish spring festival of *Lag ba-Omer* to support the hospital, *El Comersial* appealed to its readers to attend: "It is then our duty to prevent the failure of this philanthropic institution and to demonstrate to [its] devoted administrators that the Smyrniot Jew is always ready to respond generously to every call for help." The paper continued, "when it is a question of the poor, one must not hesitate, one must save them in any way possible."[139]

Brandishing its typical sarcasm, in 1910 the satirical Ladino newspaper *El Soytari, or The Joker*, published an article entitled "*Izmir ermozeado*," or "Beautified Izmir." It celebrated Izmir's dramatic urban transformation, pointing to its electricity, telephones, boulevards, tramway lines, and gardens as proof that the city had made enormous progress "in all that regards civilization."[140] Surveying each of these innovations, the article showcased not the manner in which they improved daily life but rather their inefficiencies, unrealized potential, and even laughable grandiosity. *El Soytari* described electric tramways, for instance, as being run by "half-dead horses," allowing travel to the Punta[141] in less than two hours. Lacking the necessary cranks and speakers, Izmir's telephones were compared to tiny boxes attached with string, while plans for grand new boulevards were lampooned for existing only "in the mind[s] of architects." Completing its tour of Izmir's changed landscape, *El Soytari* concluded sardonically that "civilization is forging ahead like the spear of Pinhas."[142]

"*Izmir ermozeado*" captured the sense of upheaval that likely accompanied the city's rapid reconfiguration as a modern municipality. As this chapter has shown, the heavily impoverished Jewish community navigated this upheaval most intimately not in its technological or infrastructural changes but in its reordering of social norms. Communal elites purposefully recategorized the presence of Jewish poverty on the city's streets, ardently seeking to remove it from public view. They abandoned raucous Purim carnivals and beggars' processions, encouraging their coreligionists to adopt rituals more in step with the culture of the changed landscape. They saw in their communal hospital proof of their commitment to a shared public good. Through all of these efforts to manage poverty and its presence in public, Izmir's Jews understood that they were marking both themselves and their city as modern.

{ CHAPTER 2 }

KUALO ES LA VERA KARIDAD?
WHAT IS TRUE CHARITY?

The Jewish community of Ottoman Izmir was home to a robust and mixed economy of charity. Dozens of associations tended to those in need, among them the *Mohar u-Matan*, which helped provide young poor girls with dowries; the *Rofe Holim* and *Bikkur Holim* societies, tending to the needs of the sick; and the *Malbish Arumim, Bigde Kodesh, Magen David*, and *Oel Moed* societies, all of which helped to clothe the naked. Numerous more associations provided assistance to travelers, impoverished brides and grooms, and women in childbirth, among many others. Alongside these associations were institutions such as Izmir's Jewish hospital and the *Lazareto*, a shelter providing housing for hundreds of destitute families. Additionally, multiple charitable initiatives punctuated the community's annual cycle of religious holidays. The winter festival of Hanukkah saw the celebration of *Shabbat Albasha*, a Sabbath devoted to providing clothing for the students of the *Talmud Tora*.[1] The *kojitas* of Purim helped sustain both individuals and the city's numerous charitable associations, while Passover saw an annual distribution of matza to all those who could not afford it. In addition, both institutions and individuals received charity through the vehicle of *hekdeshim*, or trusts, which paralleled the Islamic *vakif*, or pious endowment. As one visitor to the community would remark in the late nineteenth century, "there is no other city where one lives so calmly and protected by so many associations, all of which see to the good of the poor and the nation in general."[2]

As this chapter demonstrates, starting in the late nineteenth century, this landscape of charitable endeavors underwent significant transformation, as new attitudes to poverty changed how the "good of the poor" was interpreted and addressed. From rationalizing reforms that centralized the collection and distribution of communal charity to new initiatives aiming not to alleviate but to fully eradicate poverty from society, both alms-givers and recipients alike had to learn and navigate a new set of obligations to each other. No less consequential than the impact of this evolving economy of charity on individuals was its impact on the community as a whole, as leaders came to regard it as a crucial metric of its own "progress."

Modern Charity

The beginnings of modern Jewish philanthropy can be traced to the port cities of the early modern western Sephardi diaspora. The circulation of new ideas regarding poverty coupled with a steady influx of Ashkenazi Jews seeking refuge in cities such as Amsterdam led Sephardi Jews to adopt a rationalizing approach to charity and a general "striving for efficiency." For example, the Jews of Bordeaux centralized the distribution of charity through the maintenance of a "poor register" and regularly inspected the neediness of petitioners, while in 1664 the Jews of Amsterdam forbade all private donations of charity to the Ashkenazi poor who had continued to stream into the community.[3]

Similarly, it was a financial threat that led the Ottoman state to reform its *vakifs*, or pious endowments. Functioning as pillars of Islamic charity, the *vakifs* of the Ottoman Empire numbered approximately twenty thousand by the late eighteenth century and generated income equivalent to one-third of the state's total revenues.[4] Yet given the numerous players involved in their establishment, such as founders, managers, and religious authorities, as well as the sheer diversity of their purposes, locations, properties, and beneficiaries, *vakifs* eluded state control for centuries. With the aim of redirecting revenue to increasingly depleted state treasuries, in 1826 Sultan Mahmud II centralized all of the Empire's *vakifs* under the control of the *Evkaf-i Hümayun Nezareti*, or "Ministry of Endowments," requiring that all income be directed first to the state, which would reallocate it as deemed appropriate.[5] Abdülhamid II (r. 1876–1909) would further transform Ottoman charity with the creation of new institutions such as the *Darülaceze*, the empire's first "poorhouse," and the *Hamidiye Etfal Hastahane-i Âlisi*, its first modern hospital for poor and needy children.[6] As has been demonstrated, Abdülhamid II deliberately exploited the symbolism of such modern charitable initiatives to bolster his own sultanic authority and legitimacy and neutralize the political threat he recognized in the increasingly powerful Young Turks.[7]

Like their European Jewish coreligionists as well as their Ottoman governors, the Jews of Izmir transformed their distribution of charity in the hopes of quelling a deeply menacing threat: the shame yielded by the preponderance of Jewish beggars on the streets of Izmir. As we have seen, elites established the *Gabbaé Sedaka* Society in 1878 as a response to this threat, centralizing the flow of communal charity through a new system of monthly subscriptions from alms-givers and weekly disbursements to the poverty-stricken. As the *Alliance* director Semtob Pariente noted in 1879, these measures had "surpassed all expectations," as "all those in the habit of giving rushed to subscribe," secure in the knowledge that their "charity would be used properly."[8]

Just as significant as the association's drive to rid Izmir of Jewish beggars was the way in which, through its activities, *Gabbaé Sedaka* restructured not only charity but the very category of poverty itself. From its earliest days, the association's administrators and supporters insisted that begging had become so prevalent because it manipulated and obscured a crucial distinction: that between "imposters who [beg] as speculation" and "the truly poor."[9] Presenting the achievements of his association to the communal leadership in the fall of 1879, Behor Yomtov Danon highlighted how it had "centralized assistance through contributions made by each wealthy member of the community such that the truly poor receive what they need through our care."[10]

The efforts of *Gabbaé Sedaka* to identify and alleviate the plight of the "truly poor" were certainly not the first expression of a taxonomy of poverty in the Jewish world. In the medieval period, a distinction prevailed between those who could not support themselves, such as widows, orphans, the elderly, and the infirm, and those who had been thrust into poverty as a result of certain circumstances, a phenomenon that modern historians have classified as the difference between "structural" and "conjunctural" poverty.[11] Such a distinction informed medieval Jewish charity as well. As has been demonstrated in the case of medieval Egypt, such a distinction is evidenced by the frequent usage of the term *mastur* in describing petitioners who were "conjuncturally" poor. Meaning "concealed," *mastur* conveyed the sense of shame that a previously self-sufficient petitioner experienced when forced to accept charity.[12] While the distribution of charity in medieval times was an individualized process, documents from the Cairo Geniza collection suggest that it was not only the "structurally" poor who received charity, but the "conjuncturally" poor as well, as many professions appear on alms lists under both "beneficiaries" and "recipients." This suggests that it was not uncommon to be in a state of flux between these two categories, indicating that many self-sufficient people hovered just above a state of poverty.[13]

What, then, did *Gabbaé Sedaka* mean by *los verdaderos povres*, or "the truly poor"? Did this term refer to the traditional distinction between the indigent and the *mastur*? Or was it informed by more modern sensibilities about poverty and its roots? A careful examination of the association's only extant *defter de reklamos*, a rich repository of claims made by the poor over the four-year period from 1879 to 1882, helps reconstruct the answer. Comprised of hundreds of petitions for charitable assistance as well as the decisions made by administrators in each case, the register provides a rare glimpse into the lived experience of poverty and an unmatched point of entry into the mobilization taxonomies of poverty and "deservedness" in the modern Sephardi world.

Unsurprisingly, the register demonstrates that the "structurally" poor were almost always granted assistance, either in the form of a stipend or an allowance of bread. Those who had "fallen" into poverty were also granted assistance. Such was the case of the wife of a Saul Esperanza, whose weekly stipend was increased by two *okkas* of bread to help support her family, as her husband had fallen ill; the case of Raphael Huli, a tinsmith, who was given 29 *kuruş* to help cover the expenses of a new baby; and the case of Raphael Niego, a porter who simply could not make ends meet, who was given 16 *kuruş* for the week.[14]

At the same time, a significant number of "conjunctural" claims were redirected to the *Gemilut Hasadim* Society, the association responsible for tending to the "shamefaced" poor. Such was the case of a Moses Algazi, a tanner who had fallen ill and had been bedridden for a month; an Ashkenazi painter claiming he was "very poor"; a Menahem Halevi of Burnabat, whose family was "dying of hunger"; a Behor Ruso, whose wife and five children were "going hungry"; and a Moses Arditi, who "was ill and bedridden at home" and needed a weekly stipend "to be able to survive." Most reflective of this pattern was the request for a weekly stipend brought on behalf of a maker of sacks. "Given that he has a profession," concluded the administrators, the case would be referred to the *Gemilut Hasadim* Society "so that he might request a loan as he can make a guarantee."[15] Notably, none of these cases were reported by the petitioners themselves, but rather by acquaintances or neighbors, underscoring the continued shame associated with having "fallen" into poverty. Yet such deferments to the *Gemilut Hasadim* Society reflect how for the administrators of *Gabbaé Sedaka*, "true" poverty meant a life of indigence marked by no other possible remedy.

While many shamefaced poor were referred to the *Gemilut Hasadim* Society, *Gabbaé Sedaka* employed a distinctly modern approach, refusing charity to those who were perceived to be able-bodied and finding them work instead.[16] For example, when a seller of secondhand clothes petitioned for assistance, administrators wondered, "why is he not working in selling?"[17] A greengrocer complaining of decreasing demand for his produce was turned away, with administrators deciding that he was "not to be given anything,"[18] while a maker of notebooks was granted assistance only when he was not able to work.[19] When the widow of a Benjamin Shuhami petitioned for support, claiming that she "[had] nobody, was suffering a great deal and lacked the strength to do hard labor," the association first decided that her son could support her, then revised its decision and contended that "she should take up work as a servant."[20] There is some evidence to suggest that even those in a state of "structural" poverty were urged to find support from able-bodied relatives. Such was the case for a widow who, although unable to work herself, was urged "to support herself through her children."[21]

Just as *Gabbaé Sedaka* mobilized new taxonomies of poverty in withholding charity from the able-bodied, so too did it restructure taxonomies of "deservedness." Traditionally, it was not the local poor but foreigners who had to justify their worthiness for inclusion in the local public dole.[22] Such an approach persisted in Ottoman Izmir, as the efforts of the *ve-Aavtem et a-Ger*, or "You Shall Love the Stranger" Society, demonstrate. Founded in

1888 with the goal of "coming to the aid of every foreigner in need," its statutes mandated that such aid be contingent upon a process of examination.[23] In accordance with this directive, the Society petitioned the chief rabbi for help in April 1891, asking that eight families be given matza for Passover. "Having been embarrassed to come and claim matza, those listed below have gone without it until now," the letter stated. "We declare that they are deserving and may justly be given matza."[24]

Given that *Gabbaé Sedaka* had excluded all foreign beggars from its purview from its very inception, the *defter* points here to a significant rupture with traditional forms of distributing charity. Many of the decisions recorded by administrators reflect that native petitioners were also subjected to strict criteria of deservedness. Marking a shift towards rationalization, *Gabbaé Sedaka* dispatched its own administrators to verify both the poverty and the condition of its claimants. After approaching reliable sources such as family members, neighbors, or business associates, administrators reported back to the leadership, making recommendations based on their findings. Referred to as *tomar informasion*, or "collecting information," this process was a key part of *Gabbaé Sedaka's* decision-making.

In the case of the widow of a certain David Morati, administrators deemed it necessary to investigate the profession of her son.[25] The case of a poverty-stricken public crier who was father to twelve children was investigated via his neighbors,[26] while in the case of Abraham Falkon, a greengrocer who had injured his foot, administrators decided to "call upon his son and investigate."[27] As notes recorded by administrators demonstrate, the investigation of claims was not merely a formality but a thorough process of vetting with profound consequences. In deciding the case of another greengrocer who had fallen ill, administrators noted their inclination to provide a remedy as "Senyor Behor Amado has very good information that he is needy."[28] In the case of a widow, administrators contacted multiple sources to investigate her claims, as the first source was reportedly not able to provide "good information."[29] One petitioner, who asked for assistance in supporting four orphaned children, was required to first furnish proof of the money left to them, after which point the case would be reviewed.[30] Perhaps anticipating such investigations, petitioners sometimes brought supporting documentation to help bolster their claims. Such was the case of the wife of one

Abraham Akohen, who brought the signed testimony of four witnesses attesting to her husband's having "become Greek," which had presumably left her bereft of financial support.[31] Both the information gathered and the credibility of its source could yield dramatically different results for petitioners. For example, the case of one petitioner who claimed to be "very poor [and] without food" was ultimately denied due to information gathered from a certain Isaac Dayan, as administrators decided she was "not entitled to receive" assistance.[32] By contrast, information collected regarding the situation of Moses Mizrahi, who claimed he was "very poor," was deemed legitimate and administrators "agreed to grant him" assistance.[33]

While administrators and their supporters frequently touted their new approach as proof of the community's "progress," this "progress" was not a particularly welcome change for those in need. Dismissing mounting complaints from petitioners who had been denied assistance, *La Buena Esperanza* defended the association, insisting that it was "verifying with great care the status of each one so as not to leave them wanting for anything." Concluding that such people had made living on charity "into a profession," the newspaper bemoaned how some were simply "not willing to abandon at any price that detestable business of stretching out one's hand and living on public charity."[34]

Further demonstrating its rationalizing methods, the *Gabbaé Sedaka* Society implemented a range of formalized allowances. Once a claim was accepted as being both within the association's purview and valid, administrators determined the type of allowance to be given, which varied according to its composition and frequency. The most common type of support was the *semanada*, or "weekly" stipend, typically comprised of approximately ten to fifteen *kuruş* and an *okka* or two of bread. An example of a case that successfully qualified for a *semanada* is the wife of a certain Mordekhai Eliezer. Having attacked her with a knife, Eliezer had been imprisoned, leaving her with no "protector." She beseeched *Gabbaé Sedaka* for a *semanada*, and was granted nine *kuruş* a week until her husband was released.[35]

In line with its drive to direct charity only to the most indigent, *Gabbaé Sedaka* showed itself to be conservative in granting *semanadas*, usually opting for less frequent allowances. A man claiming he was no longer able to support his family, as his wife had been bedridden for five years, was denied a weekly stipend and offered an "occasional allowance" instead.[36] Perhaps aware of the potential difficulty of securing a *semanada*, a town crier who argued that he had not made any requests in two months but now found himself very distressed, asked instead for "anything." Administrators in turn agreed to award him an occasional allowance.[37] Perhaps the petition of a certain Isaac Sarfati most clearly demonstrates the complicated nature of securing *semanadas*. A seller of secondhand clothes, Sarfati asked for a loan to enable him to support himself in his profession, promising to relinquish his *semanada* in return. Despite *Gabbaé Sedaka*'s practice of referring requests for loans to the *Gemilut Hasadim* Society, Sarfati's request was granted.[38]

In addition to these weekly and occasional allowances, there were also one-time gifts, or *regalos*, which were commonly awarded to those facing specific and temporary financial hardships. For example, a certain Jacob Habif was granted 1 *mecidiye* (equivalent to twenty *kuruş*) to enable him to buy bread, allowing him to comply with his doctor's orders to consume a more robust diet.[39] Expenses relating to *kazar ija*, or marrying off one's daughter, must have been particularly burdensome, as numerous parents, both mothers and fathers, sought assistance in this regard. For example, the wife of a certain Raphael Shaul was granted a sum of 60 *kuruş* to marry off her daughter,[40] and the widow of a Joseph Kohen was granted five *mecidiyes* for the same purpose.[41] Even requests for such assistance from those capable of earning a livelihood were granted: the wool seller Abraham Halevi, for example, was given 40 *kuruş*.[42]

The decisions rendered by *Gabbaé Sedaka* had additional implications for petitioners that far surpassed the actual charity they received. An official designation of neediness as determined by *Gabbaé Sedaka* served as a public mark of legitimate poverty across the community. In 1899, the association, now functioning as the *Ozer Dalim* Society, printed the names of those it deemed worthy of charity in a public circular. The circular listed 256 people—nearly half of whom were widows, and each of whom represented a family of between six and eight people—along with the monetary allowances they had been granted. The average monetary allowance was approximately nine *kuruş*, while the average amount of bread was just over one *okka*.[43] The same year, the list was used in distributing a lump sum of funds for the poor received from the Central Committee of the *Alliance*,[44] while in

1901, reforms implemented in the levy of the *bedel* tax specifically exempted "the poor recognized by the *Ozer Dalim* Society."[45] Those lacking an official designation from the association were not relieved of the burden.

Upending traditional patterns of giving charity, *Gabbaé Sedaka* sought to centralize its collections across the community through a system of monthly subscriptions known as *mezadas*. Although administrators believed that this method would lend the association financial stability, a budget from its early years demonstrates that subscriptions generated only between ten to twenty percent of its revenue, with the remainder covered by the monthly subsidy received from the Communal Council, gifts from major donors, and special events. During the week of 17 Adar II 5642 (March 8, 1882), *Gabbaé Sedaka* reported that revenue from monthly subscriptions amounted to just eleven percent of its total budget, while revenue from the *kojita de Purim*, or annual Purim charity collection, accounted for more than three times that amount. A week later, revenue from *mezadas* amounted to only seven percent of the total budget, while funds raised through the association's annual Purim soirée represented forty-three percent.[46] Events such as soirées, special holiday collections, and lotteries would continue to supplement the association's revenue for the rest of its history.

Gabbaé Sedaka's adoption of impersonal, private, and bureaucratic methods did not lend it the stability it had envisioned. Its mobilization of new categories of deservedness and new mechanisms such as subscriptions met with an uneven reception across the community. As early as December 1881, administrators complained that *Gabbaé Sedaka* was at risk of failure due to a "lack of members,"[47] and just a few months later, the Communal Council officially dissolved it. Announcing its decision in a public bulletin, the Communal Council recounted how people had resisted paying their subscriptions and rejected the association's determinations of worthiness. Although it had found among its beneficiaries "people who were not needy enough to qualify for an allowance," the Communal Council recognized that suspending their allowances would be seen as *haksızlık*, or "injustice." Concluding that "it is impossible to run this association going forward without the desire and support of the people," the Council, along with the rabbinical establishment, formally ordered people "to go out and collect as they used to" and reminded community members to "give *sedaka* kindly, without showing disgust."[48]

Yet only a year later, the preponderance of Jewish beggars on the streets had once again led a group of notables to reestablish the association, this time under the new name of *Ozer Dalim*. Blaming its prior failure on the reluctance of subscribers, *La Buena Esperanza* embarked on a broader campaign to educate Izmir's Jewish public in the ways of modern charity. "It is clear that *Ozer Dalim* cannot and should not help those young men who, though they work the entire week, learn to eat the bread of laziness and go out to houses and stores," the paper explained, adding that helping such types would be "encouraging the vice of collecting [charity] and contravening [the biblical maxim] 'you shall enjoy the fruit of your labors.'"[49] It also instructed its readers of their new duties, reminding them that "upon seeing these types of people go out to collect [charity], community members should not encourage them, but push those who have not been given anything [by *Ozer Dalim*] to go and work. The *kupa* refuses to give allowances after having examined [their circumstances] and determined that it is not just for them to usurp the right of the poor person."[50]

The awareness that Izmir's Jewish public needed to be instructed and coaxed in the ways of modern charity persisted over the association's long history. In 1899, framing anonymous charity as being compatible with Jewish tradition, administrators reminded the community that "the best charity, that which is most pleasing in the eyes of God, is the charity practiced by our holy association. The hand that gives never sees the hand that receives. This is what is most humane [and] most noble in charity."[51] *La Buena Esperanza* in particular emerged as a staunch advocate for the association, publishing countless articles emphasizing its merits and warning of the dangers if it were absent. A 1903 article claimed that "charity, such as it is practiced today, is but an enticement to laziness," and described how charity had often been misdirected to those working men and women who shamelessly relied on begging to supplement their income for frivolous expenses while "the suffering poor, the truly poor," who only asked for charity with the greatest embarrassment, found themselves ignored.[52] Celebrating the reestablishment (yet again) of the association that year, *La Buena Esperanza* exhorted the Jews of Izmir to pay their subscriptions regularly and to avoid being "indulgent or pious in helping the lazy who ask you for *sedaka*. Some do not want to work, while others want twice as much as what the association determined is fair to give them. If you do not give to them, some will go to work, while the others will be content with what the members of *Ozer Dalim* conscientiously accord them."[53]

Yet the tendency to give charity to any and all beggars on the street, regardless of the vetting of *Ozer Dalim*, persisted. In 1913, the association printed a public announcement in *El Pregonero* expressing regret at the public's continued willingness to give charity to beggars on the street. "We ask the public," wrote the administrators, "to turn a deaf ear to these false beggars" and report them, so that appropriate measures could be taken.[54] As *La Buena Esperanza* had previously advised, "the only answer you should give, and that you must always give, is: Go to the Association!"[55]

For all the enthusiasm of its administrators, the association was haunted by marked financial instability, as it was dissolved and reconstituted five times between 1878 and 1903. *La Buena Esperanza* in particular promoted the narrative that the association's troubles were the result of indifference on the part of its subscribers, castigating them for going "entire years"[56] without honoring their subscriptions and "trying to speculate with the *sedaka* they used to give to the poor."[57] Yet the more likely cause was the reality that many subscribers probably hovered just above a state of poverty themselves. In addition, as the 1898 circular points out, in a short span of four years the number of families supported by the association had ballooned from 100 to 280, an increase of 180%, while the number of subscribers had stayed flat.[58]

The association's fragility led some to question its methods. Amid preparations to reestablish the association in 1888, *La Buena Esperanza* cautioned against reliance on voluntary subscriptions, recommending the use of traditional sources of revenue such as the *gabela* tax on kosher meat instead.[59] The Communal Council promptly rejected this proposal, likely due to the constant controversy stoked by the regressive tax. Yet it did implement other measures to incentivize payment of dues, and it declared certain communal services, such as circumcisions, contingent upon having no debts to *Ozer Dalim*.[60] In the wake of the association's fourth failure, in 1893, the Communal Council again debated earmarking tax revenue from the sale of matza and *ketubbot*, as well as prohibiting charity collections by other associations.[61]

This financial instability also led *Ozer Dalim* to rethink its ambitious mission. At least twice, the association weighed limiting allowances to only the structurally poor, such as the infirm and the elderly as well as women.[62] Yet the increasing number of Izmir's Jewish poor in the late Ottoman period made such solutions impracticable. Limiting allowances would not only prevent *Ozer Dalim* from removing every Jewish beggar from the streets,[63] but would also betray the long tradition of communal charity that was the hallmark of the *kehillah*. As administrators noted in 1898, "the idea of helping only the elderly and infirm could not be maintained for long. The poor struggled to support their children and make a living, and unfortunately the doors of *Ozer Dalim* needed to open monthly, weekly, and even daily to a greater number of them. Heads of households, widows supporting children, orphans with no father or mother, all asked for help, even a piece of bread. How could we ignore such a cry?"[64]

The struggles *Ozer Dalim* faced in staying afloat should not obscure nor diminish its profound historical significance. Despite its numerous dissolutions and reconstitutions, the association remained a firm part of the communal landscape, either concretely through its activities or symbolically through the pronounced anxiety and shame expressed in its absence. Against the backdrop of an increasingly impoverished community, the comprehensive restructuring of charity as envisioned by the cadre of "enlightened" administrators of *Ozer Dalim* stands as a critical metric for how Izmir's Jews negotiated the demands of the modern age. Continuously celebrated as a source of honor and pride unique in the Ottoman Jewish world, the existence of *Ozer Dalim* proved that the Jews of Izmir could not only remove its poverty from public view, but also reshape larger values and mores undergirding charity for both its givers and recipients alike. As communal administrators noted in 1912, "*Ozer Dalim* is a source of such honor [and] does its duty with justice and order" through "help[ing] the deserving poor."[65]

Rationalization

The modern principles prizing order and rationality not only animated new associations such as *Ozer Dalim* but transformed long-standing institutions as well. As early as the 1880s, frustration had surfaced over the preponderance of *kojitas*, or "collections," whereby representatives from numerous charities approached shops, homes, and private family celebrations asking for donations.⁶⁶ In a manner similar to the distaste that came to characterize public opinion of begging, people not only found that the ever-expanding number of charities and causes was disruptive and a "bother," but also believed that they deprived the "truly" needy of charity. In 1885, responding to mounting complaints, the rabbinic establishment took the drastic step of banning *kojitas* on Purim, though they had been a centerpiece of the traditional observance of the holiday. While the typical community member wanted to "fulfill the obligation of sitting in his doorway and giving charity to the poor, each according to his ability, the arrival of twenty associations leaves the head of the household embarrassed and leads him to close his door." Ruling that "no administration nor any association, whether small or big, may go out on Purim as is the custom," the rabbis hoped to protect the "true poor person," as they feared that "gradually, he will not find any open doors."⁶⁷ Echoing a similar sentiment, in 1893 *La Buena Esperanza* complained that the "disturbances" of collections by the most minor and even unheard-of groups at private celebrations would one day force people to "reject even those collections of charities whose mission is beneficial and humane." The paper called on the Communal Council to ban such collections, even if it required the help of local police.⁶⁸

The Communal Council did try to address the problem. Communal statutes drafted in 1884 called for the creation of three separate commissions to address the various needs of the poor; these were merged and formalized as the "charity commission" in 1897, when the statues were approved.⁶⁹ Reflecting the rationalizing spirit that characterized modern Jewish philanthropy, the internal statutes of the new commission defined its role as the "control and inspection of all charitable associations and institutions," the "dissolution of those whose revenues only anger the public and whose charity is of little importance," and the "merging of associations that work for the same goal." Further underscoring the responsibility of charitable institutions towards the public that sustained them, the statutes required that they present their budgets for approval on an annual basis and declared their official "recognition" dependent on the "authorization" and "approval" of the Communal Council.⁷⁰

Yet the *kojitas* seem to have continued unabated. In 1908, complaints about the burdens of ever-increasing *kojitas* surfaced again, with one reader of *El Comercial* noting that "as long as there is no label to distinguish between the real and the fake, I will not give a cent. I hope that everyone does the same, so that the matter can be better ordered."[71] Yet another denounced the ever-growing number of subscriptions: "In the name of 'human solidarity' they make the public suffer," the letter said, denouncing them as "charity by force."[72] Demonstrating the ongoing limitations of reforms in changing the reality on the ground, a few weeks later the Council again reminded the public to refrain from supporting the collections of any association beyond the five that it had formally recognized.[73]

While the impact of such reforms remained weak, they did play a part in constructing a new ideal of communal charity based on public accountability and transparency, an ideal that the Ladino press in particular helped disseminate. In 1905, both *El Novelista* and *El Meseret* demanded an investigation into the finances of *Ozer Dalim*,[74] which later revealed "certain financial and administrative irregularities."[75] To earn trust, *Ozer Dalim* soon began to make its budgets public, printing them in both *La Buena Esperanza* and *El Comercial*.[76] *El Novelista* remained particularly active in pressing for accountability across the community's charities. In 1907, the paper declared that "no one knows anything about their management, the type of charity they do, or to what they devote their revenues. One does not know who its members might be, who chooses them, who authorizes them to spend public funds with no supervision or accountability . . . each operates according to its own preferences."[77] Calling for the rationalization not only of charities but of the entire communal administration, the newspaper argued that "all of the friends of the poor would return to take care of them with ardor, as they have in the past."[78] In 1908, *El Novelista* published a series of articles under the headline "Why *Ozer Dalim* Is Not Making Progress." Penned by a former administrator who had recently resigned, the series opened with a criticism of nearly every aspect of the association's functioning, from its oversight of the budget, through its record keeping, down to the bread it sourced. Writing under the pseudonym David Arditi, the author expressed an urgency in making his case, speaking as someone "who knows the pain and suffering of honest people in earning a living." "They cannot be left to walk in the darkness," Arditi argued, insisting that they "know how the association they support is run."[79]

While the complete reconfiguration of charity for both beneficiaries and donors was almost universally seen as essential to the community's overall progress, it did not go entirely uncriticized. In 1910, the satirical newspaper *El Soytari* published an article announcing that in a break with tradition, the Communal Council would no longer distribute matza to all of the needy but only to those registered with *Ozer Dalim*. Mockingly emphasizing the suffering not of the poor but of overburdened donors, the article decried how taking bread out of one's own mouth for "any and every so-called needy person" would make beggars of the whole community. Passover especially offered a "pretext" for such impostors "to become brazen and give the appearance of a needy person" and take advantage of communal generosity. Sadly, the "nuisance" caused by matza distribution had put communal administrators in terrible straits, making them the targets of the "insults and threats of any and every vagabond who had been refused matza for the second and third times." Accusing the poor of selling their matza for a profit, the article recommended suspending the distribution indefinitely, advising the poor to either eat rice and potatoes or mill wheat, grind it into flour, and make matza on their own. Poking fun at both the modern equation of poverty with laziness and the reverence for self-sufficiency, the article concluded:

> This is what the Jews did when they left Egypt. They did not approach the Communal Council or anyone else, but made small fires and baked the *yovkas* dough like the Turkish nomads do. Do this yourselves and free yourselves from the Communal Council, pull yourselves out of this agonizing poverty that you got yourselves into with your own hands to be able to qualify for free matza. Work, exert yourselves, help yourselves, by yourselves, for yourselves, and you will see that the heavens will help you.[80]

Eliminating Poverty

Alongside efforts to rationalize the collection and distribution of charity, there emerged a complete reenvisioning of the very purpose of charity. Breaking with the traditional presumption that the poor were an essential part of the social landscape, communal leaders began to experiment with a range of strategies aimed at stamping poverty out completely. In searching for its root causes and debating how best to address them, they operated under the prevailing assumption that the community's endemic poverty was subverting its potential for "progress."

Chief among the solutions elites proffered was the introduction of vocational training. By the mid-nineteenth century, productivization had emerged as an important step in the larger project of "regeneration" that accompanied the emancipation of western and central European Jewries. The push for "occupational restructuring" in the Jewish world intersected with post-Enlightenment ideologies that emphasized the importance of utility to the state and the moralizing and ethical impact of work on the individual.[81] European *maskilim* promoted a broad range of productivization strategies that varied according to the economic position of their Jewish communities, with the poor being prodded especially towards artisanship, crafts, and agriculture.[82] In France, for example, by the mid-nineteenth century, Jewish philanthropists had established numerous apprenticeship programs and vocational schools in places such as Paris, Strasbourg, and Mulhouse.[83] The assumption that Jewish communities required such restructuring also shaped the efforts of French Jewish philanthropists in the East, as *Alliance* administrators and supporters found in productivization a powerful antidote to the "stagnation" they sought to combat.[84] By the early twentieth century, Izmir, Istanbul, and Edirne were all home to *Alliance*-sponsored apprenticeship programs for boys and workshops for girls.[85]

Ottoman Jews saw the state implement similar initiatives for all of its subjects. Between 1862 and 1899, the state established over thirty *islahhanes*, or orphanages for vagrant and destitute children (literally "houses of reform"). *Islahhanes* provided orphans and poverty-stricken children in cities across the empire with sustained and intensive vocational training, intended to create a new generation of skilled Ottoman workers who would be saved from a life of begging while reinvigorating the Ottoman economy and boosting its urban manufacturing.[86]

Among Izmir's Jews, debates over vocational training centered on the *Talmud Tora*, a community school where poor children were given a religious education according to traditional methods. In addition to schooling, the *Talmud Tora* also provided its students with food and clothing; for orphans, it also provided housing. Its teachers were often poverty-stricken themselves, and were given room and board at the school in exchange for their work. A pillar of the community, the school enjoyed a hallowed status. As *El Novelista* would comment, "for the Smyrniot, the most holy and beloved institution is the *Talmud Tora*."[87]

By the 1870s, however, the *Talmud Tora* was in dire shape, with approximately three hundred and fifty students under the care of only eight teachers. So poverty-stricken were the children that many families reportedly sold the clothes they received from the school in order to be able to feed them.[88] According to the *Alliance* administrator David Cazès, those who had clothing were "very poorly dressed, in rags, and one only rarely sees socks on their feet. While some wear shoes, others cannot afford this luxury and simply go barefoot."[89] The situation worsened over the following years, as the increasing numbers of students, which soared to six hundred in 1886, exacerbated the school's poor hygienic conditions.[90] In 1880, calling the school's state "deplorable," its director Haim Amado wrote that students of the *Talmud Tora* were "languish[ing] in ignorance, crammed haphazardly into infected, humid and lowly rooms without serious supervision."[91]

The nineteenth century saw continued critiques of the school's deteriorating sanitary conditions and overcrowding. However, it was the notion that the *Talmud Tora* was doing more to perpetuate poverty than eliminate it that most worried locals and Western observers alike. In 1873, David Cazès remarked that upon their exit from the school at fourteen years of age, children were "abandoned to their own devices with no support or guide, becom[ing] beggars, thieves, or even worse."[92] The school's director later noted that children left the school "just as ignorant as when they entered, in possession not of a primary education that would pull them out of difficulties over the course of their lives, but rather vices that will have a disastrous effect on their future."[93] Narrating the history of the institution in 1906, *El Novelista* recalled how truancy was the order of the day, with students typically ending up as shoe shiners.[94]

As early as the 1860s, the association that administered the *Talmud Tora*, known as *Mahzikei Ani'im*, or "Sustainers of the Poor," had attempted to establish a vocational school for its students.[95] The association saw in the arrival of the *Alliance* in 1873 the potential for a powerful ally in bringing such a project to fruition. In 1875, *Mahzikei Ani'im* urged Cazès not only to reform the school's religious curriculum but to "ensure the livelihood of the

FIGURE 4. Façade Principale du Talmud Thora, Smyrne [nd].
Source: Photothèque de l'Alliance israélite universelle (Paris).

poor children of the *Talmud Tora* by opening an establishment for learning trades."[96] Cazès, who had previously founded a successful vocational training program in the Jewish community of Volos,[97] was initially amenable to such involvement and reported that local leaders were "fairly willing to accept the joining of the *Talmud Tora* to our school."[98] *Mahzikei Ani'im* also planned to enroll Jewish students in a new government-run vocational school once it opened, provided that kosher food could be secured for them.[99]

The administrators of *Mahzikei Ani'im* understood that their vision of charity was a new one that would have to be explained and justified to Izmir's Jewish public. In the summer of 1875, the association organized a major celebration for the *Talmud Tora*, which was covered in detail in a special supplement to *La Esperanza*. The event was attended by numerous rabbis, among them Chief Rabbi Abraham Palacci, and featured speeches in Hebrew emphasizing the importance of religious education. Following these remarks, the program shifted to "the question of trades."[100] Two orphaned students of the *Talmud Tora*, named Simon and Levi, then recited a Ladino poem in the style of Sephardi *coplas* meant to instruct the audience in the mutually reinforcing nature of Torah study and learning a profession. Levi began, reciting, "My brother, with my little knowledge I have understood / and with the little Torah that I have studied, I understand what is obligated and what is to be avoided," and concludes, "keep me far from evil and such indignities / I must first learn well and [only] later move on to a trade." Eager to correct him, his classmate Simon explained how such an understanding was not just misguided but even sacrilegious:

> My brother, my brother! You blaspheme!
> You have saddened my soul
> The right thing to want to do
> is learn the Law and soon have a trade.
>
> A trade helps a man support himself with honor
> A calm soul praises his Creator.
> He praises and sings with much joy
> That he supports his family by the work of his own hands.

> We want to eat by the work of our own hands
> We want nothing to do with begging for charity
> We want to support ourselves through work
> We put all of our hope in this.
>
> We want honorable trades to be our portion
> For all of the work that you have dedicated to us
> If your wishes come to fruition
> It is the poor and the orphaned who will benefit.

Turning to the audience for help, Levi explained, "our directors want to do this / yet they have not the money they need. They await the help of our brethren / So they might see us work in their lifetime."[101] Visibly moved, the audience reportedly held "handkerchiefs in their hands to wipe away the tears that flowed from their eyes."[102]

In reproducing the poem for its readers, *La Esperanza* sought to instruct Izmir's Jewish public in this new type of charity, declaring *Mahzikei Ani'im* worthy of praise for "recognizing that one of their first obligations to the poor and orphaned students of the *Talmud Tora* is to teach them a trade so they can support themselves with honor and will not be forced to ask for charity."[103] The charity demanded of Izmir's Jews thus shifted its moral benefit from the giver, where it had long resided, to the receiver. Labeling it "a humane endeavor,"[104] *La Esperanza* made clear that when successful, such charity would eventually render itself obsolete.

Similar efforts to demonstrate the compatibility of the modern impulse to remove poverty from society with Jewish tradition continued as *Mahzikei Ani'im* sought to reform the *Talmud Tora*. One observer noted that "our sages of the Mishnah said and advised—'fitting is learning in Torah along with a craft,' [and] 'if there is no sustenance, there is no Torah learning.'" Where, then, is the sustenance and the craft of these children?"[105] *La Buena Esperanza* also marshaled traditional sources to bolster arguments in favor of vocational training, reminding its readers of the Mishnaic principle that "all learning of Torah which is not joined with labor is destined to be null and cause sin."[106]

Mahzikei Ani'im did manage to introduce some reforms to the *Talmud Tora*, such as the addition of Turkish language instruction, which it deemed "very necessary in the present century."[107] Yet overall, the gains it made in bringing vocational training to the students of the *Talmud Tora* were modest. While *Mahzikei Ani'im* had welcomed the *Alliance* as a potential partner in reshaping the *Talmud Tora, Alliance* administrators preferred to operate independently, prioritizing their own schools and programs. Some advances were made in 1892, when the *Gemilut Hasadim* Society announced that it would shift its mission from helping "fallen families" to "the praiseworthy goal of teaching trades to the orphaned and the son of the poor man."[108] Approaching the *Alliance* for help, *Gemilut Hasadim* proposed the merging of the two institutions' vocational programs. Although Gabriel Arié of the *Alliance* refused to cooperate outright, he did arrange for a yearly pledge of five hundred francs to help sponsor the program.[109] By 1895, *Gemilut Hasadim* had seen some incremental progress and had managed to sponsor the training of eight apprentices at the *Talmud Tora*.[110]

Vocational training efforts at the *Talmud Tora* saw some improvement after the *Alliance* assumed direct control of the school in 1898,[111] increasing the number of apprentices from eight in 1895 to forty in 1901.[112] That year, Arié reported that the program was operating according to plan and, reaffirming his earlier reluctance to work with local leaders, relayed to his supervisors in Paris that "the community has nothing to do with it; [the program] is run under my supervision by a distinct committee."[113] While the institution was confronted with major challenges, among them the financing and construction of a new building that was finally inaugurated in 1908, vocational training remained firmly on the agenda. In 1909, administrators appointed a commission to study the issue, which affirmed "the importance of the goal" and the need "to do everything to advance this endeavor."[114] In appealing to the chief rabbi of the empire for financial assistance later that year, leaders described the school as a safe haven for five hundred poor and orphaned students who received a "serious" religious education alongside instruction in the "language of the country, French, and then a manual trade that will enable them to earn a living with honor."[115]

Ultimately, the *Talmud Tora* did not emerge as the training ground for self-sufficient artisans that so many leaders had envisioned. Nonetheless, the new meanings invested in the role and purpose of this traditional institution reflect the socioeconomic dimensions of the community's modern

FIGURE 5. Photo of Students and Teachers, Talmud Tora, 1900s. Source: CAHJP, Tr/Iz. 819, Central Archives for the History of the Jewish People, Jerusalem.

transformations. A reformed *Talmud Tora* in Izmir was reenvisioned not as an institution devoted to harmonizing secular and religious knowledge but primarily as a trade school that might remake the socioeconomic structure of the community as a whole. As *El Novelista* appealed to its readers in 1905:

> Give to the *Talmud Tora*! Give to the trades initiative of this institution, and then there will be no need for the *Ozer Dalim*. Let us educate men who understand their duty to work to avoid being the charge of others. Let us educate workers who can support their children. It is in this way that we will uplift the economic status of our community ... it is with instruction that misery will end.[116]

Alliance Productivization

More successful were the apprenticeship programs run directly through the *Alliance*, which, as an institution, commanded much more authority and financial support than did the *Talmud Tora*. By 1876, the *Alliance* had

FIGURE 6. Le bâtiment de l'école de garçons, Smyrne 1910.
Source: Photothèque de l'Alliance israélite universelle (Paris).

managed to place six of its students in Izmir's *islahhane*,[117] and two years later it had drawn up plans for its own vocational training program in a building already belonging to its school. In a dedicated space consisting of three workshops and a studio, the *Alliance* planned to train at least twenty students in cobbling, carpentry, and tailoring, and the school received a substantial loan from *Mahzikei Ani'im* in support of the endeavor.[118] In 1884, the *Alliance* established a workshop for young girls, training them in laundering and ironing.[119] In the following years, the girls' program was expanded, with the addition of training in the cutting and making of dresses and coats, sewing, embroidery, and the manufacture of various laces.[120]

By the 1890s, vocational training at the *Alliance* school had made significant strides. In 1895, Gabrie Arié proudly reported that "two hundred poor families no longer beg for charity; they are supported by young workers who were our apprentices,"[121] and concluded that "from both a humanitarian and a practical point of view, in the Orient our apprenticeship programs are more useful than our schools."[122] In 1897, Arié reported that the *Alliance* had so far sponsored the training of a total of two hundred and thirty-five apprentices in forty-two different trades, the most popular being carpentry, cobbling, tailoring, metalworking, and blacksmithing.[123] Although only one hundred and three of these apprentices remained in their positions for the long term,[124] Arié remained hopeful, arguing that the moralizing influence of working with one's hands was far more important than the trade itself. The Jews of Izmir had finally come to appreciate the "nobility of manual labor," as Arié claimed that placement in an apprenticeship had become the "dream" of four-fifths of the *Alliance*'s students.[125] "The Jews of the Orient—of Izmir especially," Arié noted in 1897, were "ready to embrace manual work with ardor."[126]

Yet, as with the *Talmud Tora*'s plans, Arié's grand hopes for the Jews of Izmir were never fully realized. As happened in numerous other Ottoman Jewish communities, the *Alliance* ultimately failed to create the artisanal class that it had regarded as essential to the "regeneration" of Eastern Jewry.[127] Multiple historical factors relating both to the empire as a whole and to its Jewish communities in particular combined to undermine the success of such projects. The pronounced economic instability of the Ottoman Empire, coupled with the persistence of an ethnically fractured marketplace, made it difficult for newly trained Jewish apprentices to penetrate the market.[128] These fracture lines were particularly salient in Izmir, where so many sectors of the city's commerce were dominated by Greeks. Compounding these unfavorable economic circumstances was the lack of a strong artisanal tradition among Ottoman Sephardim, which led Jewish students and parents alike to question the ultimate benefit of pursuing such trades. Productivization efforts had but a meager impact on the larger socioeconomic status of the Jews of Izmir, as the overwhelming majority of the community remained in petty trade.[129]

Commercial Education

Given the position of Izmir in the Ottoman economy, more prudent strategies for restructuring the economic profile of the city's Jews were based not in artisanship nor agriculture but in commerce. As we have seen, by the late nineteenth century, Izmir dominated the trade of the entire western Anatolian region, with its robust connections to world markets making its economic prowess in the Ottoman Empire virtually unmatched.[130] Describing the consummate Izmirli and his position in the global economy in 1914,

El Meseret observed that "the Izmirli works with capital; the Anatolian works with his hands."[131]

Although many of Izmir's Jews did indeed "work with capital," they largely did so as street hawkers, petty tradesmen, and peddlers and were thus alienated from the larger-scale markets of the port. As *La Buena Esperanza* put it, "all of us know that the social and economic position of the Jews of Izmir is totally unsatisfactory," noting how the lack of Jewish commercial and industrial establishments meant that with "very few exceptions, the Jew of Izmir struggles, suffers, and too much."[132] For some, it was this disjuncture between Izmir's commercial prowess and the diminished status of its Jewish population that needed to be targeted most urgently in addressing the root causes of Jewish poverty. A lawyer named Albert Tarica, who had received his training in France, was particularly active in elevating the issue into a broad communal concern. In 1903, he delivered a sweeping lecture to the *Alliance* alumni association on the history and importance of commerce, declaring that "nothing could be more relevant right now." Surveying commerce from its very origins up to his day, Tarica explained how the exchange of goods and services evolved into a complex and elaborate system based on the instruments of capital, credit, and banks and impressed upon the audience how "commerce develops with the progress of humanity."[133] Tarica made the case not only for the connection of commerce to "civilization" but for its impact on individuals, as its principles reinforced the virtues of hard work and economy in one's personal finances. Emphasizing the importance of commercial education for Izmir's Jewish youth, Tarica offered free courses in political economy as well as others that would "contribute to the development of commerce and the wealth of nations."[134]

The notion that Izmir's Jews were in desperate need of such an education inspired Tarica to publish *El Komersio* the next year, at once a sweeping history of commerce and a contemporary how-to manual. "Many of our coreligionists are ignorant of the ABCs of commerce, even while practicing it," noted Tarica, a lamentable fact that "frequently causes them to be deceived and harmed." Tarica promised his readers full instruction in all of the economic and legal complexities of modern commerce, making every effort to "be as clear as possible and to introduce concepts without using many technical terms." *El Komersio* is divided into three separate sections, the first of which provides a comprehensive overview of the mechanics of commerce, covering topics such as buying and selling, brokerage, commissions, stock exchanges, methods of transport, insurance, and customs. The second section, entitled "Commercial Instruments," discusses different types of currency, credit and exchange, banks, bills of exchange, promissory notes, and checks, while the third, entitled "Companies," explains the mechanics of corporations, partnerships, and trademarks. Speaking directly to the Jews of Izmir, Tarica includes valuable information about the workings of their port in particular, explaining the movement of goods through its quays, its specific customs duties, and the rules governing its stock exchange.[135]

Reflecting the desire that his work be "useful and indispensable to all, and above all, to the Jewish merchants of the entire Orient," Tarica deliberately explains commercial transactions using scenarios that would be familiar to his readers. In discussing how to draw up a bill of exchange, for example, Tarica writes:

> How does one negotiate a bill of exchange? To negotiate a bill of exchange means to sell the bill. Paul of Izmir draws up a bill of exchange for Simon (let us mix foreign and Hebrew names, since commerce is international), of Constantinople, for the benefit of Reuben. Does Reuben need to show up himself to collect on it? This would nullify the utility of the bill of exchange. But no! Reuben can collect these funds very easily without leaving Izmir. He can approach a person who is going to Constantinople and sell it to him, while of course giving him a profit. This profit will consist of interest and a small commission.[136]

The text abounds with other such examples, as Tarica seeks to make Izmir's commerce legible for its Jews.

Others shared Tarica's call for a reinvigoration of Jewish commerce. In 1907, the Ladino press reported on efforts by the local business leader Haim Polako and others to develop a Jewish commercial association. This association, which the press simply called "the project," would help reintroduce Izmir's Jews into the city's robust commercial life and was touted as the only initiative that would truly "serve the moral and material uplifting of all of our coreligionists."[137] The full details were announced in June of that year. "Unfortunately, the economic and social situation of the Jews of Izmir is not brilliant," the founders lamented, noting that only a very meager number of Jews occupied notable positions in the world of business. The reason for this, they claimed, was quite simple: Jews lacked "means, funds, capital." The answer was therefore simple: the Jews of Izmir needed to band together to pool intellectual and financial resources. Only collective action would enable Izmir's Jews to "progress in the struggle for life."[138]

To make it possible to accomplish these lofty goals, the organizers provided a detailed blueprint. The Jews of Izmir would form a wide-ranging corporation, the accumulated capital of which would support "the advancement of all Jews at all levels of commerce, finance, and industry." Crucially, its organizers sought the broadest reach possible for the corporation and structured its mechanisms in service of this principle. They deliberately dispensed with requiring down payments, which would have worked against the corporation's primary goal of serving "the masses of the public, and especially the poor." Shares, priced at 45 Turkish *liras* each, would be amortized over the course of nine years, meaning that weekly payments would come to between five and eight *metalikas*.[139] "There is no doubt," they wrote, "that this modest sum is within the reach of all classes: old and young, merchants and employees, the rich, the middle class, and even workers and girls in service."[140]

Most prominently addressing the needs of aspiring entrepreneurs, the corporation would provide essential banking services such as loans and advances and would also boast a physical headquarters where young people could rent desks, establish offices, consult with advisors, and cultivate the essential connections that help solidify partnerships. At the same time, the corporation was not just envisioned as a resource for entrepreneurs. Parents could buy shares and ensure their financial security upon the marriage of their children. Widows and orphans could invest their small savings and benefit from the interest. Instead of wasting their income on "useless things," young working girls could invest in the association to establish stable dowries for themselves. Even those who could not afford shares could derive some benefit, as they could set up savings accounts with as little as five *kuruş*. Craftsmen and manual laborers could rely on the association for small loans, while even "great capitalists" could benefit from investing their wealth in the corporation, where it would be "better placed and managed." "We can say," the corporation's initiators stated, "without fear of exaggeration, that this can remedy today's situation. It can enable us to take giant steps in the path of progress, and it can help us procure the means necessary to securing vital positions in the great commercial and financial center of Izmir."[141]

Distinguishing itself from other attempts to combat poverty in Jewish Izmir, this project demonstrates a keen awareness of what truly effective "productivization" might have looked like locally. Instead of training would-be cobblers, tailors, and farmers, the initiative was based on a deep knowledge of the pulse of the city and its economic horizons and an intimate and realistic understanding of the stumbling blocks to upward social mobility that Izmir's Jewish poor encountered daily. Speaking to the plight of an aspiring textile merchant, the organizers reflected, "how can you fulfill the order of your partner in London or Marseille when you do not have the money or necessary credit to be able to buy the clothing they order?" Reflecting the struggles faced by employers and their female employees alike, the project founders wondered "who has not seen those painful moments that so many employers experience when their servant girls get married and they owe them many weekly and even yearly payments?" Organizers were equally sensitive to the difficulty "working people, peddlers, artisans, and active, honest, and hardworking people" typically faced in securing loans for lack of a "solid guarantee or collateral," as well as the struggles many others faced in saving any money at all. Promising to see to all of these typical situations, and many more, the administrators found in their innovation a solution uniquely suited to the needs of a community that had been failed by past efforts:

> Until now, we have not reflected upon the ever-increasing demands of modern civilization, nor have we done anything for our own advancement; we never think of our destiny or our future. The time has come to wake up and to see to our destiny and future with great ardor. Let us join hands, pool our strength and our capital and strive together for the same ideal—the moral and material uplifting of us all.[142]

While it does not seem that this "grandiose project" ever evolved beyond the initial planning phase, there is evidence to suggest that it sought to institutionalize new patterns in communal life that were already emerging. In March 1907, for example, *El Comercial* reported the foundation of two new Jewish commercial ventures—a bank, "Franko, Yisrael, Alaluf i Komp.," and a manufacturing house called "Tarica, Yisrael, Franko i Komp." Urging investment in each, the paper reminded its readers of the "absolute need to join forces to succeed in the struggle for life."[143] In July 1907, the owners of Lahana i Shuhami i Komp., sellers of both ready-to-wear and custom clothing, reported their company's transformation into a public venture, urging people to buy shares,[144] while in December of that year, the entrepreneurs Nissim Yisashar and Jak Algrante formed a new company dealing in commission, representation, and consignment.[145] Perhaps the clearest reflection of how these new ventures sought to improve the status not only of their individual investors, but of the whole community, can be seen in the August 1908 foundation of Jacob Ninyo and Company, an outfit dealing in the manufacture of socks, clothing, textiles, and perfume. Urging people to buy shares, Ninyo wrote, "Sirs, you have grown tired of handing your money over to lotteries. You have seen how, short of a miracle, no one has gotten rich or even made two *paras*. But here [with a share in the company], you can save twenty or thirty liras without even realizing it. Don't close your doors ... now is the time to invest so that both we and our country can progress."[146]

Against the backdrop of the fourth failure of the *Ozer Dalim* Society in 1903, *La Buena Esperanza* published a multi-article series entitled "*Kualo es la vera karidad*?" or "What is True Charity?" The newspaper embarked on an impassioned educational campaign to instruct its readers in the goals of true charity, among them the "taking in of its poor" and the "fortification of its institutions."[147] Most revealingly, however, *La Buena Esperanza* defined "true" charity as all that which permits a community "to continue its journey on the path of progress."[148] As this chapter has demonstrated, such was the animating principle behind a complete reenvisioning of Jewish charity in Izmir, from its collection through its distribution to its larger purpose. Modern charity, as envisioned by the administrators of *Ozer Dalim* and their supporters, required not only the removal of Izmir's Jewish poor from the streets but their vetting and insertion in a broader apparatus of verification and classification rooted in new conceptions of "deservedness." Breaking with centuries of tradition, communal leaders proffered numerous strategies for "productivizing" Izmir's Jewish poor, from vocational training to education in the basics of commerce. As these varied initiatives demonstrate, at stake for the community was not only removing Jewish poverty from the city's streets but also its ability to control, solve, and ultimately eliminate a new and pernicious social "crisis" that had only recently been created.

(CHAPTER 3)

"MAKE A *MONSIEUR* OUT OF HIM!"

A boy has barely finished school with a modest accumulation of knowledge and his parents have but one wish: Make a *monsieur* out of him! Finding him a job as a writer or an agent is an almost impossible proposition. What becomes of this young man? If some succeed, how many others find only a wall in their future, and miserable prospects, while yet others [see] mediocrity for all of their lives? What can you expect from a people made of employees? If some of them barely manage to clothe themselves—oh the irony! they need to dress well—what help can they possibly offer the community?

Such was one answer submitted to a 1905 essay contest sponsored by *La Buena Esperanza* asking readers to explain Izmir's Jewish community's "economic decadence." Locating the root of the problem in the increasingly commonplace desire among Izmir's Jews to make "*müsyö[s]*" out of their sons, A. Kuriel blamed the *Alliance* in particular for having encouraged them to pursue liberal professions instead of more practical and "lucrative" ones. Given the difficulty of finding employment for such students upon completing their education, Kuriel argued that instead of facilitating upward social mobility, the *Alliance* had instead "increased the number of *déclassés* among us."[1]

Kuriel was right that the upward social mobility so central to the *Alliance* program was largely unattainable for most of Izmir's aspiring Jewish *monsieurs*. The realities of economic life in late Ottoman Izmir made the "liberal professions" that were encouraged by an *Alliance* education particularly ill-suited to the mission of "productivization" it sought to bring to the Jews of the East. The pulse of Izmir's economy was rooted in its robust commercial activity, and it was notably Izmir's Greeks, of both Hellenic and Ottoman extraction, who predominated across all sectors of the port's commerce, from trade to shipping to banking.² The proliferation of ethnic segmentation in the marketplace made it difficult for Jews to exit petty trade and unskilled labor, fields where they been clustered since the early eighteenth century.

Given that access to bourgeois culture demanded in part "a secure economic status, well beyond the subsistence minimum: means, space, and time,"³ for most of Izmir's Jews the prospect of becoming a *"müsyö"* was out of reach. Yet, as this chapter demonstrates, for a small upper crust, this new cultural ideal was attainable and was expressed through a range of new patterns of residence, socialization, associational life, and leisure. Reported on and encouraged by the reformist editors of Izmir's Ladino press, these practices were also undergirded by a changing discourse of gender, as Izmir's Jewish women in particular negotiated a host of new expectations governing their lives in both public and private. Notably, unlike their coreligionists elsewhere, Izmir's Jewish bourgeois often saw increased social mixing with their non-Jewish neighbors, pointing to the ascendancy of class over forms of religious and ethnic belonging in a late Ottoman port city.

Looking beyond this upper crust, this chapter will reconstruct the very fraught nature of embourgeoisement and its possibilities and frustrations for the wider community. Following the work of Pierre Bourdieu, class is perhaps best conceptualized not as a strictly economic faction but rather a specific position that is consciously cultivated in a larger and shared social space. The deliberate aesthetic choices made in service of this position reinforce its nature as a "rank to be upheld or a distance to be kept"⁴ and are "often constituted in opposition to the choices of groups closest in social space, with whom the competition is most direct and immediate, and, more precisely, no doubt, in relation to those choices most clearly marked by the intention (perceived as pretension) of marking distinction vis à vis lower groups."⁵ For Bourdieu, the working class functions largely as "a foil, a negative reference point, in relation to which all aesthetics define themselves, by successive negations."⁶ For Jews striving for upward social mobility in Izmir, economic constraints both complicated and compounded the pressures of constructing and maintaining this crucial symbolic distance from the petty traders and unskilled laborers that predominated in the community.[7] Moreover, the pronounced Westernization of the late Ottoman period made the construction of such social boundaries all the more complicated, entailing as it did a delicate negotiation of the perceived opposition between life *a la turka* and life *a la franka*.[8] For many Jews in Izmir, becoming bourgeois, an enterprise beset by contradictions and anxieties, was ultimately about navigating the *"dezeo de 'pareser' kuando no pueden 'ser,'"* or the "desire 'to appear' [a certain way] when you can't 'be' [that way]."[9]

The Emergence of Karataş

By the 1890s, upwardly mobile Jews from Izmir had begun relocating to the suburb of Karataş, just south of the city. They were motivated in large part by a desire to escape the grittiness of Izmir's traditional Jewish quarters, believing that the waterfront suburb of Karataş offered a more sanitary and healthier existence. This demographic shift in the Jewish community was a product of the larger process of urban expansion during the late Ottoman period. By the late nineteenth century, the areas of Karataş and Göztepe had been integrated into Izmir proper through connections by boat as well as by new tramway lines.[10] Once belonging to the outskirts of the city, Karataş was home to Izmir's oldest Jewish cemetery, a plot of 100 *dunams* (25 acres) located in the once isolated area of *Bahri Baba*.[11] By 1885, Halil Rifat Pasha had forbidden new burials in *Bahri Baba* to facilitate the municipality's construction of new roads linking Karataş and its environs with the city center, and ultimately relocated the entire cemetery to the less-traveled area of Kan Çeşme.[12]

In 1890, there were seventy-seven Jewish households in Karataş and Bahri Baba,[13] but by 1900, the neighborhood was home to approximately five or six thousand Jews, or roughly one quarter of Izmir's total Jewish population.[14] In 1894, a local committee in Karataş sought a subsidy from the Communal Council to establish an *Alliance* school in the neighborhood,[15] a plan that was realized a year later. In 1905, the community sought the state's permission to construct a new synagogue in the neighborhood.[16] Grand Vizier Ferid gave them permission to proceed with building the synagogue,

FIGURE 7. Fond du golfe de Caratache et Guez-tépé, Smyrne. Postcard. Collection of the author.

which would become *Kal Kadoş Bet Israel*, at an estimated cost of one thousand two hundred Ottoman gold *liras*, which was covered in full by the community.[17] Karataş also became home to the Rothschild Hospital: In 1911, when plans to build a new hospital stalled, the businessman and taffeta merchant Nissim Levi donated a large house in the neighborhood to serve this function and designated it as a *vakif*, or pious foundation.[18]

Despite being at a geographical remove from the rest of Izmir's Jewish neighborhoods, the Jews of Karataş were regarded as part of the city's larger Jewish community. Communal budgets show, for example, that Jewish institutions in Karataş, such as its *Alliance* school and synagogue, received regular communal subventions.[19] At the same time, the Jewish community of Karataş operated independently as well. The Ladino press consistently referred to the area as *un foborgo*, or a "suburb" of the city,[20] typically listing "Izmir" and "Karataş" as separate categories of subscribers to local charitable associations.[21]

Yet more significant than its spatial distance from the city's densely populated Jewish neighborhoods such as *Irgat Bazar* was Karataş's social distance from them. In 1896, Gabriel Arié described the suburb as an area "where more and more of the intelligent and rich elements of the Community are taking refuge."[22] In 1900, he noted that the vast majority of the Jewish inhabitants of Karataş were "well-off," observing that "anyone who rises above an average level of comfort moves towards this quarter."[23] Using the neighborhoods of Istanbul as a reference point, Arié compared the "aristocratic" Karataş to the capital's upscale and heavily European Galata, while characterizing the rest of Izmir as "a sort of *Hasköy*, where only the poor population is left."[24]

In marked contrast to the situation in Izmir proper, most students at the *Alliance* school in Karataş did not receive scholarships but were paying students.[25] The neighborhood was home to well-patronized cafés, among them the *Café l'Abri*, which catered specifically to the needs of its Jewish customers. Out of respect for the summer holiday of *Shavu'ot*, in 1908, the café advertised that it would refrain from hosting live music, while the week after that it promised six nights of musical performances in Turkish, Arabic, and Ladino under the direction of the Jewish musician Haim Efendi.[26] In announcing its plans for the summer season a few years later, the *Café l'Abri* promised nightly sea swimming, fresh fish and cold *raki*, and daily live music, except on Tuesdays and the Sabbath. "For residents of Izmirna, all it takes is 2 *metalikas* on the tramway to have the same diversions as Karataşlis," noted *La Boz de Izmir*.[27]

There was perhaps no better reflection of how Karataş, as a space, embodied upward Jewish social mobility than the *Asansör*. Built by Nissim Levi in 1908, this water-powered public elevator saved Karataş residents the "long and arduous" climb from the street up to the residential areas in the hills. The innovation, which made coming and going on a daily basis much easier,[28] was hailed as a clever solution to the problems resulting from urban expansion in a city with mountainous topography.[29] Yet even more striking is the symbolism of how the *Asansör* allowed the Jews of Karataş to ascend not only the city's hills but its social ladder. After a short ride to the top, riders could enjoy a café and observation deck, where they could take in a spectacular view of the Aegean and the city. *El Novelista* declared the elevator, which was seen as proof of the city's progress, to be "one of the monuments that enhances the splendor of our city."[30] Its public opening was attended by numerous city officials, Jewish communal leaders, editors of local newspapers, and many "ladies of distinction."[31] After the elevator ride to the top, guests heard speeches and enjoyed refreshments on a deck "magnificently adorned and arranged for the occasion, with good taste and intelligence."[32]

The upward social mobility that marked the quarter contributed to a rift between its residents and the rest of the Jewish community. While Karataş was home to its own coeducational *Alliance* school, many preferred to send their children to Christian schools instead, a pattern that Gabriel Arié dismissed as the "unjustified preference of a class of upstarts."[33] Parents in Karataş opted for Christian schools, Arié observed, because they "wanted different peers for their children, another milieu than that of the poor Jews who comprise the vast majority of our school population."[34] While Arié disparaged this as a form of "snobbery particular to the Orient,"[35] the pattern reflects how socioeconomic categories of belonging came to supplant religious ones among a segment of Izmir's Jews. The impulse to spurn a Jewish education, even the "enlightened" one offered by the *Alliance*, in order to foster what were perceived as superior relationships for one's children demonstrates the care that the Jews of Karataş took to cultivate and protect their new social status. As *El Pregonero* observed in 1913, the quarter was home to all those who "want to insert themselves in the aristocracy, who want to look down on those from Izmir," and who "exude an air of honor and greatness for no other reason than their residence Karataş."[36]

A Modern Culture of Philanthropy

A key feature of embourgeoisement as it unfolded in Jewish Izmir was the rise of charity balls and special events organized to benefit local communal institutions such as the *Talmud Tora*, the Rothschild Hospital, and the *Ozer Dalim* Society. Referred to as "balls," "dancing soirées," and "evening parties," these frequent events were represented in the Ladino press as elegant and brilliant affairs both sponsored and attended by the upper echelons of the community, usually emanating from the ranks of the communal leadership and Izmir's small number of Jewish mercantile elites, two groups with significant overlap. For example, an 1876 ball for the benefit of the *Eskola Nasional* was sponsored by Mr. Jacques Sidi and his wife,[37] well-known notables of *franko* origin who were instrumental in establishing the *Alliance* presence in Izmir, while an 1889 ball for the benefit of the *Ozer Dalim* Society was sponsored by Nissim Habif (co-owner of Izmir's Habif and Polako department store) and his wife.[38] A banquet held in honor of Semtob Pariente upon his departure from Izmir in 1893 was attended not only by the chief rabbi and numerous members of the Communal Council, but also by representatives of Izmir's major Jewish charitable institutions, two newspapers, and the leaders of the French and Ashkenazi communities,[39] while a 1907 ball held for the benefit of the *Alliance* was attended by Chief Rabbi Bensenyor, all of the Communal Council, and numerous other Jewish "notables."[40]

While the Ladino press often mentioned communal leaders and notables by name in covering these events, it referred to other attendees in broad and all-encompassing terms. In 1883, the "aristocracy" of Izmir reportedly attended a party for the *Alliance*,[41] and in 1887, *La Buena Esperanza* described how a soirée for the *Ozer Dalim* Society had been attended by "the most aristocratic families of our community."[42] The audience for an 1892 theater production for the benefit of *Ozer Dalim* was comprised of "the finest families of our community,"[43] while the crowd at a 1907 party for the *Alliance* was as "numerous as it was exclusive."[44] Ticket prices help make concrete the affluence of these "aristocratic" crowds. Available for purchase at the upscale Habif and Polako store, a ticket to the 1889 *Ozer Dalim* Society ball, for example, cost three *mecidiyes*,[45] equivalent to sixty *kuruş*, or approximately three weeks' pay for a laborer such as a porter.[46]

On the surface, these balls were held first and foremost to raise funds for local charities. Yet charity events such as *Ozer Dalim*'s annual Purim show or the Rothschild Hospital's annual *Lag ba-Omer* festival operated on a symbolic level as well. In addition to providing a real financial boon to often troubled charitable associations, such events promoted a profound association between two cornerstones of bourgeois life—philanthropy and "respectable" leisure. A discourse emphasizing the harmony between these two values pervades the earliest mentions of charity balls in Izmir's Ladino press. Advertising upcoming balls held by Izmir's Greek and Armenian communities in 1878, *La Esperanza* claimed that "alongside entertainment there is also charity."[47] In reporting on the festivities marking the inauguration of a new building for the *Alliance* school in 1883, the paper lauded those who made their attendance at the event "*un plazer i dover*," or "a pleasure and a duty."[48] Guests at a soirée for the *Ozer Dalim* Society in 1887 were, again, recognized for having made their attendance at the party "both a pleasure and a duty,"[49] while *El Novelista* invoked the same discourse in 1908 to praise guests attending an evening of theater and cinema for the benefit of the *Talmud Tora*.[50]

This dual discourse was employed not only to characterize the philanthropic intentions of the attendees but to frame their experience of such events. While the 1887 soirée held for *Ozer Dalim* reportedly enjoyed significant "material" success, the accomplishment was matched by the "moral" success of the evening, which saw dancing continue into the early hours of the morning "with the same joy, brilliance, and tranquility."[51] Similarly, an *Alliance* theater production during the Purim season of 1892 reportedly enjoyed "great success from both a moral and material perspective."[52] Packed with patrons who had purchased tickets for the show, the school was "illuminated like daylight" as actors skillfully delivered their Turkish and Ladino lines and the *Sosiedad Muzikal Israelit* played enjoyable pieces. *La Buena Esperanza* underscored how the public left incredibly content, already demanding that the actors stage another performance during the upcoming Passover holiday.[53] In 1906, *El Novelista* lauded the women's charity *Nashim Sadkaniot* for hosting an elegant soirée, remarking that the "moral and material benefit" of the evening was "very brilliant,"[54] while a year later the paper promoted a literary and musical evening benefit for the *Ozer Dalim* Society by reminding attendees that their "act of charity" would be enriched by a "few hours of pleasant and instructive entertainment."[55]

The focus on the "moral" impact of such events for those in attendance belies the recognition that philanthropy encompassed much more than a pure humanitarian devotion to charitable causes. Scholars have demonstrated that modern philanthropic activities were informed by a host of political, social, and cultural considerations. Research on nineteenth-century philanthropy in cities such as New York and Leipzig has shown how philanthropic activities allowed previously marginalized groups to establish and assert "new positions of cultural and social power."[56] In a similar manner, Izmir's Jewish bourgeois attended soirées and balls to cement their new social status. The public nature of such events and their frequent coverage in a supportive Ladino press only amplified their performative nature and the significance of their "moralizing" impact. In this way, Izmir's growing bourgeois class mobilized new forms of modern philanthropy to regenerate not only the poor, but themselves as well.

Tracking the spaces where such events were held points to growing footholds of bourgeois taste in the community. In 1882, for example, the Communal Council rejected a request to use the *hahamhane*, or offices of the chief rabbinate, for a soirée sponsored by the Rothschild Hospital, dismissing such events as a "frivolous" use of "a place of honor for the whole community."[57] Yet only a few years later, the *hahamhane* had begun to host such soirées for religious institutions, such as benefits for the *Keter Tora* School[58] and the *Ozer Dalim* Society.[59] The *Talmud Tora* school also hosted such events, though not without some controversy. In 1910, discontent surfaced over how social gatherings had interrupted study, damaged the building, and even desecrated the Sabbath, all of which "are not in accordance with the name of the *Talmud Tora*." Meeting to discuss the matter, administrators decided to ban such festivities outright, ruling that "no celebration with dancing or food will be permitted by any means." They further agreed that any future events would need to bring material benefit to the institution while assuring that study would not be disturbed.[60]

Later, the emergence of new institutions afforded the community new spaces for functions that straddled the Jewish and emerging bourgeois orbits. By the 1880s, the *Alliance* had begun to host charity events for its schools and associated institutions such as Izmir's new *kabineto de lektura*, or reading room,[61] and was approached by the *Talmud Tora*.[62] By the mid-1890s, *Alliance* facilities had become an attractive option for charitable associations outside of its purview, such as the *Malbish Arumim* Society, which requested the use of its space for a benefit in 1894.[63] Demonstrating both the prestige of the *Alliance* as a venue of bourgeois respectability and the frequency of such events, school director Gabriel Arié rejected the request despite its worthy cause for fear of being "inundated by all of the charitable associations of Izmir."[64] Between 1890 and 1905, in addition to the *Alliance*, the Jews of Izmir could also hold events at the *Cercle Israélite*, a new gathering place for "enlightened youths,"[65] where the *Mahzikei Ani'im*, for instance, held its dancing soirée in 1902.[66]

During the course of Izmir's urban transformation in the late nineteenth and early twentieth centuries, the city's Jews were also sometimes able to

FIGURE 8. Le Sporting Club, Souvenir de Smyrne. Postcard. Collection of the author.

access venues external to the community for its celebrations. Among the most famous of these new venues was the Sporting Club, a grand waterfront building built in 1893 devoted to the practice of numerous sports.[67] Membership in the club was selective and comprised of Izmir's upper-class Europeans, Greeks, and Armenians. The actual practice of sports was eclipsed by the club's stature as an exclusive gathering place for Izmir's mercantile elite.[68] The Sporting Club also included a theater, which hosted numerous productions put on by traveling European theater and opera companies. On a typical weekend in 1907, *El Novelista* advertised that the opera star Suzanne Munte and her Parisian troupe would perform three French comedies at the Sporting Club, *Le Voleur*, *La Passerelle*, and *Le Bonheur Mesdames*.[69]

Again reflecting the aspirational nature of Jewish embourgeoisement, Jews do not seem to have been prominent among the Sporting Club's membership.[70] Yet by the turn of the century, they had begun renting the venue for their own communal events. Most notable among these were the semi-annual theater productions staged for the benefit of the *Ozer Dalim* Society. In 1905 and 1907, *Ozer Dalim* used the venue to host its annual Purim show,[71] while during the fall holiday of *Sukkot* in 1906, the association staged

Ladino productions of *El Galeriano Inosente* and *Los Embarasos de un Avokato* there.[72] In 1907, the *Talmud Tora* rented the theater at the Sporting Club to host a particularly grand "evening of drama and music."[73] A year later, the local Ottoman press reported that the *Talmud Tora* would host a *sinematoğraf temaşası*, or movie screening benefit, at the Sporting Club.[74]

Joining the Sporting Club was Izmir's new Kraemer Hotel and Palace, which also became a preferred venue for communal functions. A luxurious hotel with an attached glass brasserie, the institution was celebrated as a "princely palace" and characterized as a "splendid edifice surpassing many great European hotels in luxury and elegance."[75] The status of the Kraemer Palace as a gathering place for Izmir's elite was highlighted by its inauguration ceremony, which was reportedly attended by "the elite of the Smyrniot population." Situated on Izmir's newly constructed quays, the hotel boasted twenty-five "luxuriously furnished" guest rooms, a dining room, a vast ballroom, and dedicated smoking rooms. Its height as one of the tallest buildings in the area afforded visitors "one of the most pleasant panoramas of Asia Minor" and "a picturesque view of the city with its innumerable buildings." The building also boasted an automatic elevator that transported visitors the distance of the one hundred and twenty-five steps leading to the third floor in what seemed to be "less than one second."[76]

In 1906, the brasserie of the Kraemer Palace was the site of a grand ball held by the *Nashim Sadkaniot* Society. Comprised largely of former *Alliance* students, the association functioned as the women's section of the *Bikkur Holim* Society.[77] *El Comercial* described the festivities as reflecting the height of bourgeois style, not least because it was enhanced by its now famous location:

> The ball given last Sunday night in the halls of the great Kraemer Brasserie enjoyed the most brilliant of successes. The halls were splendidly illuminated and decorated with refined and attractive taste.... Upon entering the room [attendees] were overcome with excitement and joy.... [The] starry sky of a thousand electric lights moved [even] the most unfeeling.... The excitement became greater and greater at each moment, and after each dance, the buffets were quickly filled with those having refreshments or some dessert. The committee of women who ran the party shared with each and every guest

gracious words and kind greetings. Everyone got along as though they were family and enjoyed themselves until a very late hour of the night.[78]

New Patterns of Socialization

Even more significant in reconstructing patterns of embourgeoisement among the Jewish community of Izmir than the frequency of their charity balls or the symbolism of the venues in which they were held is the way in which associational life reshaped vertical relationships with representatives of the state. For the Jews of Izmir, charity balls facilitated socialization not only among Izmir's Jewish bourgeois but with other elements of the city's upper crust. Numerous Jewish charity balls were attended by local officials, whether Ottoman or foreign. For example, in reporting on a ball for a Jewish school in 1876, *La Buena Esperanza* reported that numerous officials had "honored this Jewish ball with their presence" such as the governor general of the province of Aydın, the head of the provincial treasury, the president of the Commerce Tribunal, and multiple foreign consuls.[79] Given its stature as a French philanthropic organization, the *Alliance*'s festivities often drew diverse crowds. An 1883 ball celebrating the inauguration of its new school illustrates this, boasting a "numerous" and "exclusive" crowd.[80] In attendance were not only the local *vali*, army and police officials, the director of the Ottoman Bank, and the director of the new Izmir-Kasaba railroad,[81] but the local Catholic archbishop as well, along with the consuls general of America, France, Persia,[82] Austria, Italy, Greece, Portugal, Sweden, and Norway, most of whom came with their wives and entourages.[83] Notably, a special room had been prepared for the harem of the governor general of the province, who attended the party because his sons attended the *Alliance* boys' school.[84] Later *Alliance* events enjoyed similar successes; an 1892 multilingual theater production, for instance, counted local police officials, the inspector of public instruction, and "other Muslim dignitaries" among its audience.[85]

The presence of Ottoman and foreign officials at such balls fostered a sense of pride among the balls' organizers and provided opportunities for Jews to demonstrate their loyalty to the state.[86] In reporting on an 1884 ball, *La Buena Esperanza* highlighted the fact that Ms. Polako's "graceful" outfit was adorned by a handkerchief embroidered with "Long Live the Sultan."[87] Despite coming on the heels of a devastating cholera epidemic, an 1894 ball for the benefit of the *Talmud Tora* was attended by a "large and elegant crowd"[88] that included the local *vali* himself. "The presence of our honorable and enlightened *vali* lent a particular brilliance to this charity gala," reported Gabriel Arié. "Around midnight, when His Excellency was getting ready to leave, the national Hamidian hymn began to play and hearty hurrahs! along with cries of 'Long Live the Sultan' filled the room."[89]

Perhaps even more significant than new patterns of vertical socialization was how such associational life bridged the ethnic and religious divides that continued to permeate late Ottoman society. While Izmir's role as one of the empire's most active ports had always facilitated interaction among mercantile elites of different religious groups, the changing physical landscape of the city along with new social norms in the late nineteenth century gave rise to socialization beyond the world of commerce. As we have seen, the newly developed *Kordon* attracted the upper class of all of Izmir's ethnic groups with its cafés, clubs, hotels, and theaters, while its promenade in particular was enjoyed by Izmir's bourgeois as a much-needed place for *flânerie*.[90] Upper-class Muslims were known to participate in Izmir's numerous European *cercles*, and new boating races in the Gulf of Izmir and outdoor film screenings were among the numerous events that drew mixed crowds.[91]

Against the backdrop of this changing environment, affluent Jews in Izmir experienced increased socialization with their non-Jewish neighbors, particularly within the realm of philanthropy. The presence of upper-class Greeks, Muslims, and Armenians at Jewish charity events became commonplace in the late nineteenth century. For example, the 1883 ball marking the inauguration of a new *Alliance* building was attended not only by numerous officials and foreign consuls but also by the "aristocracy of Izmirna," which included "many notables and great dignitaries from the Muslim, Jewish, and Christian communities."[92] The same discourse was employed to describe the success of an 1884 ball given for the benefit of local Jewish schools.[93] Held in the palace of the governor general, its rooms were filled with "the most aristocratic classes of Izmirna," including numerous foreign consuls and Ottoman officials and "great merchants and bankers from our city." *La Buena Esperanza* celebrated the fact that "our Jewish compatriots contributed much to the success of this ball."[94] The notion that a well-executed ball served not just to raise charity but to enhance the overall reputation of the

Jewish community is further demonstrated in the press coverage of an 1887 soirée for the *Ozer Dalim* Society. Reporting that many "Christian notables" were in attendance, *La Buena Esperanza* noted with pride that "they continuously praised the particularly fine and elegant manner in which [the party] was organized."[95] A particularly revealing example of how philanthropy increased socialization across ethnic lines was a 1907 benefit for the *Talmud Tora* school. Held at the exclusive Sporting Club, the event was to feature live music, theater, and poetry readings. Forming the honorary committee were the president of the municipality, the director of political affairs for the province, and the chief of police, along with a host of elites from Izmir's Greek, European, and Armenian communities.[96] As for the performances, a Mademoiselle Cohen recited "Pour les pauvres," by Victor Hugo, which was followed first by a duet sung by two Greeks and then by a monologue recited by an Armenian. Closing the entertainment was a duet, "Aimer c'est vivre," performed by two women—one British, the other Italian. Thus, a charity event for a Jewish school, a long-standing communal institution where nearly five hundred destitute students were instructed in religious texts according to traditional methods, was, in the words of its French-language invitation, to be enjoyed by "the most refined enthusiasts of the Smyrniot public."[97]

This kind of diversity of patronage seems to have been reciprocal, as Jews attended non-Jewish charity events as well. *La Buena Esperanza* reported on the profits generated by non-Jewish events[98] and frequently encouraged its readers to attend them. In 1876 (when it was still *La Esperanza*), the newspaper announced a masked ball for the benefit of Izmir's Armenian schools, calling upon its readers to contribute to "this civilizing and philanthropic endeavor."[99] In 1878, the paper advertised two balls, one given by the Greek community for the girls' school of San Demetri and another benefiting local Armenian charities, instructing its readers on where and how to purchase tickets.[100] The proliferation of balls in all of Izmir's ethnic groups can be seen in *El Novelista*'s advertisements for its printing press. Boasting capabilities in Greek and French in addition to Turkish and Ladino, the press advertised its ability to print invitations to weddings, balls, and theater programs.[101]

There is also evidence to suggest that alongside the proliferation of ethnically based balls, there was an emergence of citywide philanthropy as well. Informed by the universalizing discourses of charity and emerging notions of the "public good," upper-class Jews began to attend balls supporting humanitarian causes not specific to religious associations but involving the city as a whole. In 1903, for example, a charity ball was given for all of the poor of Izmir "regardless of religion."[102] Held in the salons of the *Cercle Européen*, the ball was sponsored by the wife of the French consul and reportedly enjoyed "brilliant success."[103]

Apart from illuminating the porous nature of ethnic and religious boundaries among the upper classes in late-Ottoman urban society, tracking the patterns of embourgeoisement among the Jews of Izmir helps to nuance our understanding of the process in the wider Jewish world. Long rooted in the Central and Western European experiences, scholarship on embourgeoisement has typically emphasized the need for Jews to abandon their particularism in order to become middle class. In the case of German Jewry, for example, Marion Kaplan has argued that "since class formation demanded visible means of distinguishing those belonging to different classes, Jews needed to be visibly middle-class. But they also needed to be invisibly Jewish."[104] In surveying the grand themes of modern Jewish history, Todd Endelman has argued that in Western Europe, acculturation was typically not accompanied by the social mixing it sought to facilitate, noting that even "baptized Jews" associated closely with one another.[105] The Ottoman Sephardi world yields a different model of embourgeoisement encountered by Jews in the modern period—one framed by the continued legitimation of religious particularism.

Gender

Central to the process of embourgeoisement among the Jews of Izmir was a reframing of traditional gender roles. The construction of bourgeois womanhood was marked by its emphasis on the private sphere, demanding the cultivation of a pristine domestic environment and a commitment to a motherhood that prized morality, piety, and responsibility.[106] Izmir's Jews received intimate instruction in these ideals through their education at the city's three *Alliance Israélite Universelle* schools. Idealizing the social type of the *mère-educatrice*, or "mother-educator," *Alliance* teachers demonstrated a keen awareness that the ultimate success of Westernization was largely reliant on changes effected in the home.[107]

FIGURE 9. Shlomo Algranati and Family, Izmir, c. 1905.
Source: © Beit Hatfustot, The Oster Visual Documentation Center,
Tel Aviv, Courtesy of Samuel Bisbachar, Israel.

Many of Izmir's Ladino newspaper editors reinforced this discourse of gender, expanding its reach to a broader audience. The highbrow *El Comercial* took a particular interest in the role of women, publishing numerous articles on the subject over its three-year span. Admitting that women had not yet produced an "Aristotle, Archimedes, [or] a Pasteur," *El Comercial* nonetheless insisted that "one must recognize that in the domain of sensibility, woman is superior to man. She possesses a more developed sense of tact and much greater capacities for affection and devotion."[108] The paper gave fuller expression to the ideal bourgeois type in an article entitled "Let Us Respect Women":

What is a woman's role? Is it not sublime and grandiose? Is it not women who pursue the noble and holy mission of raising the family? Is it not into their hands that the future of humanity is entrusted? Is it not with a remarkable vigilance and true heroism that women undertake such a difficult yet delicate mission? It is she who must bring up her children, it is she whose mandate is to educate noble citizens—human men in the real sense of the word—it is she who sees to inculcating in children, from the cradle, ideas of health, principles of good education, [and] the seed of virtues and noble qualities. What role could be more important than this? What mission is more noble than that of women?[109]

Jacob Algrante of *El Novelista* agreed. Idealizing the role of the woman as "providence in our youth, consolation in our illness and in the most critical moments of our life, and our blessing in moments of happiness," his paper argued that "it is she who forms our soul, who leads us to goodness. She is our moral and religious education. She supports us with her virtue and faith."[110]

As the *Alliance* graduate and Izmir native Graziella Benghiat would reflect in a lecture on "feminism" that she delivered to fellow alumni in 1913,

FIGURE 10. Première classe de l'école des filles, Smyrne, 1910.
Photothèque de l'Alliance israélite universelle (Paris).

"nature had certainly gifted men and women the same dose of intelligence, but one different in quality.... What remains, then, is for us to know how to share work and give to each one the task that best suits each of us in life."[111] Characterizing women as more tender and sensitive by nature, she argued that it made no sense at all for a woman to pursue a career outside the home, as this would "rob her of dignity," "strip her of the respect" she was due, and distract her from "the role that she is meant to play in the evolution of the world." "In the theater," she wondered, "do we not give each actor the role that suits him best?"[112]

The attribution of such characteristics to women ably facilitated the notion that they were particularly well-suited to charitable endeavors. Endowed with qualities of "grandeur of heart, sensibility, sweetness, and piety," the Jewish woman, according to *El Novelista*, was naturally predisposed to serve as "consolation for the poor, a refuge for the miserable, and a loving mother for the orphan. Oh, how capable are these women of alleviating the suffering and pain of the unfortunate."[113] So well-suited were women to engaging in charity that it was cast as a domain where they might even be superior to men. Addressing readers who might be frustrated by "inequality," *El Novelista* insisted that it would be "ridiculous" for a woman to try to "shine" as a man does. Instead, women needed to take pride in the distinct and separate role that nature had allotted them, a role "lacking neither grandeur nor dignity":

> The only place where a woman can walk alongside a man or dispute his steps is in the domain of charity.... Among her attributes are love and devotion. Where is there not a wound to heal, an unfortunate to help, a tear to dry? It is upon the underprivileged that the affections filling women's hearts can be spread.[114]

By the 1870s, the Ladino press had begun to profile women it found worthy of praise for their commitment to charitable causes. In 1874, *La Esperanza* highlighted the efforts of Madame de Leon Sidi during the *Shabbat Albasha* season, a time when numerous communal charities clothed the poor children of the *Talmud Tora*. Detailing her role in the clothing distribution, the paper crowned her "the mother of the poor and orphaned, the sustainer and consolation of widows and rabbis."[115] Underscoring the imagery of a benevolent bourgeois woman caring for the needy, *La Esperanza* declared that "it was a great pleasure to see the orphans leaving the house of this blessed and humanitarian woman with clothes and money, their tender hearts thanking God Almighty ... as they are sustained by her great generosity in each season and occasion."[116]

Many women began to follow Madame Sidi's example. By the 1880s, numerous Jewish women's charitable associations had emerged in Izmir, such as *La Buena Veluntad*, *Nashim Sadkaniot*, and the *God's Will Society*, as well as women's sections of the *Bikkur Holim* and the *Talmud Tora* Societies.[117] Soon, long-standing communal initiatives, such as those that clothed the children of the *Talmud Tora*, came to be regarded as the exclusive province of newly formed women's charities. In 1902, for example, the Women's Committee of the *Talmud Tora* sewed and distributed clothing for its students during the *Albasha* season. "One must see the joy on the faces of these little, unfortunate children," *La Buena Esperanza* proclaimed, "when they are called by their brave female protectors who give them [each] a shirt, pants, handkerchief, *sisit* [four-cornered ritual garment with fringes], and, to some, shoes."[118] A similar discourse was used in framing the activities of the Women's Committee in 1907. Arriving at the *Talmud Tora* bearing the undergarments the women had sewn for the children, a Madame Levi was reportedly "very moved to see the pitiable state of these little beings, and with tears in her eyes she congratulated the Women's Committee for the care that it provides for these little orphans, who have found second mothers in these women of the committee."[119] Encountering the students just after the clothing distribution in *Irgat Bazar*, the market district in the heart of Izmir's Jewish quarter, Joseph Romano, an editorialist for *El Novelista*, reflected that "it is difficult to describe the immense joy that these children felt on that day." Again reflecting the connection between bourgeois femininity and charity, Romano lauded those "guardian angels" whose "social position would permit them to stay at home and remain indifferent to the outside world." "If the prisons curse our women for snatching away future prisoners," Romano concluded, "humanity and the heavens bless them."[120]

Somewhat paradoxically, the Ladino press singled out the anonymous nature of some women's philanthropic activities as particularly deserving of praise. This attitude was rooted in the image of a mother-protector who instinctively senses where human suffering lies as well as how to alleviate it, and women active in charities were therefore celebrated for their modest and inconspicuous care for the poor. As a profile of Madame Dudu de Polako of the women's section of the *Bikkur Holim* stated:

> The first departures of the swallows having barely announced the arrival of the strong season, the winter having just begun, every year, you will see her tending to the poor and bedridden, to the elderly handicapped women, who underneath their rags, complain of pain and cold.... The beating of the very sensitive heart of Madame Polako calls her to duty. We say a duty because a habit becomes a duty. Leaving behind the warm stoves, enveloping coats, thick and comfortable rugs, she takes to the street, in search of suffering. She finds it. Her heart knows where it is. With a remarkable benevolence, with a tender nobility, she provides consolation and shelter.[121]

The "natural" ability of women to seek out suffering was regarded as especially well-suited to serving the needs of the shamefaced poor, or those thrust into poverty due to particular circumstances. Protecting the anonymity of such cases was seen as paramount, as is demonstrated by the work of the *God's Will Society*, a women's group that had come to the aid of numerous "fallen families" in advance of Passover.[122] Lamenting that "the stronger sex neglects this sort of charity," *El Novelista* marveled at how "a group of girls [with] tender hearts, future Jewish mothers, fulfill this need."[123]

The reshaping of Jewish philanthropy in late Ottoman Izmir also gave rise to new complexities regarding the changing role of women in the public sphere. In 1875, a benefit featuring public speeches delivered by both communal leaders and *Talmud Tora* students was held over the course of two days, to accommodate separate events for men and women.[124] Yet only a year later, *La Esperanza* reported that the presence of women and young ladies at a ball for a Jewish school had lent it "a more splendid form."[125] The notion that the presence of women served only to enhance such events found numerous echoes over the coming years. Reporting on an 1884 ball, *La Buena Esperanza* highlighted how "the elegant clothing, fine jewelry, and grace of the women lent a greater brilliance to this ball that left nothing to be desired,"[126] while in 1887, it proudly reported that more than seventy women and young ladies had attended the soirée for the *Ozer Dalim* Society.[127] So valuable was the presence of women at charity balls that in 1907, a proposal surfaced to allow them to attend balls free of charge. In favor of such a step, one contributor commented that "all of our readers can attest to the fact that the brilliant success of any ball is due to the feminine sex," arguing that without women, such an event "could not be called a ball."[128]

While the presence of women at balls was not particularly contentious, their participation in philanthropic theater performances sparked significant debate. There was a certain uneasiness in the community with respect to the detrimental impact of theater on women and their virtue, given people's mixed attitudes towards theater in general as well as discomfort with the intimate contact between the sexes that inevitably took place on stage. *El Comercial* ardently took up the issue, arguing that true "progress" would not arrive until "the old ideas that currently predominate regarding the theater disappear."[129] While allowing that theater had "shocked social conventions," *El Comercial* still insisted that "the time has come for us to give a little more freedom to our young women," and "with the instinct that guides the finer sex, they will know how to carry themselves. . . . If she is an honest girl, she will always remain an honest girl."[130] In later articles, *El Comercial* treated the ability of women to appear on the stage for charitable purposes as not only desirable but a requirement of modernity itself. Permitting women on stage would serve only "to awaken their enthusiasm for generous and useful causes [and] encourage them to do praiseworthy acts." The paper criticized opponents of the idea for disseminating "backwards ideas from old times" that were "incompatible with the needs of the current age" and urged its readers to accept that "the twentieth century is a century of progress and civilization, a century in which men and women must think, reason, and act in accordance with its demands."[131] Only a couple of weeks later, the newspaper triumphantly reported on a ball held for the benefit of the *Alliance*, celebrating how women "did not hesitate to take to the stage."[132] This happy news demonstrated that Jewish Izmirlis were "slowly familiarizing themselves with the demands of life in the present day."[133]

The advent of *baylar a la franka*, or "European-style" dancing, proved to be another arena in which new philanthropic activities sparked internal debate. Alexander Benghiat, editor of *El Meseret*, emerged as a staunch critic of such dancing and used his newspaper to discourage the practice. In 1901, he criticized those "so-called *frankeados* who dance not with their sisters or wives, but with the daughters of their neighbors or with distant acquaintances."[134] Insinuating that such dancing encouraged inappropriate contact between the sexes, Benghiat concluded that "European-style dancing is horrible for us Levantines." The only protection against the "scandalous scenes that take place every day in the big cities of Europe" was the "calm and peaceful manner of living that we have in these parts," he wrote.[135]

The popularity of charity balls and theater performances also intersected with increasing concern regarding appropriate dress. Given the function of dress as a visible and public marker of class, attendance at such events demanded not only a certain comportment but appropriate clothing and accoutrements as well. The Ladino press was particularly engaged in encouraging Ottoman Sephardim to remake their attire along European lines, printing copious advertisements for specifically bourgeois goods such as hats, suits, and corsets.[136] While such goods were likely too expensive for most, there is evidence to suggest that demand for Western clothing was indeed increasing in the community. Whereas census records from the 1840s label those working in tailoring simply as *shastres*, records from the mid-1880s begin to employ the category of *shastre franko*, or "Western tailor."[137] Later tax records from 1890 demonstrate an intensifying differentiation between the two modes of dress, as alongside *shastre franko* the term *shastre turko* begins to appear as well.[138]

As was the case for many of their fellow Ottomans, for Izmir's Jews, adopting bourgeois practices demanded the careful navigation of these two modes. In announcing a ball for the *Alliance*, to be attended by both Jewish and Christian business leaders, the organizing committee requested that attendees arrive "in style."[139] Explaining that men would be required to wear all black and women could wear their usual ball attire, *La Buena Esperanza* alerted its readers that anyone wearing "Turkish-style clothing" would be barred from entering.[140] Respecting such a dress code would ensure that the ball "would be praised by all parties" and demonstrate that Izmir's Jews bore a strong "national love."[141] Further underscoring the public nature of dress as a marker of class as well as the importance that Izmir's Jews attached to appearing middle class in the eyes of their neighbors, such demands to arrive "in style" were absent from announcements for the 1892 "national soirée" held for the *Ozer Dalim* and *Mahzikei Ani'im* Societies. "Given that this soirée is but a party for families [and] is purely national," the organizers declared, "men and women may come dressed without going to great expense."[142]

A reliable critic of Westernizing change and its displacement of tradition, Alexander Benghiat of *El Meseret* again used his newspaper as a forum to discourage the adoption of new patterns of dress, particularly among women. In 1901 Benghiat attacked the *decolleté* chosen by many women attending balls, with its shorter sleeves and open display of the neck, upper chest, and back.[143] Surprised that such a style had become popular, Benghiat wondered how "an educated and intelligent woman who calls herself honest could go to a ball in such revealing clothing with the idea of pleasing men." Placing the blame squarely on the influence of the West, Benghiat remarked that "civilization has required us to dress ourselves, but too much civilization is causing women to get rid of some of their clothes." "I do not believe that they are obligated by any 'fashion' to come half naked to a ball," Benghiat continued, concluding that "more important than fashion is good sense."[144]

New Patterns of Leisure

The advent of charity balls and theater performances reflected not only the emergence of a culture of modern philanthropy, but also a new culture of leisure. In Ottoman lands, Western notions of "edifying leisure" were nourished by Orientalist discourses asserting the laziness and nonproductive nature of a monolithic "Eastern" culture. Particularly troubling to Westernizing reformers in Jewish Izmir were the widespread practices of socializing in cafés and gambling. In 1902, Daniel Angel described how families and neighbors gathered together most evenings to play games. Noting that "the countryside and long strolls were the privilege of the few," Angel remarked that "the café is the rendez-vous of the majority." "During these beautiful winter days in our sunny cities," he continued, "young people stay there, condemning their limbs to inertia" in a noxious atmosphere contaminated by tobacco smoke to play cards and dominoes.[145] *El Novelista* argued that undignified behavior was bound to happen at such places, given the mixing of "people of a thousand types, of a thousand social conditions, and of a thousand natures."[146]

Such an environment was not conducive to intellectual exchange. With so many people drinking, yelling, and smoking, it was only "natural that one would not have a conversation summoning concentration and attention."[147]

Similarly, popular diversions such as card games, dominoes, and backgammon were cast by the press as vices serving no edifying purpose or, as *El Novelista* put it in 1906, "a waste of time."[148] Even more pernicious was how such games undermined bourgeois notions of sobriety and economy. Emerging as a relentless adversary of gambling, *El Novelista* treated it as a curse afflicting both the gambler and his entire family. As a result of the inevitable debts he amassed, his daughters would have no choice but to become "streetwalkers," and his wife would likely also begin to gamble. The paper concluded: "gambling is powerful. It is attractive. It does not leave its victims alone. It boils the blood. It destroys the flesh. Despite this, they all gamble. They ruin themselves morally and materially. Without shoes on their feet, they gamble. Without money, they gamble. Without honor, they gamble!"[149]

To supplant such trends, the Ladino press encouraged alternative forms of leisure that would facilitate, rather than stifle, the process of regeneration. In 1877, *La Esperanza* encouraged its readers to attend an art show held at the Jewish hospital. The famous artist, a "Professor Imanuel," was to stop in Izmir on his travels, display his artwork at the hospital, and donate the proceeds of the show to the institution. "We invite our compatriots who would like to spend their time on these long winter nights to take advantage of this occasion to see the beautiful and captivating works of this famous artist, as well as to help our hospital with a small sum."[150] Again mobilizing the dual discourse of "obligation and leisure" that so frequently framed calls for charity, *La Esperanza* highlighted "the obligation of those who recognize the holy mission of the hospital to help its blessed cause with a little money while enjoying themselves at the same time."[151]

Pointing to the recent surge Izmir had seen in the foundation of clubs and recreational associations, one reader of *El Novelista* argued that instead of spending time aimlessly in cafes, "why not create a commercial club, a café or a center where our young people and merchants can meet in the afternoons and on rest days?"[152] Such an establishment would be "indispensable" to those who "are not of the sort that needs to drink a few *rakis* in the afternoon, but rather those who do not see gambling as the foundation of their existence." At such a club, "everyone would find a companion, make a new acquaintance, develop new relationships, find out that so-and-so is in need of a correspondent or that someone else needs an agent, and they could recommend themselves to each other and help remedy each other's situation."[153]

New opportunities to fill one's evenings in a respectable manner were also created by Izmir's new *kabineto de lektura*, or "reading room," which opened under the name *La Jeunesse Israélite* in 1884. The institution was headed by a group of "honest and enlightened men"[154] such as the *Alliance* school director Semtob Pariente and the local merchant Nissim Habif. Membership in the reading room was to be limited to those seventeen years of age and older who could both write and speak at least one language.[155] At the ceremony marking its opening, Matitya Kohen offered sweeping remarks extolling the virtues of reading as an avenue for personal betterment and a near salvational tool for the entire community. Addressing his eager audience of young men, Kohen remarked that "this Jewish population, which has remained, I say with much bitterness, in the obscurity of ignorance, is setting its sights on you, and expects everything from you. Because of you, I am convinced that they will certainly not lack for noble role models." Kohen went so far as to ascribe to reading a world-historical importance, arguing that those committed to the project were working for the "salvation of Israel" and would earn the "support of those who love and honor humanity, brotherhood, and civilization."[156] A catalogue detailing a major donation of books to the institution on the part of S.H. Goldschmidt, president of the *Alliance Israélite Universelle*, likely reflects the nature of its holdings. Among the books donated by Goldschmidt were many works of history, science, general reference guides, and numerous travelogues of the Middle East and the Levant.[157]

A new public lecture series initiated in 1895 by the *Alliance* created additional opportunities for edifying leisure. Held on a monthly basis at the *Alliance* school, these lectures were deliberately planned for three o'clock on Saturday afternoons, which was precisely the time when "all of the Jews [were] free and crowded the streets and quays."[158] In November 1896, Gabriel Arié reported the attendance of a few hundred people at a recent Saturday lecture and listed "A Glance at the History of the Jews of Spain," "Perseverance and Its Influence in Life," "Hygiene and Antiseptic Treatments in the Case of Illness," "Music Among the Jews," and "Izmir, its History and the History of the Jewish Community of the City" among the future lectures to be held.[159] In later years, a Sunday lecture series emerged as well, known as *Alhad Literario*, or "Literary Sunday." In January 1905, the *Sala de Lektura*[160] sponsored a lecture on balloons. Held at the *Alliance* school, the event featured the honorable Senyor Habif, who delivered the talk in "pure and elegant language."[161] The audience, which was comprised of numerous members of the association, accompanied by their wives, offered copious applause and were said to have left the event "extremely content."[162]

New forms of leisure were not only intended to enrich the mind. The turn of the century saw a marked resurgence of interest in the benefits of fresh air and physical exercise, as sporting and recreational clubs proliferated in Izmir. Against this backdrop, Western discourses calling for the physical regeneration of European Jewry combined with discourses asserting the atrophy of Eastern populations to paint a dismal portrait of an inherent "physical laziness" that needed urgent attention.[163] Reform-minded elites in Izmir proffered multiple solutions to the problem. For *Alliance* leader Daniel Angel, the answer lay in establishing a panoply of societies dedicated to physical exercise, among them gymnastic, soccer, and tennis clubs as well as cycling courses.[164] Some contributors to *El Comercial* agreed. Signing his name as "the naturalist," one reader described his recent attendance at a soccer match in glowing terms. "Oh! What a beautiful morning, and how wonderful I felt: on my right a green field sowed with barley, in front of me Mount Pagus that dominates our city, in the middle of which vines beginning to flower; in a word, I enjoyed an immense panorama in which the purity of the sky and the glowing rays of the sun added a happy note."[165]

Others promoted daylong outdoor excursions to Izmir's countryside, where people could take in the fresh country air and participate in numerous sporting events. One such event was an excursion to Tire sponsored by the *Sala de Lektura* in 1906.[166] Attendees would depart the city at six o'clock in the morning on the train from the Caravan Point. Once in Tire, "excursionists," as they were later called, would spend the day engaged in walks, cycling, and soccer as well as music, dancing, and other "amusements." Tickets could be purchased in diverse neighborhoods, among them the upscale *franko mahala* as well as the working-class *Irgat Bazar* and *Udon Bazar*.[167] A similar countryside excursion to Aydın took place in 1907. "A compact multitude of people impatiently awaited the arrival of the train from the Punta," reported the journalist covering the event. "Pleasure and happiness were clear on everyone's faces.... They had been waiting for this happy day to get away from the preoccupations and worries of our everyday life." In Aydın, the excursionists enjoyed "a thousand and one recreations" such as soccer matches, track and field games, and dancing.[168]

While such leisure activities were frequently promoted by elites in the press, it bears repeating that they remained out of reach for most. A spring picnic organized by the *Alliance* alumni association in 1898 reflects this. Held not in the countryside but locally, in the gardens of the Ottoman Water Company with their "delightful trees and large lake of pure and clear water," the picnic featured musical performances by adults as well as children of the *Talmud Tora*. With, most likely, few expenses for attendees, the event was very well-attended by a broad cross-section of the community, a fact that *El Meseret* found particularly newsworthy. "Until now, never has our youth been gathered this way in the same place. The banker with the shopkeeper, the employer with the employee, the merchant with the worker, all were in each other's company, all celebrated together," the paper observed. Such events served to "strengthen the good sentiments of brotherhood between people of all classes in our community."[169]

Bourgeois Respectability and Self-Restraint

Bourgeois values of economy, sobriety, and self-restraint found a particularly sharp resonance in a population already grappling with the supposed "backwardness" of its own Eastern culture. In 1899, Gabriel Arié remarked that the community's "taste for luxury," "disproportion between the resources of each person and the needs he creates for himself," and "spirit of improvidence and total absence of habits of economy" were among the main causes of its decline.[170] Given their role as the central arbiters of embourgeoisement, attention was focused disproportionately on educating women in "habits of economy" and their strict implementation in the home. Calling a new bride arrived in the home of her husband "a queen in her kingdom," one contributor to *El Comercial* discussed the attributes of a new social type, "*la buena nekuchera*," or "the good housewife." Though she bore those qualities specific to women such as good judgment, foresight, and sweetness, she also needed to "descend from her pedestal" and master the art of "domestic accounting." Such an art required the careful management of a household budget with its numerous expenses such as rent, taxes, insurance, and utilities, as well as saving for unforeseen events. While each housewife would necessarily approach this responsibility differently based on the size and means of her family, each needed to be governed by "one rule only," namely, "economy." "Only spend in accordance with the needs of your family," he urged, cautioning housewives to remain especially vigilant with respect to small expenses that repeat themselves continuously and quickly accumulate. Citing the wisdom of Benjamin Franklin, *El Comercial* recommended that housewives check the bills for all of their purchases and pay close attention to the weights and measures used in the marketplace. "Young woman," the article concluded, "no detail, no matter how small, should be above your notice."[171]

The centrality of a woman's meticulous management of the home was emphasized by the *Liga de Pas i Solidaridad*, an association founded in 1909 with the goal of preventing the communal conflict that had roiled the community for so many decades. In a lecture delivered in March 1914, member Nissim Kuri explained the obligations that its members and their wives bore not only towards humanity but towards each other. Calling the wives of the League's members "sisters," Kuri stressed the value of women's intrinsic propensity for sweetness, tenderness, affection, comfort, and consolation in "life's struggles" and highlighted the Baroness de Hirsch as the ultimate female role model. "The strength of a man is in his mind and arms," Kuri posited, while "the strength of a woman comes solely from her heart." Insisting that he was indeed a "partisan of the emancipation of women," Kuri argued that such emancipation needed to harmonize with the framework that suited women's nature best, in work that "ennobled the soul" and "sweetened the heart." "Women, remain women!" Kuri exclaimed. "Do not seek to become half-men."[172]

Kuri went on to say that sisters of the League could most ably demonstrate their acceptance of its values in their mastery of "domestic economy," the "part of conjugal life belonging entirely to the woman." Again we see the portrait of a conscientious homemaker paying meticulous and constant attention to her family's income and expenses. Guarding against the excessive social pressures of "modern habits," sisters of the League were advised to "eat and dress according to the status of [y]our wallets." Such frugality would have benefits far beyond the home. The transformation of each individual Jewish household at the hands of a capable woman would have profound consequences for the community as a whole. Situating women as the ultimate bulwark against the community's unconscious "physical and moral decadence," Kuri concluded, "you cannot imagine the serenity, the calm of both mind and soul that reigns in a well-run and wisely balanced household. The economic uplifting of an entire people depends on it."[173]

The idealization of bourgeois "simplicity" for women led to a preoccupation with the temptations of luxury and its associated vices, a trend that has been documented among Izmir's Greeks as well.[174] Again, dress proves an instructive metric for how Jews negotiated such tensions. In 1883, for example, *La Buena Esperanza* lamented the slow and uneven pace at which Izmir's Jewish women were abandoning their traditional garb. While they had begun to adopt some Western fashions, some continued to don the *tokado*, an elaborate headdress specific to Sephardi women. *La Buena Esperanza* denigrated the practice as a "veritable scandal," claiming it negated any "progress" achieved through wearing Western attire. "Why bother going to dressmaker after dressmaker? Why spend so much money while wearing a *tokadiko* of a thousand wonders?" the paper wondered.[175]

Yet Izmir's Jewish women could not win. As Western-style ladies' hats became increasingly common as the decades wore on, the women who donned them were criticized for excessive extravagance. Their obstruction of the audience's view during theater performances became especially contentious and, as a result, charitable associations began to ask that women refrain from wearing such accessories during benefits. In 1906, the *Talmud Tora* stipulated that women patrons planning to attend the association's upcoming show "come without hats,"[176] and in 1907 *Ozer Dalim* followed suit.[177] Later that year, an impassioned editorial appeared in the pages of *El Comercial* on the subject, with its author remarking that ladies' hats had become "veritable gardens of Babylon." Recognizing the need to "harmonize the exigencies of fashion with the community of spectators," he offered numerous solutions largely emanating from the great halls of Parisian venues such as the *Opéra*, the *Opéra Comique*, and the *Comédie Française*. In such establishments, he argued, not only had new rules been imposed regulating ladies' hats but the general attitude towards such elaborate headgear had changed. It had gradually become acceptable for women to wear lace or scarves instead of opulent hats, and he pointed out that the famous stage actress Sarah Bernhardt had banned such hats at her performances.[178] A year later, women were encouraged to join a leisurely excursion to Aydın as a way to abandon "their hats as high as the pyramids of Egypt, gala dresses, luxurious robes, and froufrou skirts."[179] Spending the day engaged in wholesome field games and activities out in the countryside, women could truly demonstrate that they were "adherents of simplicity."[180]

Yet another revealing critique of women's luxury was put forth by a young seamstress. She first lamented that the "demands of life today" had increased the cost of living such that fathers could barely maintain their households and made the "caprices of their daughters" nearly impossible to satisfy. The seamstress sarcastically described how she worked tirelessly "to increase the profits of the department stores of Frank Street" and expressed shame at occupying herself "only with exterior adornments." The seamstress also criticized the demands her clients made upon her own patterns of dress. "Obligated as I am to be in frequent contact with my aristocratic clients, forced to accompany many of them in buying clothes, I must be as well-dressed as they are, with artfulness, taste [and] refinement, otherwise, my clients would undoubtedly abandon me." If women would only "give the best example of simplicity," the seamstress continued, others would quickly follow their example and dress "according to [their] position." The seamstress concluded by exhorting the newspaper to continue its commitment to "the movement begun in support of the suppression of luxury," adding that it could lead to "important reforms."[181]

While women were central to such debates, men were not immune to the renewed focus on the virtues of sobriety and dangers of luxury. In 1900, *El Meseret* cautioned its readers against amassing debt, calling it a source of embarrassment and anxiety.[182] Later that year, the paper declared that the "enlightened times" demanded an embrace of "economy" to safeguard against "the evil visit (of poverty)."[183] By 1908, the awareness that "economy" had become "an obligation" had spurred interest in savings associations. Noting the difficulty with which regular employees managed to save even the smallest portion of their salaries, writer Solomon Mizrahi opined that new savings accounts could educate holders about the roots of debt and combat "negligence, carelessness, and the wasting of money."[184]

El Pregonero embraced these middle-class values while couching them in the language of Jewish tradition. "The way a man uses money, in saving it or wasting it, is one of the best mirrors of the wisdom of his conduct," the paper argued. To illustrate this point, *El Pregonero* cited the example of King Solomon, who "did not ask God for riches but for industriousness," along with other traditional texts such as Proverbs 30:8, "Give me neither poverty nor riches, but provide me with my daily bread," and Ethics of the Fathers 4:1, "Who is strong? He who overcomes his desire."[185]

Belying a belief that embourgeoisement could not be authentically achieved in the East, the Jews of Izmir were criticized by their observers for adopting Western tastes and habits disingenuously. In 1904, *Alliance* teacher J. Attias reduced the expansion of bourgeois habits, pastimes, and even philanthropies among the Jews of Izmir to a collection of shallow performances executed solely for the sake of appearance. Notably, Attias argued that such superficiality was common to all Smyrniots:

> It is the characteristic sign of the Smyrniot, regardless of his religion or class. Everyone organizes their life around rivalries of luxury and an insatiable need to keep up appearances. At first, one might be, however, tempted to take the Smyrniot for an idealistic and sentimental specimen. But appearances are deceiving. . . . At the root of all acts of Smyrniots, even those that seem the most unselfish, one discovers a simple desire to keep up appearances, to make people talk about oneself. . . . One goes to the theater here to see such-and-such a play not for the love of art, but because it seems in good taste to see such-and-such a play. True *moutons de Panurge*, Smyrniots follow the current of the day; they easily renounce their own beliefs in order to come to terms with the most recalcitrant of people. . . . One must strain to find noble sentiments among Smyrniots.

Dismissing them as "*moutons de Panurge*," or sheep blindly following each other, Attias thus disparages Smyrniots for having deftly mastered and mobilized the "simple desire to keep up appearances."[186] Yet this critique in fact demonstrates not the superficiality of embourgeoisement in Izmir but its authenticity. Research has shown the art of "emulation," defined by the *Grand Dictionnaire universel* not as mere imitation but as "a sentiment of rivalry that leads us to equal or better our peers," to be a foundation of European bourgeois life.[187] Over the course of the late nineteenth and early twentieth centuries, a significant percentage of the city's Jewish population witnessed major changes in residential patterns, as well as manners of associational life, dress, and leisure. Izmir's Jewish women in particular saw their roles transformed according to bourgeois ideals of motherly protection, propriety, and simplicity. Demonstrating the local specificity of such processes, this chapter has shed light on how the appropriation and expression of bourgeois ideals among upwardly mobile Jews in Izmir was shaped by the Westernizing discourses of the day. Channeled in large part through the "civilizing mission" of the *Alliance*, embourgeoisement for Izmir's Jews demanded a deliberate shedding of the "Eastern" culture that had hindered their development of sobriety and industry. Thus, lectures at the *Sala de Lektura* began to unseat backgammon and card games as appropriate leisure activities. Traditional clothing was gradually replaced by gala dresses and elaborate hats. Excursions to the countryside would remedy the "laziness" to which Izmir's Jews had grown accustomed.

Yet as this chapter has further shown, in addition to the Westernizing inflections of embourgeoisement, the process was equally nurtured by the plural environment that marked Ottoman Izmir in particular and the continued affirmation of religious distinctiveness that marked the Ottoman Empire as a whole. In a process that stood in contrast to European models of Jewish embourgeoisement, upwardly mobile Jews in Izmir engaged in increased interaction and socialization with their bourgeois neighbors of different religious groups across a range of activities and pursuits. Seen from the perspective of Izmir's aspiring Jewish bourgeois, marking oneself as modern required a negotiation of the values not of Judaism but of the ascendant middle class.

《 CHAPTER 4 》

SUSTAINING THE *KEHILLAH*:
TAXING *EL PUEVLO*

Siervos fuimos al kasap en Izmir.
"We were slaves to the butcher in Izmir."[1]

This was the claim of the *Agada de la karne*, or "Meat Haggadah," in the Passover edition of the satirical newspaper *El Soytari* in 1909. Using the *magid*, or "telling" section of the Haggadah, as a model, *El Soytari* recast the traditional biblical narrative of the Israelites' oppression, enslavement, and ultimate liberation as the ongoing struggle for freedom from the injustices of Izmir's kosher meat industry. Such a comparison would surely have resonated deeply with its readership, for the industry in Izmir had been a near-incessant source of communal and class conflict for much of the modern period. By the time *El Soytari* published its *Agada de la karne* in 1909, Izmir had seen deeply polarizing conflicts over the ritual slaughter, inspection, pricing, and sale of kosher meat in 1840, 1846, 1865, 1879, 1888, and 1899, with countless smaller controversies in between.

While such crises frequently punctuated life in Jewish Izmir, the city was certainly not alone in this regard in the eastern Sephardi diaspora. The kosher meat industry in Istanbul also saw instability during this period,[2] as did the community of Salonica.[3] Nor was Izmir unique in the wider Jewish world, as numerous communities such as those of Paris,[4] Kiev,[5] New York,[6] and St. Petersburg,[7] also witnessed controversies over various aspects of the kosher meat industry.

While seemingly mundane, the complexities of the kosher meat market in Ottoman Izmir are rich in historical significance. First, tracking the sale of kosher meat and, in particular, the tax on it known as the *gabela* uncovers a significant contributing factor to the poverty that plagued so many of Izmir's Jews and captures the realities of everyday Jewish life in a Mediterranean city. More important, however, is the way in which the *gabela* and its trajectory in the nineteenth and twentieth centuries illuminates a broader Sephardi engagement with modernity. Far from being a symptom of internal decay, the *gabela* and the conflicts surrounding it catalyzed the emergence of a vibrant public sphere in Izmir's Jewish community—a space where people discussed, debated, protested, mobilized, and even organized politically around a common concern. Furthermore, while this sphere functioned within the Jewish community, the discourses characterizing it reflect a mutually reinforcing relationship between the *kehillah* and the Ottoman state through the dissolution of the Ottoman Empire.

Community Finances

Despite the Ottoman Empire's gradual adoption of centralizing reforms in the nineteenth century, its multiple religious groups continued to manage their internal affairs with little state intervention. Among the many dimensions of communal life that remained firmly in the hands of the religious communities was the management of finances. For the Jews of Izmir, the multiple responsibilities of the *kehillah* included the assessment and levy of external taxes due to the Ottoman authorities, most notably the *cizye*, or poll tax, and the *ariha*, or income tax. To cover its own internal expenses, such as the support of charitable organizations, payment of rabbinic salaries, and maintenance of institutions such as schools, synagogues, and cemeteries, the community levied a set of sales taxes on kosher goods such as meat, wine, and cheese.[8] These sales taxes were known as *gabela* taxes, a term used for various forms of taxation in Spanish, French, and Italian.[9] While social unrest surrounding tax collection predated the modern period in Izmir,[10] by the mid-nineteenth century the collection of *gabela* taxes, which were at their core regressive sales taxes that heavily and unevenly burdened the poor, had become a source of relentless communal strife.¹¹ According to Abraham Galante, the pioneering scholar of Ottoman Jewry, one rabbi had referred to the *gabela* using the Hebrew acronym *gimel-bet-yod*, corresponding to the first letters not only of "cheese-meat-wine" but also to the word's appearance in Psalm 129:3, *al gabi horshu horshim*, or "plowmen plowed across my back."¹²

Stakeholders and Corruption in the *Gabela* System

Despite the critical role that *gabela* revenue played in sustaining the community, the administration of the system was plagued by constant instability. A key reason for this was the ability of multiple groups, each with a vested interest in the system, to influence its implementation. These groups often operated outside of the purview of the Communal Council, skirting its authority and ignoring its directives. Primary among these groups were the *shohatim*, or ritual slaughterers. Due to their specialized skill in performing the ritual slaughter of animals according to Jewish law, an essential service for the community, the Communal Council paid the *shohatim* handsomely. Multiple budgets demonstrate that payment of the *shohatim* was frequently among the community's largest expenses.¹³ Continued reliance upon the meat *gabela* as the community's main source of revenue thus necessitated not only the consistent consumption of kosher meat, but also the willingness of the *shohatim* to provide it. Their specialized knowledge made them an exceedingly powerful faction in communal politics, and they frequently leveraged their skills against the numerous attempts by the Communal Council to regulate the local kosher meat industry more tightly, both in the slaughterhouse and in the marketplace.

A second interest group were the *gabeleros*, or men who bought the *gabela* tax outright and subsequently collected it from the larger community. The farming of the *gabela* mirrored the Ottoman system of *iltizam*, whereby the privilege to collect certain taxes was sold to the highest bidder.¹⁴ The abuses that habitually plagued this tax farming system across the empire surfaced within the Jewish community as well, as the *gabela* was subject to frequent mismanagement and extortion at the hands of wealthy *gabeleros*. No less problematic were the kosher butchers, or *karniseros/kasapes*, of Izmir, who constituted a third group with a stake in shaping meat *gabela* policies. Charged with the sale of kosher meat to consumers in the marketplace, they

FIGURE 11. Rabbi Elazar Halevi Slaughtering a Lamb, c. 1920s. © Beit Hatfustot, The Oster Visual Documentation Center, Tel Aviv, Courtesy of Haim Ashbal, Israel.

often had a hand in the corruption that plagued the system, given their ability to set prices unofficially, manipulate weights and measures, and control the quality of the product. Butchers were also on the front lines when conflicts spilled over onto the streets of Izmir's *djudería*. And though their precise role remains somewhat opaque, the sources also reflect the presence of yet a fourth group, known in Izmir as *kayafes*, with a role and stake in *gabela* policies. The word is likely a variation on *kahya*,[15] a communal representative to the state in matters related to taxation; among the multiple activities in which the *kayafes* were involved were communicating the municipality's directives regarding pricing,[16] obtaining meat from the *shohatim*,[17] and selling the meat after slaughter.[18]

Even in the absence of corruption, attempts to reconcile the often conflicting demands of the *shohatim*, *gabeleros*, *karniseros*, and *kayafes* with the needs of the community yielded a pattern of ad hoc decision-making on the part of the lay council in levying and collecting the tax. Nor was the meat *gabela* itself a predictable fixture of the landscape, as communal leaders frequently suspended it when controversy dictated. The presence or absence of the meat *gabela* at any particular moment was often referred to in terms of the *kuchiyo*, or the proverbial communal "knife," and the vacillation between *kuchiyo libero* (the suspension of the *gabela*) and *kuchiyo atado* (its reinstatement) was a frequent preoccupation.[19] This broad array of players, policies, and competing interests surrounding the kosher meat tax in Izmir made it a near-constant source of instability. Solutions to *gabela* impasses were almost always temporary as well as controversial. In fact, the volatility that characterized the *gabela* in Izmir was not a betrayal of an otherwise coherent system, but the foundation of the system itself.

Mechanics of "Traditional" Communal Autonomy

Conflicts surrounding the meat *gabela* reflect the tensions embedded in the way in which an increasingly impoverished community allocated resources among its members. Yet the system is also revealing of the often messy mechanics of Jewish communal autonomy on the Ottoman scene throughout the modern period. The continued expectation of undisturbed religious autonomy dictated that the Jewish community independently finance practically all facets of its communal life. Though the system was not in use when

Izmir's Jewish community was first established in the seventeenth century,[20] budgets demonstrate that by the nineteenth century, the funds generated by the kosher meat industry constituted by far the largest revenue stream for the community. For example, budgets from both 1886[21] and 1899[22] indicate that a staggering ninety-five percent of communal revenue was generated from the sale of kosher meat. Ultimately, it was the meat *gabela* that enabled the community to function, allowing it to pay its rabbis, maintain its cemetery, educate its children, and feed its poor. Though this was prohibited by Jewish law, communal leaders also occasionally relied on *gabela* revenue to cover external debts, such as taxes due to the Ottoman authorities, as well. Simply put, despite its tenuousness, the meat *gabela* was the lifeline of Izmir's Jewish community. As *El Pregonero* wrote in 1909, "this is the meaning of *hahamhane* [the chief rabbinate]: meat, slaughterers, and butchers. Or, in a word, cattle."[23]

The centrality of the kosher meat industry to communal autonomy is evidenced by the way in which various factions harnessed it for their own gain. In 1888, for example, against the backdrop of unrest fomented by mounting tax debts to the Ottoman state as well as a growing dissatisfaction with the lay council's administration of communal affairs,[24] a small but vocal group vowed to introduce a "foreign" *shohet* [singular of *shohatim*] into the community in order to "ruin the *gabela*."[25] The Communal Council promptly retaliated, threatening to excommunicate anyone who might patronize an Ashkenazi *shohet*, declaring such meat "completely *taref*" (ritually unacceptable), and warning that "those who eat this meat will be excluded from our community, as, according to our law, they are excommunicated."[26] While the rebel faction tried to circumvent this ruling by recruiting a Sephardi *shohet* from neighboring Aydın, the threat of excommunication in fact failed to deter many Sephardi consumers from patronizing the unsanctioned Ashkenazi butchery system, which, in just one week, caused a deficit of five hundred francs in communal revenue.[27] Semtob Pariente, the administrator of the local *Alliance* school, opined that "it is in cutting off their food supply that parasites who abuse their powers can be made to see reason."[28] Though the parties ultimately reached a compromise, which, among other stipulations, required a five-year moratorium on any additional meat taxes,[29] the truce was short-lived: violence over meat erupted in the *djudería* only a few months later.³⁰ It would appear that Pariente was right when he observed that Izmir's meat *gabela* was "a revenue the community could not do without."³¹

Even in the absence of conflict, the mere possibility of the establishment of butcheries external to the officially sanctioned system was a source of deep anxiety for communal leaders. Such was the case in 1897, when a group of Ashkenazi Jews in town sought to formalize their growing community by securing their own building for prayer.³² The Sephardi Communal Council reacted with uneasiness, noting with fear the potential for the Ashkenazim to eventually secure their own *shohet*.³³ Such concerns were undoubtedly fueled not only by local concerns but also by recent events in Istanbul, where the availability of meat supplied by Ashkenazi butchers had devastated communal resources.³⁴ Already in 1889, the effects of the financial instability caused by the circumvention of the *gabela* on the part of Ashkenazi butchers both in Istanbul and Izmir made it all the way up to the office of the grand viziership.³⁵ The fraught nature of the establishment of a formal Ashkenazi community in Izmir is evidenced by the protracted negotiations on the matter between the Sephardi community, the local governor, and even the consul of Austria-Hungary, who was involved due to the foreign nationality of some of the Ashkenazi petitioners.³⁶

The constant vulnerability of the *gabela* system to an array of threats, be they poor harvests, the corruption of various stakeholders, shifting consumption patterns, or competing butcheries, left the community searching for more stable mechanisms through which to finance itself. In 1911, the Communal Council experimented with levying a direct tax called the *derito komunal*, or "communal tax." Not only did it meet with opposition from butchers and other "interested parties,"³⁷ but the tax also failed to generate sufficient revenue in the following years, with communal leaders dismissing it as "pathetic,"³⁸ "slow,"³⁹ and "insignificant."⁴⁰ A census prepared in advance of the implementation of the *derito komunal* demonstrates why this was so. Of the approximately one thousand taxpayers assessed, just four percent found themselves in the highest of the four established brackets, at 200 *kuruş*. Eleven percent were assessed in the second-highest bracket, at 100 *kuruş*, while thirty percent were assessed at 50 *kuruş*. Nearly fifty-five percent of all taxpayers were assessed at 25 *kuruş*, the lowest bracket.⁴¹ Ongoing efforts to formalize the tax and distribute its burden equitably by establishing seven categories of taxpayers were further thwarted by the economic dislocations of World War I.[42] After beseeching people to pay the tax in 1916,[43] the Communal Council still met with staunch recalcitrance from those who believed that they had been assessed too much.[44] By the spring of 1917, the Communal Council had agreed to suspend the *derito komunal*, confirming its earlier suspicion that "any tax abandoned to the free will of the taxpayer will not be able to survive."[45] Thus, though constantly negotiated, contested, and reconfigured, the meat *gabela* remained a fixture of Jewish life in Ottoman Izmir. In this sense, Jewish communal autonomy in Izmir ultimately lay not in the rabbinical courts, lay councils, or synagogues, but in the slaughterhouse.

Modern Change

An array of sources suggests that by the mid-nineteenth century, Izmir's Jews had begun to engage this traditional mechanism of Jewish self-government and its vicissitudes through an expanding repertoire of new practices and discourses. Once the province of the rabbinical and lay authorities, in the late nineteenth century, a growing cross-section of Izmir's Jews contested the tax in new forums such as bulletins, pamphlets, and newspapers. Supporters and detractors of the *gabela* organized into new associations, publicizing their positions on the tax and promoting their visions for reform. The polarization engendered by the tax began to be expressed in the language of modern politics as the Jews of Izmir demonstrated, signed petitions, and boycotted goods. Taken together, these trends point to the existence of a robust public sphere within Izmir's Jewish community, in line with Jürgen Habermas's classic formulation of a "sphere of private people come together as a public."[46] As such, the case of Izmir invites an expansion of this paradigm—which has already been examined in Ashkenazi case studies such as the Russian Pale of Settlement[47] and the Kingdom of Poland[48]—to the Sephardi world.

The view from Jewish Izmir also has implications for the study of civil society in the late Ottoman context, particularly with respect to its multiple ethnoreligious groups. Recent scholarship has revised the long-held assumption that a strong central state necessarily precluded the development of a vibrant public sphere in the Ottoman Empire in the modern period,[49] pointing instead to how semi-official institutions, such as aid societies, allowed a "new elite" an expanded field of political participation.[50] Yet even the very term "public sphere" suggests a unity that is belied by the Ottoman Empire's plural nature and continued affirmation of communal autonomy. The story of Izmir's engagement with the *gabela*, then, suggests the simultaneous evolution of multiple publics that frequently overlapped and, in the Jewish case, ultimately reinforced each other. In addition, the story of the *gabela* provides a contrasting view of the process by which civil society developed on the Ottoman scene. It has been shown, for example, how the wealth of nineteenth-century Greek merchants allowed them to mobilize in the non-state arena, which ultimately laid the groundwork for a vibrant civil society in western Anatolia.[51] For the Jews of Izmir, however, it was not the wealth of the upper classes but the poverty of the masses that ultimately catalyzed and sustained such a sphere.

Bulletins and the Press

Oversight of the *gabela* had once been the sole province of lay and rabbinic authorities. Yet in the nineteenth century, the *gabela* was discussed and criticized in an expanding range of new forums and venues. The 1847 publication of *Shavat Ani'im*, or "The Cry of the Poor," a searing condemnation of Izmir's lay oligarchs for their iniquitous administration of communal finances and manipulation of *gabela* taxes, stands as an instructive turning point. Published anonymously, *Shavat Ani'im* recalls in great detail the deeply polarizing conflicts over *gabela* taxes that had plagued Izmir in the early 1840s, conflicts that were punctuated by bitter rabbinic contestation, the consumption of non-kosher meat, the formation of an independent Jewish community, and even apostasy.[52] Written from the perspective of Izmir's Jewish poor, *Shavat Ani'im* stands as a rare portal into the injustices that undergirded the community's traditional *kehillah* structure. Noting that many of the community's power brokers were *frankos*, or "foreign" Jews of Italian extraction, *Shavat Ani'im* decries how the poor had long been "oppressed and humiliated" and "dishonored and abused"[53] at their hands. Such resentment against *frankos* was common in the Sephardi world, as the privileges they enjoyed due to their extraterritorial status often set them apart, making them immune from local taxes and legal rulings.

Even more striking than the view it grants into the social cleavages wrought by the extraterritoriality of the *frankos* is the way *Shavat Ani'im* gives voice to the increasingly potent cleavages wrought by socioeconomic disparity. This broadening class consciousness is evidenced from the pamphlet's opening lines, which speak in the collective name of "the Jewish poor, residents of Izmir."[54] Such language permeates the entire text, as the pamphlet frequently voices the grievances of a unified poor and its "manipulation by the rich."[55] Further underscoring this mobilization is the way the text employs the first person plural, which communicates a shared sense of grievance among Izmir's Jewish poor and expresses their growing self-understanding as a group distinct from the city's other social strata. This sense of alienation was further concretized through the formal separation of the poor from the established *kehillah* and their formation of a new one. As the text states, "we made our frustrations with the rich known, [but] to no avail," and further explains, "among us are elderly people who remember the conflict between our poor and the rich during the time of Rabbi Mayo and Rabbi Hazan. And Rabbi Hazan sided with the poor, ruling that they be permitted to separate from the rich." "We no longer want to associate with the oligarchs," the pamphlet declares, "those who align themselves with the rich rabbis."[56]

This newly asserted group consciousness is perhaps best encapsulated by *Shavat Ani'im*'s use of the term *el puevlo*, or "the people," which appears in the text, remarkably, more than thirty times. In describing the plight of the poor, *Shavat Ani'im* decries how "the people found themselves so manipulated." In explaining the consequences of their formal separation from the *kehillah*, the pamphlet narrates how "the people witnessed dishonor" and "the people would be unwilling to live in the city or sustain Judaism" without Rabbi Hazan at its head. At one point, *Shavat Ani'im* even uses the phrase "we the people, the *esnafes* [guilds] and the poor."[57] In other words, the pamphlet presumes not only that *el puevlo* exists, but that it functions as a collectivity with agency that negotiates on its own behalf, controls its own fate, and criticizes the establishment.

This vehement critique intensified over the following decades. The year 1879 again saw conflict erupt over the *gabela*, which had recently been suppressed due to the efforts of the *Gabbaé Sedaka* association to stem the increasing scourge of public begging. To defend its platform, the association issued a series of bulletins in the spring of 1879 detailing its strategy for financing the community without recourse to regressive sales taxes. Through these bulletins, *Gabbaé Sedaka* articulated a clear vision of a reformed communal administration, proposing in detail the necessary changes in the assessment, levy, and collection of taxes that would ultimately, in the words of one bulletin, "deliver us from this evil *gabela*."[58]

In a manner similar to *Shavat Ani'im*, the bulletins also point to the role of socioeconomic class in catalyzing the emergence of a public sphere in Izmir's Jewish community. The administrators of *Gabbaé Sedaka* underscored not only their message regarding the *gabela*, but also their insistence that the *gabela* be debated "in public."[59] In a bulletin called "Salvation," *Gabbaé Sedaka* argues that it has a duty to "inform the honored public about the disgrace in which we find ourselves"[60] and calls upon "rabbis, supervisors, presidents of the *kupot* [charitable associations], notables, [and] all of our readers" to recognize the evils of the kosher meat tax.[61] In "The Blare of the Horn Grew Louder and Louder,"[62] its administrators "swore in public that we have not done this for glory nor honor."[63] In another, *Gabbaé Sedaka* condemns its detractors, who "do not even show themselves in public to say this is who we are, and these are our differences," and urges that "if they have some demands, let them put them in a bulletin in public."[64] Perhaps the best expression of this expanded public sphere can be found in the association's insistence that "we are in a time in which everything can be seen clearly, and the least significant Jew can understand the way things are happening."[65] As Semtob Pariente noted, "before such disagreements were fought with physical force; this time they are being fought with printed bulletins in which each side exposes its grievances to the public, more or less with moderation."[66]

The expanding public sphere evidenced by this flurry of bulletins was further enriched by a booming Ladino press. By the late nineteenth century, Izmir was home to three major Ladino newspapers, *La Buena Esperanza* (1871), *El Novelista* (1891), and *El Meseret* (1897). By 1918, these three had been joined by numerous others, such as *El Comercial* (1906), *El Pregonero* (1908), *La Boz del Puevlo* (1909), and *La Boz de Izmir* (1912). The role of the Ladino press as an agent of social change in the eastern Sephardi diaspora has been demonstrated by scholars[67] and is reflected in the diverse ideological commitments of Izmir's Jewish newspaper editors. Given its longevity, *La*

Buena Esperanza was arguably among the most influential, with its editor, the reformist and *Alliance* supporter Aaron Joseph Hazan, envisioning it as "an instrument of progress."[68] Also professing a "love of progress" was the editor of *El Meseret*, Alexander Benghiat who sought to make his paper "a sort of tiny school."[69] Yet, for *El Meseret*, the "love of progress" also yielded the decision to publish part of the paper in Turkish so as to "serve as an interpreter between the Jewish people and the Ottoman authorities."[70] For the editors of *La Verdad*, progress demanded a strict commitment to literature and science, to the exclusion of local politics,[71] while the editor of *El Pregonero*, Rabeno Couriel, promised to advance a "conservative" agenda, positing that his paper would show that religion could never present "[even] the smallest impediment to emancipation and the free development of mankind."[72]

This growing field of newspapers provided a new outlet for discussion of the *gabela* and its vicissitudes. Izmir's Jewish press reported frequently on the essentials of the local kosher meat industry, such as its fluctuating prices and associated taxes, as well as the constant stream of impasses that it yielded. Yet the casting of journalism as an inherently "beneficial"[73] endeavor easily facilitated the emergence of the press as a venue for criticism. In 1879, notably, *La Buena Esperanza* expressed frustration with the lifting of the *gabela* tax, arguing that it allowed butchers to manipulate pricing in the absence of communal oversight. "What is the advantage for the public and what does our community gain from this famous 'free knife' [policy]? Now that 'free knife' is in effect, these famous butchers have enslaved an entire community, selling meat at whichever price they like."[74] In 1886, by contrast, the paper scolded its readers for complaining about the high price of kosher meat, reminding them that if the Communal Council were to rely on a proportional income tax instead, "there would be no schools, no *Talmud Tora*, no Hospital, and the cemetery would turn into a pile of stones.... Unfortunately, no one gives [money] freely and it must be collected in another way."[75]

Debate became only more amplified as more Ladino newspapers joined *La Buena Esperanza* in the following years. In an article entitled "*Una kesha*," or "A Complaint," *El Novelista* demanded a system in which "the public does not suffer whatsoever" and criticized Izmir's Jewish butchers for "tyrannizing the public" by "charging more than the price set by the community."[76] In 1908, the paper issued a detailed strategy for lifting the *gabela*, arguing that if the strategy was implemented, "the public that had turned its back on the *djudería*, either because of the abuse of the butcher or the high price of meat, [would] return to buy kosher meat."⁷⁷ *El Comercial*, a highbrow journal addressing itself to the mercantile elite, participated in the conversation in 1908 when it condemned two members of the Communal Council for slaughtering a cow illegally in order to destabilize communal finances. "Jewish public! Do not allow the evil designs of these nefarious men to be realized. . . . Our Council must be strong, it must know how to impose its will; otherwise, disorder will always reign."⁷⁸ In 1914, the conservative journal *El Pregonero* defended the recent reinstatement of the *gabela*, arguing that a growing deficit had left the Communal Council with no alternatives. "Our only revenue comes from meat, and if this revenue is lessened, our community cannot exist." While admitting that Izmir's kosher butchers would disfavor this, "we lean towards the public good."⁷⁹

The increasing empowerment of the press in checking the abuses of the meat industry is best evidenced by a scandal that stunned the community in 1896. In February of that year, Jacob Algrante, the editor of *El Novelista*, published a scathing attack on the communal administration. Seeking to expose the reasons behind the notably inflated price of kosher meat, which at ten and a half *kuruş* per *okka* was nearly double the price of meat in the Greek community, Algrante accused three communal figures of orchestrating an elaborate scheme whereby they pocketed 4500 *kuruş* of revenue every week.⁸⁰ While corruption in matters related to the *gabela* was nothing new, the reaction to this episode certainly was. Reporting that Izmir's Jewish community had been plunged into "revolution," the *Alliance* official Gabriel Arié remarked that a "newspaper article has turned everyone upside down."⁸¹ In response to the attack, Chief Rabbi Abraham Palacci ordered Algrante's excommunication, a decision that was announced in all of Izmir's synagogues and transmitted to all communal leaders. Yet the chief rabbi's order seems to have accomplished the reverse of what was intended, as Arié reported: "everyone the community counts among its intelligent and influential [members] is with Algrante against the Communal Council. . . . Things have become heated [and] it seems that a duel between the public and those who govern it has begun. This obscure journalist of yesterday has all of a sudden become the idol of the community."⁸²

The conflict was ultimately solved by an *Alliance*-brokered compromise, which entailed the lifting of the excommunication, a reduction in the price of meat, and an examination of the communal books of the five previous years.[83] Yet the significance of the conflict and the resulting compromise extend far beyond these measures in their illustration of the empowerment of the Ladino press. Upon the publication of Algrante's editorial in early 1896, the Communal Council condemned his "evil conduct," declaring that the only goal of his "baseless" accusations was "rousing the honored public."[84] Recognizing a potent threat in Algrante in the fall of 1896 the council summoned him to its regular meeting, demanding that he "no longer publish in his newspaper on any provocative question relating to his eminence the chief rabbi, any of the rabbinical establishment, nor any prior administration, in order to prevent discord and unpleasantness."[85] Accepting that Algrante may "write as much as he wants about our way of managing the affairs of the community," the council asked that he first approach its members before publishing on any sensitive issues so they might "try to meet his demands."[86] While the conflict of 1896 eventually abated, *El Novelista* would persist in publishing criticism of communal institutions. A decade later, the paper drew the attention of the Ottoman authorities, who sought to warn the paper to refrain from "publishing on irregularities in the chief rabbinate."[87]

The injustices of the *gabela* also affected patterns of associational life, mobilizing existing associations and catalyzing the emergence of new ones. Calling it "a source of tremendous abuse that favors a small minority to the detriment of the majority," the *Gabbaé Sedaka* association made reform of the *gabela* system central to its mission, lobbying vocally for its removal and attempting to reorganize communal finances to that end.[88] Fearing the association's increasing power, which had been bolstered by an agreement formalizing its control over communal finances, a new opposition group emerged calling itself *Ahdut*, or "Unity." *Ahdut* accused *Gabbaé Sedaka* of "wanting to play an outsized role in the community in opposition to the will of a great number" and urged its subscribers to withdraw their support.[89] *Gabbaé Sedaka* dismissed its adversaries as partisans of "the old regime of abuse and depredations."[90] Yet *Ahdut* proved a formidable opponent, as its efforts thrust *Gabbaé Sedaka* into a deficit, which led to a bitter stalemate that was only successfully resolved by the intervention of an *Alliance* intermediary.

Similar frustration with the *gabela* contributed to the formation of a new association in 1888. After leading a push to patronize Ashkenazi butchers, the lay council's detractors established their own independent butchery, arguing that such a strategy was the "best way to force the hand of the Communal Council and chief rabbi."[91] Reorganizing itself as an association called *Madrikhei Yosher*, or "Guardians of Ethics," the rebel faction gave its sole objective as being "the pursuit of honesty and the prevention of all injustice in our community." To that end, it promised that under its oversight, "the head of a family in the community could easily eat good and affordable meat slaughtered by Sephardi *shohatim*."[92] Unburdening Izmir's consumers of kosher meat was the centerpiece of the association's proposed communal budgets[93] and a key negotiating point in the agreement it reached with the Communal Council in November of 1888.

Further underscoring the vibrancy of this emerging Sephardi public sphere, associations like *Gabbaé Sedaka* and *Madrikhei Yosher* made ample use of the Ladino press to communicate their grievances to a broader audience. By 1880, for example, *Gabbaé Sedaka* had established its own *komision de karne*, or "meat commission," which had run into conflict with local butchers as well as some in the leather industry. Justifying its position in *La Buena Esperanza*, the association's meat commission beseeched the newspaper's editor to ensure that "his paper serve as the crier amongst the people."[94] When *Madrikhei Yosher* started its independent butchery, the *shohatim* it hired justified their reasons for working with the association in *La Buena Esperanza*,[95] while the association itself published its demand not only that the *gabela* be abolished but a host of other reforms as well in the pages of the paper. Demanding the improvement of the *Talmud Tora*, restoration of subsidies to the *Alliance*, and fairness in assessment of *bedel* taxes, *Madrikhei Yosher* published its program "so that all of the people may be aware and judge [the issues] in question."[96]

Politicization

No better proof exists of the way that the *gabela* catalyzed the emergence of a public sphere in Izmir's *kehillah* than the conflict over rabbinic succession that roiled the community over a two-year period between 1899 and 1901. The story begins in the winter of 1899, when Chief Rabbi Abraham Palacci died after thirty years of leadership. Palacci had been a revered figure and prolific scholar, and Izmir's Ladino newspapers celebrated his rabbinate as a time marked by "gigantic steps toward progress,"[97] praising him as "the first to applaud every new endeavor of instruction, progress, and civilization."[98] His funeral was reportedly attended by an enormous crowd, including many state officials and representatives of Izmir's other religious communities, and was reported both in the local Jewish as well as the Ottoman press.[99]

Conflict over the appointment of a successor ensued immediately, with Gabriel Arié surmising that filling the post would "be as difficult and would spill as much ink in Izmir as the Dreyfus Affair."[100] While multiple solutions were debated in the initial days after Palacci's death,[101] by the spring of 1899 a group supporting the candidacy of Palacci's son, Solomon had taken the provocative step of bypassing the Communal Council and pronounced him chief rabbi. To solidify this move as a new reality, the group almost immediately sent its own *shohatim* to the abattoir, instructing them to begin slaughtering animals on behalf of the new administration with Shlomo Palacci as its head.[102] This move left the Communal Council scrambling to enlist its own *shohatim* and meant that in effect, Izmir's Jewish community had two dueling administrations.[103]

After Solomon Palacci assumed the position of chief rabbi, the Communal Council wrote to the *haham başı* of the Ottoman Empire, Moshe Halevi, describing the emergence of "a movement in favor of the Palaccis."[104] This budding "movement" was anchored in a critique of the contentious *gabela* tax, energizing its supporters around a common goal. Explaining his position to Gabriel Arié, Solomon Palacci underscored how irresponsible lay leaders had compounded the community's reliance on the *gabela*, which had increased tenfold in recent years, from fifty thousand *kuruş* per year. This increase in turn had dramatically reduced the consumption of kosher meat, as the inflated prices put it out of reach for impoverished Jewish families.[105] Arié reported Palacci as explaining:

> What right do we have to crush the poor with taxes, and force others to irreligion? In a community where there is no direct personal tax, the poorest have more of a right to the direction of communal affairs than the richest, given that proportionally they are more impacted by an equal tax than the rich, without taking into account that the latter have the resource of truffle

stuffed turkeys, which are not subject to *gabelas*. As a result, the population has risen up as one, has declared as fallen an administration whose illegal acts are no longer binding, whose alleged financial accounts are audacious lies."[106]

Arié allowed that such abuses were commonplace. Nonetheless, he accused Palacci's camp of using them to artificially mobilize support, stating that "like all troublemakers behind coups d'état, they flatter the masses," and mocking Palacci as "the representative of the Jewish proletariat of Izmir."[107] Whether or not he was sincere, however, Palacci's message resonated with Izmir's Jewish poor. Describing the events for Rabbi Moshe Halevi in Istanbul, Izmir's Communal Council recounted how Palacci's supporters had "sought to create a major disturbance by rallying the lower classes," specifically by "tricking them" into thinking that their various tax burdens would be lightened, all while "lowering the price of meat."[108] At nightfall, after the culmination of Passover, "a good part of the lower classes" descended upon the Palacci home, proclaimed Solomon Palacci the chief rabbi, and dressed him in the *ferici*, or ceremonial cloak used by religious officials. To further emphasize the particular class dynamics at play, the Communal Council noted that among the chief organizers of the rebellion were three grocers, a cobbler, a salesman of used clothes, and a mender of sacks.[109] When Palacci was later summoned to the governor general's palace, after the turmoil had caught the attention of provincial officials, he was accompanied by, in the derisive words of Gabriel Arié, "a few hundred bums."[110]

Of course, such class conflict inflamed by the *gabela* was nothing new. Yet 1899 marks a turning point, evidencing that the Jews of Izmir had begun to experiment with the trappings of modern politics. The week after Palacci assumed the position of chief rabbi, *El Meseret* notably observed that "the community had split into two parties,"[111] each of which staked a position on the kosher meat industry. In April 1899, *La Buena Esperanza* criticized Izmir's *shohatim*, condemning how they "slaughter meat [sic] on behalf of the party opposing the *Kolel*,"[112] while two months later, *El Meseret* addressed accusations that it harbored a preference for "the party that is slaughtering with [a] free knife [policy]."[113] Ultimately, these "parties" crystallized into two distinct factions, called the *Palaccistas* and the *Kolelistas*. Positions on the meat industry emerged as the central mechanism through which Izmir's

Jews engaged with the conflict, expressing their affiliation as "Palaccists" or "Kolelists" with recourse to an expanding repertoire of political activities and behaviors.

A significant venue for the expression of these new loyalties was the communal administration. While the community's provision of kosher meat was at the heart of the conflict, other domains also saw an impact. In the wake of a devastating earthquake in September 1899 in Aydın, for example, the divide between Palaccists and Kolelists thwarted relief efforts as Jewish refugees began to pour into town. As Gabriel Arié noted, "it is impossible to find in Izmir five or six Jews who dare to form a committee and who might have a chance of being received by everyone: it will be necessary to form a Palaccist commission and another anti-Palaccist."[114] Similarly, in advance of Passover in 1900, *La Buena Esperanza* made a point of exhorting *all* of its readers, "REGARDLESS OF PARTY," to ensure that the poor would be able to purchase matza for the holiday.[115] The paper later reported on the failed negotiations between "the two belligerent parties" that threatened this goal.[116]

The communal administration allowed elites a forum for political expression. Yet the sources indicate that a much broader segment of Izmir's Jewish population also found ways to express itself politically. It is clear that by 1899, the very purchase of kosher meat had evolved into a mode of political expression, denoting one's affinity for either the Palaccists or the Kolelists. While in the early days of the conflict the Palacci faction had seized control of the meat industry, its rival faction quickly regrouped, enlisting a *shohet* from Bergama. As a result, consumers in the *djudería* now had a way to register their discontent with the Palaccis: they could now buy meat from the store labeled with a large sign: "Meat of the *Kolel*." As *El Meseret* noted, "until now, there had been two rites in the city: Ashkenazim and Sephardim. Now there are three!"[117] *El Meseret* further recounted numerous anecdotes testifying to the deep meaning now encoded in consuming meat slaughtered by one faction or the other, among them a fistfight between a man and his neighbor resulting from a mistaken purchase of Palaccist meat, and the case of one consumer who ardently monitored meat sales in the *djudería* on a daily basis, waiting to eat his lunch until the Palaccis' supply had sold out.[118] Similarly, speaking on behalf of hundreds of signatories, a 1900 letter sent to the *haham bashi* of the empire described how "the people, enraged by these injustices, decided to eat non-kosher meat in order to avoid giving two *mecidiyes* to the Palaccist party because they do whatever they want with our money."[119] Lamenting how "hundreds, if not thousands, of people of Israel, men, women and children, [were] eating non-kosher meat,"[120] the letter beseeched Chief Rabbi Halevi to intervene for the "glory of Israel" and "raise the flag of the Torah."[121]

A broad base of Jewish Izmirlis also expressed its loyalties by signing petitions. Starting from the very early days of the conflict, the Communal Council reported "great activity in the city" against the Palaccis, as well as the "collection of signatures and protests against the evildoings of these people and their party."[122] In the immediate days after Solomon Palacci assumed the position of chief rabbi, a group of young people issued a "Call to Youth and Enlightened People of Our Community," denouncing both Palacci and his supporters as "enemies of religion and progress." Addressed to "comrades," "brothers," and "friends," the appeal is a call to arms, encouraging the community to "protest the new state of affairs with indignation." Providing a blueprint for pursuing such lofty goals, the call exhorts the Jews of Izmir to "sign the protest lists that will be presented to you."[123] Such talk was not bluster. *El Meseret* describes a sort of petition fever, commenting that "this whole week, no one has talked about anything but signatures, and each person wants to know which document his friend signed."[124] Mocking the recent frenzy of petition-signing on both sides of the conflict, *El Meseret* declared, "Tired of spending so much and eating food of this sort?! So brothers, onward! Sign! Where? Wherever! For whom? For whomever! On which document? On whichever! Sign. Sign. Wherever, for whomever, and on whichever [document]." The meaning invested in the act of signing a petition is best evinced by the newspaper's mocking advice to sign each petition multiple times, arguing that "that way, you will be more fair, more passionate, more impartial, more just, more conscientious, more civilized, more advanced, more learned, and more enlightened."[125] These activities continued into the summer, when one thousand people reportedly signed a petition protesting the *vali*'s support for the Palacci faction and subsequently demonstrated in front of the palace.[126]

While the political statements encoded in boycotts and petitions are quite clear, the Jews of Izmir also expressed their views in less overtly politicized ways. In February of 1899, even before the contested rabbinic transition took place, conflict had spilled into the synagogue, disrupting Sabbath services.[127] As the discord persisted, the annual Purim carnival emerged as a deeply contested ritual. Already a source of anxiety due to its raucousness and public display of Jewish poverty, the carnival of 1900 was particularly tense due to the unfolding conflict. *La Buena Esperanza* argued that the carnival should be banned, worrying that it would give "young men from both parties a chance to rough each other up," and urged the heads of both parties to lobby the local police to prohibit the carnival outright.[128] So deep was the resonance of these affiliations that storeowners referred to them in their advertising. A 1900 ad for the Bayrakli department store, owned by Nissim Levi, for example, stated, "Kolelists and Palaccists!!! Come all to Bayrakli from Monday at 8 o'clock for the next two weeks to purchase silk, woolen, and cotton goods."[129]

These new identities, of Palaccists and Kolelists, remained a firm part of Izmir's discursive universe over the following year and a half. In April of 1900, *La Buena Esperanza* reported on the possibility of external mediation from Salonica, as long as the Kolelists and Palaccists would agree to it,[130] while a month later *El Meseret* beseeched "Kolelists and Palaccists to end their animosity with a truce" and to recognize that "we are all brothers, children of the same community."[131] Ultimately, it took the firm intervention of the local *vali* to bring about such a truce. In December of 1900, Kemal Pasha summoned representatives from each of the warring parties to his palace, demanding that they arrive at a compromise. While the subsequent appointment of Joseph Bensenyor to the post of chief rabbi finally brought the impasse to an end, its significance far surpasses the relatively short twenty-three-month period over which it unfolded. The struggle between the Palaccists and Kolelists demonstrates that Izmir's *kehillah* had become home to a vibrant political life, as its members constructed new identities and expressed them with numerous new tools for critique.

Gabela Discourses

No less significant than the bulletins, associations, and political activities that comprised this sphere are the new ways Izmir's Jews represented the *gabela* within it. A critical starting point remains *Shavat Ani'im*, the 1847 pamphlet that so vividly depicts the burden imposed on Izmir's Jewish poor by the gabela in the name of a collective *puevlo*. In numerous ways, the text is firmly

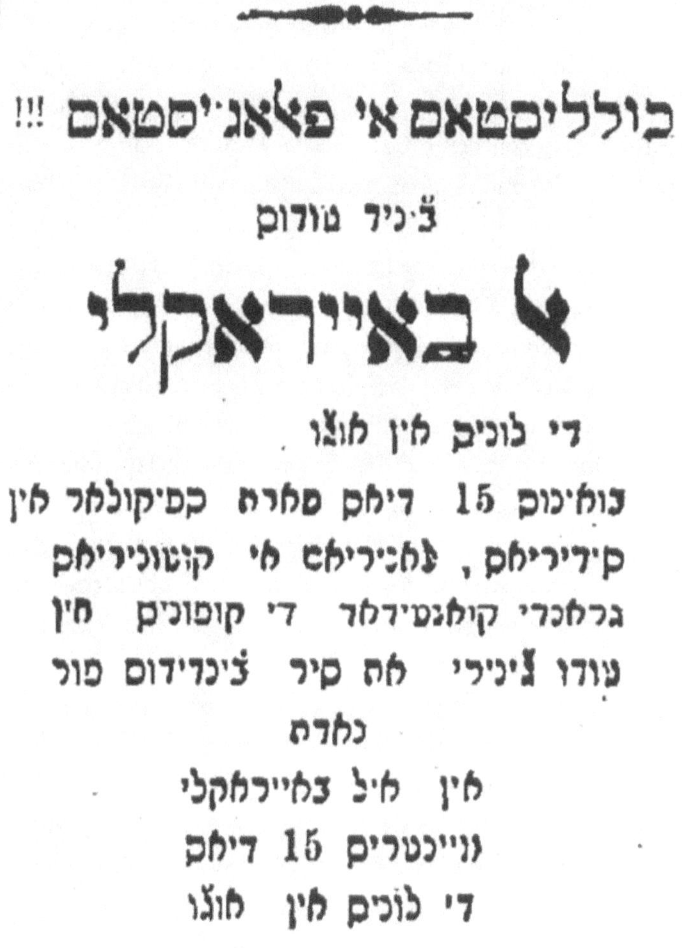

כוליסטאס אי פֿאגֿיסטאס !!!

גֿניר טודוס

א באיראקלי

די לוניס אין מוזו

טומוס 15 דיאס סאהרה קפיקולאר אין
סידיריאס, טהבֿיריאס אי קוטוניריאס
גראנדי קולנטידאד די קוטונים אין
מודו גֿיניריִ אה סיר גֿינדידום פור
נאדה
אין איל באיירמאקלי
נוייטרים 15 דיאס
די לוניס אין מוזו
לה דיריקסיון

FIGURE 12. Ad for Bayrakli Store.
Source: *La Buena Esperanza,* March 14, 1900.

rooted in the world of Jewish tradition. In its narration of the conflicts of the 1840s, the pamphlet draws upon the Hebrew Bible, claiming that communal leaders "treat the poor as slaves, taking no pity on them and abusing them much more than [we were abused during] our enslavement in Egypt."[132] Similarly, it claims that Izmir's Jewish poor were "more coerced than the *anusim* of Spain,"[133] referring to the community's early modern Iberian forebears who had been forced to convert to Catholicism. Further underscoring the text's rootedness in Jewish tradition is its preoccupation with how the *gabela* spurred people to sin. It notes with disdain how many in Izmir had "left the door of the nation" through the consumption of non-kosher meat[134] and casts a devastating fire in 1840 as a divine plan to purify the cooking instruments that had been tainted by such meat.[135] The very title of the pamphlet demonstrates its traditional nature, echoing as it does the liturgy of Sabbath morning: "hear the cry of the poor, listen to the cry of the weak and save him."

Yet mingling with these traditional elements is also language referencing the mid-nineteenth-century *Tanzimat*. While the *Tanzimat* reforms officially guaranteed the equality of all subjects regardless of religion, they also formalized the administrative structures of the Ottoman Empire's *millets* and bolstered their autonomy. In 1835, the Ottoman state had created the office of *haham bashı*, or chief rabbi. This position, which conferred a *berat*, an official document from the state granting specific privileges upon its holder, was instituted in Istanbul and across the provinces.[136] *Shavat Ani'im* takes refuge in this official reorganization of the Jewish community,[137] arguing that because of the *Tanzimat*, "only a rabbi holding a *berat* is recognized."[138] This new arrangement allowed the poor to unseat corrupt oligarchs who relied on the *gabela* with abandon, as *Shavat Ani'im* states that "we do not understand who can force us to be slaves to people we have no obligation to serve, not according to the law, nor the kingdom."[139]

The unbroken chain of conflicts caused by the *gabela* that persisted after *Shavat Ani'im* was published suggests that the impact of such state-sanctioned reform was limited. Much more durable, and ultimately consequential, than any structural changes guaranteed by the *Tanzimat* was the new vocabulary it provided Izmir's Jews in battling the injustices in their community. The text reflects that Izmir's Jews found themselves not only subject to new rules but living in a new age. Enabling the masses to reject the status quo, the pamphlet declares how "now, the poor and the middle classes have realized that as a result of the *Tanzimat-i Hayriye* [Beneficial Reforms] that our merciful king has applied to all of his reign, there are no longer any additional taxes or fines apart from the poll tax and profit tax that each person must pay individually."[140] This realization on the part of the poor led them to conclude that now "the people have the freedom of our lord king Sultan Abdülmecid [who ordered that] with the *Tanzimat-i Hayriye*, all of his flock is liberated and free. As is being said across his kingdom, only a rabbi possessing a *berat* is recognized."[141]

Critically, *Shavat Ani'im* reads this state-driven reorganization not as destabilizing of Jewish tradition but as restoring it. The text argues that because of the *Tanzimat*, "in order to be Jews, we must keep our laws according to the orders and rule of the official chief rabbi put in place by the king."[142] It celebrates the "good fortune of having the order of our lord king Sultan Abdülmecid" as his declaration that the empire's entire "flock are free of taxes, abuse, and oppression" would ultimately ensure that Izmir's Jews would "be slaves and subjects of God and the King."[143] Now able to liberate themselves from communal oligarchs, the Jewish poor could rightfully be "subject to the law of Moses."[144] Seen through the eyes of the Jewish poor, it is thus the Ottoman sultan who is the ultimate protector of Jewish law, wresting it from the corruption of the *kehillah*.

The Jews of Izmir continued to mobilize modern discourses in criticizing the *gabela* throughout the nineteenth century. In 1876, a reader of *La Buena Esperanza* reprised the discourse of *Shavat Ani'im* by declaring that the tax had "enslaved an entire nation." Reflecting the excitement surrounding the promulgation of the first Ottoman constitution that year, the anonymous author exclaimed, "we are no longer in a time of barbarism, to endure so much slavery at the hands of a *gabelero* and *kayafes*! Now is a time of freedom." If communal leaders truly wanted "the peace of the people," they needed to introduce "good reforms" and restore the *gabela* to the way it was in "olden days."[145] Again, we see how Jews in Izmir exuded confidence in the promise of a new age not for its ability to break with tradition, but for its capacity to uphold it.

The constitutional period initiated in 1876 was short-lived, as the Ottoman parliament was dissolved in 1878 and followed by the authoritarian reign of Sultan Abdülhamid II. The next time the empire would experiment with a constitution would not be until 1908, with the advent of the Young Turk Revolution. And then the Jews of Izmir attempted yet again to take refuge from the *gabela* in the promises made by the state, as evidenced in the 1909 satirical *Agada de la karne* or "Meat Haggadah." Published by Alexander Benghiat in his satirical *El Soytari*, or "The Joker," the text is part of a larger corpus of approximately forty known Ladino parodies of the Passover Haggadah. These parodies constitute a literary genre unto themselves; on the whole, they remain rooted in the traditional framework and symbols of the biblical narrative of the Exodus while, at the same time, using it as a mechanism for commentary on the array of political, ideological, and social changes facing the Sephardi community in the modern period.[146] Thus, the *Agada de la karne* tells a story of slavery and divine redemption through core elements of the traditional text, such as the "Four Questions," "It Would Have Been Enough," and the "Ten Plagues." Yet for the *Agada de la karne*, the injustices of slavery were to be found not in ancient Egypt but in the local kosher meat industry. As the text states, "in the beginning we were slaves to the *shohet* in Izmir," and continues "and God heard our voice and our troubles, and saw how much the *shohatim* were taking advantage of us."[147] In a complete reversal, the text replaces the wicked figure of Pharaoh with not just a Jewish figure, but a pillar of the community charged with upholding Jewish ritual.

The *Agada de la karne* finds the liberation from the slavery of the kosher meat industry in the promises of the recent Young Turk Revolution. Answering the question "how is this year different than all other years?" the text claims that while Izmir's Jews had previously been "so silenced and stifled," "this year, because of liberty (*hürriyet*), all of our hearts are bursting." The *Agada* further states "if the constitution had not come out in Turkey, we and our children, and our children's children, would still be enslaved with no way to break free," and "the constitution took us out of slavery, not by a messenger, and not by unknown people, but by none other than Niyazi and Enver." Just as Sultan Abdülmecid was the hero of *Shavat Ani'im* with his *Tanzimat* reforms, so too are Niyazi Bey and Enver Bey, architects of the Young Turk Revolution, the heroes of this Passover story.

The *Agada* reflects a general optimism regarding the revolution that was palpable across many cross-sections of the Ottoman Empire, expressing faith in its specific promises. Regarding the revolution's early, though ultimately short-lived, guarantee of freedom of the press, the *Agada* declares "and although we are all journalists, we are all knowledgeable, we all know the law, we were ordered by the censor not to speak. And now, God has brought us to this time." Even more pronounced is the text's emphasis on the empowerment of the *esnafes*, an imprecise term reflecting not just its literal meaning of "guilds" but a broad array of "middling classes." In its earliest days, the Young Turk Revolution was marked by social unrest, as an increasingly self-conscious working class asserted itself through a wave of strikes. Izmir itself saw the workers of both its port and the Izmir-Kasaba railway go on strike, demanding better wages.[148] A similar empowerment is visible among Izmir's Jewish *esnafes*. Though they had functioned as collectivities in Izmir before the revolution,[149] after 1908 the *esnafes* took an increasingly active role in communal politics. Functioning as a bloc that "promise[d] to be a strong force for the accomplishment of reform in the community,"[150] the *esnafes* boldly advocated for the economic interests of the community's working classes. In 1909, representatives of the *esnafes* approached the Communal Council numerous times with demands for reform, urging a more equitable assessment of *bedel* taxes based on one's profession and arguing for the instatement of *kuchiyo libero*, or the lifting of the meat *gabela*.[151] When the council still hadn't complied later that year, the heads of the *esnafes* published a bulletin "inviting the public to boycott meat slaughtered by the Communal Council."[152] Alongside this empowerment in communal politics, which continued into the following years,[153] was the emergence of a formal *Klub de los Esnafes*. Serving as a new center of gravity in the community, the *Klub* hosted many instructional lectures and enjoyed a broad base of supporters.[154]

Reflecting this increased confidence, the Meat Haggadah makes the *esnaf* the community's main power broker, investing in it the ability to effect dramatic change. In the narration of the Haggadah, it is the *esnaf* that mobilizes the community, saying "brothers, it is no longer the time to sleep," and, ultimately: "set out for the slaughterhouse." Just as the traditional Haggadah emphasizes how the ancient Israelites arrived in Egypt in small numbers but grew exponentially while enslaved, so too did Izmir's Jewish *esnaf* grow dramatically, as "with seventy souls the people of the *esnaf* went out, and now it numbers five thousand. And because of this, it is going to see the injustice, this *esnaf* is going to be fruitful and increase, and Izmir will be filled with them." Further concretizing how the Young Turk Revolution empowered the *esnaf*, the *Agada* rejoices in how "it is known that liberty allows for [free] assembly," and "it is in these assemblies that the *esnaf* works for the interest of the poor."

Like the majority of known Ladino parodies of the Passover Haggadah, the *Agada de la karne* preserves the traditional notion of divine providence. The text states that "God had mercy on us and sent us liberty, so that we might escape this evil"[155] and says "blessed is your liberty that you brought us to this moment, blessed are you who brought us freedom." At the same time, other elements of the text caution against reading these formulations as products of a certain genre alone. As discussed earlier, Jews in Izmir hoped that the new liberties offered by the state would safeguard tradition, not destabilize it. For example, in encouraging action against the *shohatim*, the *esnaf* urges the people to head to the slaughterhouse "for [the sake of] the world of your father." Perhaps the text's iteration of the *Dayenu*, or "It Would Have Been Enough," poem reflects this attitude most clearly:

> If they had lowered the number of the *shohatim* and left only half of them, that would have been enough.
>
> If only half of them were left and they had not stolen the neck [of the animal], that would have been enough.
>
> If they had stolen the neck and lowered their weekly salary, that would have been enough.
>
> If they had lowered their weekly salary and satisfied the butcher[s], that would have been enough.
>
> If they had satisfied the butcher and been made to swear not to give [him] any less, that would have been enough.
>
> If they had been made to swear not to give[him] less, and all of us had bought kosher [meat], that would have been enough.
>
> If we had all bought kosher [meat], and the butcher had behaved more appropriately, that would have been enough.
>
> If the butcher had behaved appropriately and lessened the boldness of the *shohet*, that would have been enough.[156]

The text marks not a dramatic rupture with Jewish tradition but a continuity. The ideal future it envisions is one in which a self-governing *kehillah* perseveres and, in tandem, one in which kosher meat is still slaughtered, purchased, and consumed. The *Agada* invests modern changes such as the freedoms of the press and of assembly with the power not to dismantle a traditional system but to insulate it from corruption and restore it to its rightful position. Thus, in the eyes of its Jewish observers, the Young Turk Revolution would allow the community to finally address its most potent threat, which emanated not from the state nor from its neighbors but from the *kehillah* itself.

In 1921, on the eve of the birth of the Turkish Republic, the Communal Council published a report on the financial state of the community. Just as it had been for decades, the *gabela* remained a "plague" that was "practically incurable."[157] Despite having achieved some success in controlling the meat industry over the years, the Council admitted that "measures must be taken now to replace it."[158] Yet the tax persisted. It was not until 1934 that the discourse around the *gabela* began to change, as the chief rabbinate of Turkey advised Izmir's Jewish leaders to replace the regressive tax with a general one that would appeal to a sense of duty towards the *kehillah*.[159] Non-compliance with taxation would not be punished by *herem* nor by the involvement of the authorities but would be met with the power of persuasion and ardent appeals to "the feelings of solidarity that each Jewish soul possesses."[160]

The longevity of the *kehillah* structure ultimately meant that conflicts over the meat *gabela* haunted the community for much of the modern age. Yet contrary to how these struggles have been represented—to the extent that they have been represented at all—they are indicators not of stagnation but of a dynamic encounter with modernity. Throughout the late imperial period, Izmir's Jews engaged their traditional mechanisms of self-government and its intrinsic burden on the poor in a robust public sphere marked by a growing field of tools for critique. Moreover, the discourses they mobilized in grappling with the *gabela* reflect the distinctly Ottoman inflection of this sphere, with its reinforcement and even amplification of Jewish communal autonomy. Thus, the significance of the *gabela* lies most profoundly in its emergence and persistence as, in the words of *El Pregonero*, "the question of the day."[161]

(CHAPTER 5)

AUTHORITY AND LEADERSHIP: REPRESENTING *EL PUEVLO*

In August of 1908, only a few weeks after the Young Turk Revolution, the communal notable Hiskia Franco wrote an article for *El Comercial* explaining the new rules of political engagement. With the restoration of the constitution, for the first time in three decades Ottomans would now convene a parliament. Along with their fellow Ottoman citizens, Ottoman Jews would soon be charged with electing delegates to the House of Deputies. Franco worried that though Jews might have appreciated the magnitude of the revolution, they still lacked a clear sense of their new "duties and rights" as citizens tasked with choosing who might represent them. Calling upon his readers to mobilize in order to "guide Jewish opinion and defend our interests," Franco remarked that as an entity, "[']the people['] is new in democratic life. Clear-eyed souls must lead it and put it on a strong path."[1]

Though Franco held that *el puevlo* was new in democratic life in 1908, in fact Izmir's Jews had been debating its role and authority in the context of the *kehillah*, or semi-autonomous Jewish community, for decades. Through the lens of the lay Communal Council and the rabbinate, the two anchors of the traditional *kehillah* structure, this chapter charts the reimagining of the *kehillah* as a vehicle for progress. Undergirding this progress was the expectation that a modern *kehillah* would not just manage communal affairs efficiently and rationally but would establish and protect a new social status quo in which the "the people" had widening authority. Communal leaders experimented with a range of new tools for Jewish self-governance, such as rationalized statutes and representative assemblies, and reconfigured the rabbinate as a bulwark against the exploitation of the poor. While some of these experiments were more successful than others, as this chapter will show, ultimately the most durable transformation emerged on the level of discourse, as consensus mounted that *el buen rijo*, or "good administration," was a precondition for any kind of progress.[2]

Lay Authority

In the 1860s, the rationalizing thrust of the *Tanzimat* reforms led the Ottoman state to reorganize the structure of its multiple *millets*. Central to this was the granting of organic statutes to the empire's Armenian, Greek, and Jewish communities. Seeking generally to empower the laity at the expense of the clergy, these statutes were the product of the state's efforts to prevent European meddling in the affairs of the empire's Christian populations and stem the tide of nationalism by weakening religious authority.[3] Following the Greeks in 1862 and Armenians in 1863, the empire's Jews adopted organic statutes in 1865. Known as the *Hahamhane Nizamnamesi*, the statutes delineated clear boundaries between rabbinical and lay authority and set forth regulations for their associated councils. They also called for the establishment of a mixed council, or *meclis umumi*.[4]

While the statutes made the chief rabbi of Istanbul the ultimate religious authority for all Ottoman Jews, they were officially granted only to the community of Istanbul,[5] leaving the adoption of such reforms in the provinces in the hands of local communities. And although *La Esperanza* reported on the benefits of rationalizing reforms in the 1870s,[6] it was not until 1884 that the project began in Izmir in earnest, when the lawyer Gabriel Calev proposed circulating a draft of a new *regulamento* to congregations and associations for approval. Like the *Hahamhane Nizamnamesi*, this *procheto de estatuto* sought to lend a formalized structure to the community's traditional institutions and codify distinct roles and responsibilities for the rabbinical and lay establishments. In addition to drawing clear internal boundaries between existing centers of power, the draft sought to draw new ones around the *kehillah* as a whole, establishing membership parameters for citizenship and residency.[7]

Reflecting the spirit of the statutes promulgated across all of the Empire's *millets*, the 1884 draft calls for an array of innovations aimed at increasing popular representation. Mandating regular elections and voting by secret ballot, the draft also calls for the creation of a *meclis umumi*, a mixed assembly of delegates comprised of a broad base of representatives. Envisioned as the ultimate arbiter of communal administration, the *meclis umumi* would be empowered to elect the chief rabbi and members of the religious and lay councils, review all proposals and budgets prepared by the lay council while retaining the right of refusal, and even "examine and judge accusations" leveled against the religious and lay councils through a judicial commission of nine men.[8]

Crucially, the 1884 draft reflects how in Jewish Izmir, the state's call for "reforms capable of spreading progress and prosperity"[9] demanded a reordering of social hierarchies. The new general assembly was to be composed of representatives from all local "corporations," which the text translates parenthetically as *esnafes*, a term borrowed from Turkish and signifying (as noted in chapter 4) not only "guilds" but also a broad array of middling classes. The statutes then advance a taxonomy of all Izmir's Jewish *esnafes*, breaking them into four distinct categories. In the first are members of the mercantile elite, such as "rentiers, bankers, wholesalers, manufacturers," and those in liberal professions such as doctors, lawyers, teachers, journalists, engineers, civil servants, and rabbis. The second category is comprised of brokers, retailers, money changers, pharmacists, and employees in public administration and banks, while artisans such as tailors, jewelers, hatmakers, watchmakers, carpenters, and ironworkers made up the third. The fourth, which was undoubtedly the most numerous, is the bottom rung, comprised of petty merchants such as greengrocers, spice sellers, fruiterers, bakers, peddlers, waiters, and workers such as makers of sacks.[10] Each of the four categories was to be represented in the general assembly according to a proportional formula whereby the first received one delegate for every ten members, the second received one for every twenty, the third one for every fifty, and the last, one for every hundred. While they are clearly weighted in favor of the first and most elite category, the fact that the statutes assume that the working class was entitled to any representation at all marks a dramatic rupture with the past. Theoretically, in 1884 the *meclis umumi* of the *kehillah* was envisioned as a body where both bankers and porters, doctors and greengrocers could advocate for their own interests in larger questions facing the community.

In addition to calling for their representation in the new general assembly, the 1884 statutes address the specific interests of Izmir's Jewish poor and working classes in other ways, most notably with respect to taxation. For centuries, the levy of communal taxes had been at the core of numerous conflicts fought along class lines. It was only a few years before these statutes were drafted that the community suffered a polarizing impasse over the *gabela* on meat, which advocates of the poor sought to abolish, as discussed in earlier chapters. In imagining a reformed communal administration, Calev proposed eliminating the *gabela* completely, fully replacing its revenue through the levy of direct taxes. Seeking to insulate the poorer classes from abuse, these direct taxes were to be assessed strictly according to one's profession, not wealth. Calculated according to the hierarchy of *korporasiones*, the assessment would further guard against exploitation by setting a ceiling of ten *mecidiyes* for the direct tax.[11]

The statutes, in addition to their proposals for reformed representation and taxation, also reveal how the very purpose of the *kehillah* was reenvisioned in the modern period, declaring its role as the "moral and material advancement of the community above all." That such advancement warranted new measures in managing poverty is clear in the statutes' declaration that the *kehillah* must "spread instruction and learning of the Torah, teach trades, and care for public health and the poor."[12] The draft called for three separate commissions to implement this agenda. The first would "support the teaching of trades by all possible means, [and] spread instruction in general," and supervise the *Talmud Tora* and *Alliance* schools to ensure that they were doing the same. The second would devote itself exclusively to "public health," seeing to the support of the overburdened communal hospital, sending doctors on house calls at no charge, and maintaining the cleanliness of the city's Jewish neighborhoods, "especially those where the poor class live." The third commission would see specifically to the daily needs of the most destitute, "doing everything possible to ease their plight" by securing shelter for them, supplying clothing to students of the *Talmud Tora*, and providing basic necessities for the infirm. In addition, this final commission would do "everything in its power to ensure that there are no beggars."[13]

The centrality of poverty—its management, control, and relief—to the 1884 vision for the role of a reformed lay leadership speaks not only to the social implications of "progress" for Sephardi Jews but also to the continued necessity of the Ottoman *kehillah* structure deep into the modern period. Despite the multiplying limits to the juridical autonomy of the *kehillah* in the modern period, as well as new intervening state structures such as the municipality, no other institution existed—shared, city, state, or otherwise— that would directly address the endemic, systemic poverty that plagued Izmir's Jewish public.

Once drafted, the statutes became the subject of intense debate. A broad segment of the community had an opportunity to comment on the project after a public reading at the *hahamhane*[14] as well as a distribution of the draft to Izmir's various congregations and associations.[15] The reformist *La Buena Esperanza* welcomed the initiative, praising the vision that animated the project.[16] Yet as the summer progressed, fears mounted that the statutes might allow the Communal Council to "insert itself directly into the administration of congregations"[17] and "appropriate the funds of associations."[18] The statutes were also criticized for implementing rules "that had not been seen in our ancestors' days"[19] and for running contrary to "religion."[20] After reviewing letters from various associations, congregations, and notables, the Communal Council reported that most did not accept the statutes, noting that even those who did still "objected to many things in them."[21] Two influential and generally revered members of the Communal Council, Haim Polako and Alexander Sidi, were so demoralized by the failure of the project that they resigned in protest.[22]

Yet despite their failure, the statutes of 1884 are of crucial importance in how they reflect both the profound meaning vested in the larger project of reforming Jewish self-government and the emergence of a new discourse mobilized to support it. While communal statutes were not legal codes per se, the logic animating their implementation parallels the larger push for legal codification in the *Tanzimat* era. Just as the statesmen of the *Tanzimat* embraced legal codification as a remedy for the "misrule, injustice, and disorder" that they believed resulted from a "lack of written laws as official instruments accessible to the public,"[23] so too did Izmir's Jews tout the ability of statutes to "put the management of the community in better order"[24] and ensure *el buen rijo*, or "good administration."²⁵ Similarly, Izmir's Jewish elites regarded the implementation of statutes not just as a tool for combating disorder but as a mechanism for reordering social relationships. Calling it the "ultimate signifier of modernity," one scholar has argued that "the code was an accessible, simplified arrangement of relations among subjects, and between subjects of the state, through a rational set of formulas that provided for predictability of judicial outcomes."²⁶ At the public reading of the new statutes, Gabriel Calev emphasized how they would allow people to "recognize the rights and obligations that they have toward each other in the affairs of the community" and explained that their innovations were required by "an enlightened time such as ours."²⁷ These rights belonged to all community members, regardless of rank, as the Communal Council argued that the statutes allowed "each person to recognize from where his rights emanate, from the chief rabbi to the smallest member, and [each] recognizes the respect due to them."²⁸ Calev echoed this notion in his public reading, arguing that a new code would allow everyone, "members as well as leaders," to understand the boundaries of their "powers and duties" within the community.²⁹ All in all, *La Buena Esperanza* contended that the organic statutes would enable the community to "be administered with order and justice, as the century requires," labeling them a "great step towards progress."³⁰

Underlying this modern discourse of "rights," "consent," "obligation," and "duty" was the steady empowerment of Izmir's Jewish *puevlo*. "The need for leaders is natural," Calev allowed at the public reading of his draft. Yet he insisted that such leaders needed to be those "who had earned the trust of the people."³¹ Though the word *puevlo* does not appear in the 1884 draft, it is clear that the *meclis umumi* was interpreted as the formal expression of its authority. One observer celebrated the "nomination of leaders through the votes of the representatives of the people,"³² while another highlighted the fact that the council would not be able to implement anything new "without the consent of the *meclis umumi*, meaning the representatives of the people."³³ The nature of the *meclis umumi* as an organ of *el puevlo*, and particularly its middle and working classes, is especially apparent in the statutes' implication for communal taxation. Assuaging the fears of those wary of the statutes' innovations, one supporter emphasized the crucial nature of securing the consent of the "people" in communal administration, given that the "general assembly would be comprised of representatives of all of the merchants and working people of the community."³⁴

The stake that *el puevlo* held in communal affairs continued to widen through the following decades. Even the very failure of the 1884 statutes reflects this empowerment. It was the Communal Council's decision to first circulate the draft among associations, societies, and congregations "to enable discussion among neighbors"³⁵ that ultimately proved its undoing, as it was reportedly "not accepted by the people."³⁶ Only a few years later, in 1891, the Communal Council was forced to disband as opposition mounted to its decision to reinstate the controversial meat *gabela* tax.³⁷ Defending its decision in a public statement, the defunct council called for the convocation of a general assembly that would study the budget, evaluate the meat tax, and "decide on a course of action" with respect to outstanding *bedel* debts and the possible reestablishment of *Ozer Dalim*. In an echo of the broad participation envisioned in the 1884, this assembly would be comprised of two delegates from each neighborhood, association, and guild.³⁸ After negotiations over the nomination of fifty-eight delegates and the procedures for their deliberations,³⁹ the men met to debate the divisive issues that had brought the communal administration to a standstill. Their attentiveness to the plight of the poor is clear in their decision not only to reinstate the *Ozer Dalim* Society but to reverse the reinstatement of the controversial *gabela* tax on meat. Opting to shift the burden to the production side of the market by taxing slaughterers and butchers according to the number of animals they handled, the delegates voted unanimously to unburden the impoverished Jewish consumer from a long detested form of exploitation.⁴⁰ Celebrating the move, Chief Rabbi Abraham Palacci hoped that the assembly would "prevent the 'cry of the poor' and bring about peace."⁴¹

Even more important than the assembly's decisions is how its initiators, delegates, and observers understood its purpose. Aware that communal taxation was already in practice being adjudicated through the everyday decisions of shopkeepers and consumers, the council convening the assembly declared that "the peace of the community is not served by everyone administering the affairs of the community in their stores and homes" and affirmed that "each leader, regardless of administration, works not for the interest of some but for the interest of the entire public."⁴² *La Buena Esperanza* exhorted delegates to "leave caprices aside" and to "keep in view only the interest of the public and the dignity of our nation,"[43] while the chief rabbi rejoiced that the decisions of the *meclis umumi* brought about "the contentment of all of the people in general."[44] So too did the delegates demonstrate an awareness of their mandate as public servants. While they agreed to levy a tax on alcoholic beverages to cover *bedel* debts, the delegates justified their position by arguing that they "could not tolerate seeing their brothers taken away each day to prison for being unable to pay, leaving their affairs and families without bread"[45] and promised to keep tavern owners from "opposing the interests of the public."[46] Announcing their decisions via the press, the delegates spoke of being "entrusted with a mandate" and invited the public to judge their decisions and evaluate whether they were "reasonable."[47]

Pressure mounted again in 1896 to convene a general assembly, this time for the purpose of electing the members of the Communal Council, which turned over every year. While procedures for the nomination of delegates were established in the spring of that year,[48] the continued lack of valid statutes after the failure of 1884 made any such assembly seem a hollow exercise in the eyes of some. Again the Ladino press took up the cause, urging delegates to press the case for establishing statutes. As *El Novelista* argued, "why bother with a *meclis umumi* if it will not dictate the chain of command for the leaders of the community? . . . Who would accept a nomination without knowing what he must do and how far his duties extend? When there are statutes, no one can tell him to do more or less."[49] *La Buena Esperanza* agreed: "will these new leaders have studied in university, or will they have come from Europe? Of course not! They will be of the same school and the same opinions as everyone who has run the community up until now." It was only a formal code of governance that could bring the Jews of Izmir "radical reform."[50]

Over the course of 1896, these arguments gained traction. After the assembly met and elected a new Communal Council,[51] it voted to require the new council to first and foremost draft statutes for approval. Aware of the gravity of their task, at their first meeting the newly appointed members proceeded with caution, debating the limits of their own authority in the absence of the statutes they were charged with creating. After lengthy deliberations, they agreed to prioritize the statutes above all but the most urgent of other matters, because, in the words of representative Isaac Ades, "if these foundations are not implemented, there can be no formality or regularity in the affairs of the community."[52]

In the following months, the Communal Council drafted statutes and printed hundreds of copies to ensure wide distribution.[53] Like the 1884 draft, these statutes created a new hierarchy for the administration of communal affairs, vesting ultimate authority in the *meclis umumi*. Yet in 1897, its delegates were categorized according not to their profession but to their congregation, as each synagogue was to elect ten of its members by secret ballot. Further broadening the representation of the assembly, delegates could be elected by all those in the congregation over the age of twenty-five, with no restrictions as to wealth or profession. The statutes thus transformed the traditional position of *memune*, or "appointee," into a "*delegado*," or "delegate," who was accountable to the electors of Izmir's wider Jewish public.

Also similar to the 1884 draft was the way in which the 1897 version envisioned the Communal Council as a vehicle for "the good functioning and advancement of the community," charging it with oversight of "charity," "instruction," and "congregations."[54] The statutes required direct supervision of all associations and institutions "subsidized by the *Kolel* and supported by the public,"[55] and mandated that should one dissolve, the council would ensure that its resources be redirected to works of "public utility." The statutes further stated that "all associations and institutions of public utility, whether [currently] in existence or to be formed in the future, must request authorization and approval of the Communal Council in order to be recognized."[56] "Progress" in Jewish Izmir, then, was intimately connected to the ability of the *kehillah* to serve the public.

In a manner that recalls its function in litigating the *gabela* tax, here again it was the Ladino press that reinforced and helped disseminate this notion of progress. Addressing the delegates themselves in advance of their meeting, *El Novelista* argued that "you, the members of the *meclis umumi*, must seek the benefit of the public that chose you as its representatives," declaring that "the *meclis umumi* is the people, and the people already have the right to tell their leaders how they want to be governed."[57] Similarly, *La Buena Esperanza* encouraged delegates to "dedicate themselves to the public interest," while *El Meseret* argued that "the prosperity of our community depends on the *meclis umumi*."[58]

FIGURE 13. Rabbi Abraham Palacci with Members of Jewish Community, Izmir 1896.
Source: © Beit Hatfustot, The Oster Visual Documentation Center, Tel Aviv,
Courtesy of Families Hasson, Izmir/Alexandria/Marseille.

While the statutes were approved and implemented in 1897,[59] this reformed administrative apparatus failed its first and ultimately biggest test only two years later, when the death of Abraham Palacci thrust the community into a protracted stalemate. Against the backdrop of unrelenting antagonisms over the meat *gabela*, the *Kolelistas* (or supporters of the lay administration) objected not only to the candidacy of the rabbi's son, Solomon Palacci, but also to the "illegal" way in which he commandeered the rabbinate. In the spring of 1899, a defensive Communal Council issued an announcement "fervently protest[ing] any election or nomination of a chief rabbi or interim rabbi to any religious post in our community not carried out in accordance with the *Hahamhane Nizamnamesi*" and held "accountable all those who usurped the power, privileges, and revenues of which the Communal Council is the only legal custodian."[60] Ultimately, when neither the application of statutes nor the convocation of a general assembly stabilized the situation, the Ottoman state intervened, naming Rabbi Joseph Eli to the post of chief rabbi in the summer of 1899.[61] When even this measure failed to restore order, however, the local *vali*, Kemal Pasha, compelled new elections in December of 1900.[62] Rabbi Joseph Bensenyor was elected by a vote of 13 to 2 and publicly accepted his new position in front of the palace.[63]

The crisis of 1899–1900 damaged the apparatus of self-government that Izmir's Jews had constructed only a few years earlier. In the following years the *meclis umumi* all but disappeared, with the chief rabbi appointing the Communal Council in 1901[64] and the local *vali* ordering the nomination of a new one in 1903.[65] More durable than the newly reformed structures of self-government themselves was the constant faith that communal leaders expressed in their potential. In the midst of another financial crisis, one that threatened the existence of the Rothschild Hospital and the *Talmud Tora* in 1907, *El Novelista* blamed the state of affairs on the persistent lack of reform:

> There is no order, there are no statutes. There is no law on which the administration of our community or institutions is based. There is not a single check on the Communal Council, nor on associations. There is no oversight of congregations or schools. There is no *meclis umumi* that might choose the members of the Communal Council, who, as it is known, are meant to report to the the delegates of the people. . . . Everyone proceeds as they see fit, whether they are very intelligent or not, without knowing whether what they do in the public domain is good or bad for the people.[66]

Responding to mounting pressure, the Communal Council agreed to "put an end to the indifference that is killing our institutions one by one" and convene a *meclis umumi*, with its president arguing that "if the people want a *meclis umumi*, we want it even more than they do."[67]

The Young Turk Revolution of 1908 only bolstered such faith in the promise of reform, as the fervor surrounding the promulgation of the second Ottoman constitution sparked renewed debates over the meaning and implementation of "good administration" on the communal level. The lawyer and local notable Albert Tarica, for example, argued that the 1897 statutes were fundamentally unjust in how they mandated the election of delegates to the general assembly. The statutes dictated that each congregation be allotted ten delegates but made no stipulation regarding the size of the congregations, which for Tarica was a guarantee that there would be "no proportion in representation."⁶⁸ Another observer commented that even the statutes' reliance on the congregation as a unit of representation was no longer appropriate, particularly because it would exclude young people, who had reportedly been attending synagogue in diminishing numbers. Given that the *meclis umumi* needed to be "the expression of the will of the people," he wrote, "all of the constituent elements of the community need to be equitably represented." It was the voices of young people, with their knowledge of "modern needs," that most needed to be heard. "Why allow laws from another century to put them at a disadvantage?" he wondered.⁶⁹ Exploring the alternative models being discussed in the community, the author weighed nominating delegates by neighborhood as well as by association, finding pitfalls in both methods. He concluded that the way to ensure the broadest franchise would be to reduce the number of delegates nominated by each synagogue from ten to six, yielding a total of sixty. The remaining forty delegates would then be elected in a special session to which "the youth would be invited."⁷⁰

When the *meclis umumi* finally met a few weeks later for the first time in years, the delegates themselves were perplexed not only by the manner of their election but by the continued validity and relevance of the 1897 statutes overall. Denouncing the meeting as "illegal," one delegate, Haim Levi, argued that "elections limited to congregations are not just" and dismissed the 1897 statutes as "invalid."⁷¹ Taking the opposite position was Joseph Estrugo, who explained that "any existing law can only be annulled by a new law." Until it convened a general assembly to undertake such a task, the council had no choice but to act in accordance with the statutes. Furthering his argument, Estrugo added:

> We have brilliant proof of this in front of our eyes. The Ottoman Committee of Union and Progress decreed for us the Constitution on the basis of the existing *kanun-ı esasi* even though there are certain articles that need modification. The committee left this work to the new parliament.⁷²

As for the statutes, in the winter of 1909, the *Alliance* administrator David Nabon reported that the administration had begun to revisit them in order to render them "more in line than the old ones with the new political regime of our country."⁷³ Completed by 1911, the revised statutes bore many similarities to their previous iterations, establishing clear boundaries between the Communal Council, chief rabbinate, and general assembly. They retained direct lay supervision of all matters related to congregations, education, and charity and, more broadly, affirmed lay authority over all associations and institutions of "public utility."[74] Yet the 1911 statutes also bore striking differences from their prior versions, as the debates over maximizing representation had led to a series of changes. The total number of delegates was reduced from one hundred to sixty, of whom four had to be rabbis and six had to be Ashkenazi Jews. While elections would still take place via congregations, no longer was each one allocated ten delegates. Instead, any congregation member over the age of 20 could vote on all sixty delegates, "whether from among the members of his synagogue or from others."[75] The continued emphasis on congregations as an organizational unit notwithstanding, this was the broadest franchise the community would ever implement.

Notably, whereas the 1897 statutes lacked provisions regulating the rabbinate, the 1911 version contained multiple sections regarding the role and responsibilities of the chief rabbi and rabbinical court. It was almost certainly the turmoil surrounding the appointment of a chief rabbi in 1899 that led administrators to mandate a tightly regulated and orderly transfer of power during moments of rabbinic succession. Upon a vacancy in the position of Chief Rabbi, the Communal Council, *meclis umumi,* and *meclis ruhani* (or religious council) would convene a joint assembly to elect an "acting rabbi" by secret ballot. After soliciting candidates via the local press, the Communal Council would conduct "an in-depth investigation of each of the candidates" and relay a list of candidates to the general assembly. The *meclis umumi,* the formal organ of *el puevlo,* would then "proceed to the definitive election of the chief rabbi" no more than one month after the official "close of the competition."[76]

In contrast to prior efforts, this fully articulated apparatus of reformed self-government was indeed implemented. Beginning in 1908, the *meclis umumi* convened on a regular basis, reviewing the activities of the Communal Council and questioning its decisions when necessary.[77] The biggest test for the new communal administration emerged in 1912, when it came time to replace Chief Rabbi Joseph Bensenyor, whose advanced age and failing health had made him increasingly unable to fulfill his role. A growing consensus emerged around the candidacy of Rabbi Nissim Danon, then chief rabbi of Rhodes. Yet the Communal Council nevertheless wrote to the chief rabbi of the empire asking for advice. Though eager to "benefit from the accord and harmony that reigned in the community," the council still wished to consider other candidates "for the sake of good administration" and asked for recommendations.[78] Commitment to the statutes continued to frame the process that followed, as the *meclis umumi* convened in November of 1912 to decide the matter. The backdrop of the Balkan Wars provoked protracted debates regarding the significance of the post of chief rabbi and his relationship to the state, as well as the ability of the community to finance the post. Finally, despite some disagreements, Aaron Joseph Hazan urged the assembly to "respond to the wish of the people and proceed to our vote."[79] The statutes' provisions regarding the transfer of rabbinic power were read aloud, and the fifty-four delegates in attendance moved to a vote. Rabbi Nissim Danon was elected to the post by an almost unanimous vote of fifty-two to one, with one abstention. The president of the general assembly, Behor de Chaves, then proclaimed Rabbi Nissim Danon chief rabbi of the community.

Congratulating his fellow delegates on a markedly uneventful transfer of rabbinic authority, President Behor de Chaves reflected, "we have needed this for thirteen years. The internal and external calm with which our vote today is being proclaimed will stand out in the annals of the community and open new horizons for our progress." Aaron Joseph Hazan was particularly impressed with the tenor of the debates. "Elderly people like me are, for the first time, seeing the nomination of a chief rabbi decided in an atmosphere of peace and harmony. This moment that we are experiencing together is a psychological milestone in the annals of the community and we should make the most of it."[80]

Marked as it was by constant experimentation, revision, and debate, at first glance the articulation of modern institutions of Jewish self-government in Izmir might be read as a fragile and ultimately ineffectual enterprise. As with the process that took place in the community of Istanbul, where statutes were only fully applied forty-three years after their initial promulgation,[81] the often partial and uneven application of such statutes in Izmir and their notable failure to prevent the conflict of 1899 makes such a reading even more tempting. Yet such an interpretation misses the significance of the project altogether and ultimately makes demands of historical actors that they did not make of themselves. The variegated but nearly constant efforts that Jews in Izmir devoted, over the course of four decades, to elaborating statutes and representative structures of self-government points to their belief that such innovations were preconditions for any form of progress. Reflecting the nature of codification as a "state of mind,"[82] the countless drafts, meetings, debates, and elections reflect a dynamic experimentation and relentless commitment to reconfiguring traditional hierarchies and vesting authority in *el puevlo*. Such was the attitude of those engaged in the experiment themselves, as Nissim Kuri of the Communal Council reflected, while presenting revised statutes to the *meclis umumi* in 1912: "these statutes constitute a structure that demands the work of many future councils. To be able to apply them, each council has the responsibility to add a stone for the construction of this edifice."[83]

The Chief Rabbinate

In tandem with changes in lay leadership structure, Izmir's Jewish community also saw an important transformation of its rabbinate. Although Ottoman Sephardim enjoyed significant autonomy in adjudicating internal religious matters, even before the nineteenth century there were considerable limitations to rabbinic authority. First, despite their high degree of activity, rabbinical courts bore no official recognition from the state in economic, civil, or criminal cases (religious matters were the exception) and could always be overruled by *sharia* courts.[84] In Izmir, Jews not only made ample use of *sharia* courts[85] but also frequently appealed to the state for intervention in religious matters. In 1847–48, numerous appeals were sent to the state asking for intervention in the crisis over rabbinic leadership, appeals that the state answered "unwillingly."[86] In 1889, the chief rabbi approached the ministry of justice, complaining that he was in a "difficult situation" and asking for help in requiring the community to pay the meat *gabela*. The request was soon referred to the grand viziership.[87] Similarly, in 1890 Izmir's *shohatim* appealed to the governor of Aydın province, complaining about having to pay the meat *gabela* while also being subject to the municipality's price ceiling. The governor replied that both financial instruments were necessary, reminding them that the gabela was a "religious obligation."[88] In 1913, the chief rabbi sent a telegram to the local *vali* complaining of a "scandal" provoked by the conversion of two Jewish girls to Islam. While the request for conversion itself had been denied by the Ottoman authorities due to the girls' young age, the rabbi petitioned for assistance in retrieving the girls from Muslim families.[89] As these sources show, it was not the rabbinate but the Ottoman state that served as the ultimate enforcer of Jewish law.

Beginning in the nineteenth century, the *Tanzimat* reforms had begun to chip away at this already circumscribed rabbinic authority. Once *millets* were required to submit to mixed tribunals in the 1840s and later, in the 1850s, to the French penal and commercial codes, rabbinic authority was officially limited to matters of personal status.[90] Additionally, the Ottomanist vision undergirding the reforms sought to diminish religious law in favor of a shared, secular one and therefore favored limiting the authority of the clergy.[91] As this chapter has already shown, an increasingly empowered laity in Izmir sought to curtail rabbinic authority in numerous ways. Statutes elaborated in the Jewish community required that the chief rabbi be elected by a general assembly[92] and further circumscribed his authority by making all of his activities contingent upon the approval of the Communal Council.[93]

While Chief Rabbi Abraham Palacci was a reliable supporter of rationalizing reform, not all in the rabbinical establishment shared his perspective. When debates first surfaced regarding the need for statutes in 1884, members of the rabbinic establishment initially protested their implementation. Citing fears that statutes would empower those with standing disputes against the community and foment "confusion," one rabbi labeled the statutes "a great embarrassment for our community."[94] Similar concerns surfaced in 1897, when Rabbi Abraham Palacci relayed the concerns of communal rabbis who protested their diminishing authority at the expense of the lay council. "If the revenue of the city were in their [lay leaders'] hands, this might have been correct," they argued, but "the revenue of the city comes from dietary laws and *ketubbot*, etc., which are religious."[95] In 1909, the *hai kevu'im*, a group of eighteen men who were traditionally paid to study full-time on behalf of the community, voiced similar concerns about their diminishing authority. That year, they decided to approach the chief rabbi and ask him to rule that "the power of the religious [council] is higher than that of the lay [council]."[96]

The act of *herem*, or excommunication, might be the most revealing metric of eroding rabbinic authority. Fully severing a person's social, economic, and religious ties, the act of *herem* had theoretically dire consequences and was the strongest punishment that rabbis could mete out. In Izmir, rabbis continued to make use of the instrument into the twentieth century, seeking to use it to police all sorts of activities and behavior. However, the sources suggest that by the late nineteenth century, the act of *herem* had lost much of its bite. In 1888, for example, the rabbinical establishment threatened to excommunicate any customer who might patronize Ashkenazi butchers in order to protest high *gabela* sales taxes, a threat that meant withholding circumcision, enrollment in schools, support from the *Bikkur Holim* Society, access to the hospital, and burial in the communal cemetery.[97] Yet the butchery system of the Ashkenazi community continued undisturbed,[98] as Semtob Pariente reported that "despite the excommunication, this week its [the Communal Council's] revenue has diminished by 500 *francs*. This reduction will be much more considerable next week."[99] Similarly, in 1896, Rabbi Abraham Palacci excommunicated the journalist Jacob Algrante of *El Novelista*,[100] who had reportedly plunged the community into "revolution" by publishing a scathing article alleging corruption in the levy of the *gabela* tax on meat.[101] Not only did the excommunication order fail to curb Algrante's influence, but, as we saw in chapter 4, it accomplished the exact reverse, as "this obscure journalist of yesterday ha[d] all of a sudden become the idol of the community." Observing the furor in the community, Gabriel Arié remarked that "the chief rabbi has been unanimously blamed for having used in this circumstance a fairly rusty weapon."[102]

Despite the weakening of its traditional authority, however, as an institution the rabbinate was far from irrelevant. In 1835, the Ottomans created the new office of *haham bashi*, or "chief rabbi," whose holder was to represent all of Ottoman Jewry. Both in the imperial center and in the provinces, the chief rabbinate was recast as an official extension of the Ottoman state. Assumption of the position of chief rabbi became predicated upon approval by the Ottoman authorities and the procurement of an official *berat*.[103] In Izmir, Rabbi Raphael Pinhas de Segura became the first to bear the formal title of *haham bashi* for the city in 1840. His *berat* ordered that "no one infringe upon his word when it is reasonable," and that his flock "never cease to submit and obey him in all that concerns their religion."[104]

A product of this official sanction was the expectation that the *haham bashı* serve as the community's formal intercessor with the authorities. Over the course of his thirty years in the role, Abraham Palacci did this numerous times, particularly in the realm of taxation. In 1891, for example, Palacci emphasized the need to fine those who had evaded paying taxes due to the state,[105] while in 1898, he transmitted a request on behalf of the *vali*, who was frustrated that the community had delayed in submitting its *bedel* registers.[106] In 1909, the Communal Council reminded the administrators of the *Talmud Tora* that the only way to address local authorities regarding any issue was through the chief rabbinate.[107]

Beyond the functional role of intercessor, the chief rabbinate was re-envisioned as a representative of the broader Jewish community. The 1884 draft statutes stipulated that the chief rabbi had to "be an Ottoman subject, between 35 and 55 years of age on the day of his election, be of good constitution and appearance, have a good reputation and no criminal or civil record, and have deep knowledge of the Torah, the Hebrew language (the holy tongue), and Judeo-Spanish, as well as the language of the government."[108] Upon official sanction of his nomination, a new chief rabbi would need to demonstrate his "loyalty to His Majesty the Sultan and the imperial government."[109] The 1911 statutes notably dropped the requirement of fluency in Hebrew and Ladino but added the requirement that the chief rabbi be married.[110] The public nature of the position is further evidenced by the preoccupation that surfaced in 1876 over the space that Abraham Palacci used to receive official visitors, as *La Esperanza* lamented that it did not "bring any honor to our community."[111]

Intersecting with the chief rabbi's embodiment of Jewish loyalty was the way his position simultaneously affirmed the distinct place of Jews in the broader Ottoman social mosaic. In contrast to the ongoing debates regarding reformed Jewish self-government, which invoked a discourse of "rights," the rabbinate remained a vehicle for communal "privilege." The continued commingling of these two discourses remained a hallmark of Izmir's *kehillah* in the modern age. The assumption that the office of the communal *haham bashı* ensured Jewish privilege informs the first imperial *berat* granted in Izmir to Raphael Pinhas de Segura in 1840. Through the mechanism of the *berat*, the Jews of Izmir were assured that no one would "disturb them or intervene in their religion," or "say to them 'this is permitted, this is forbidden,'" and were guaranteed the privilege of living "according to their law and ancient custom."[112] Nor could anyone intervene when the rabbinate sought to punish any who might contravene Jewish law.[113] The function of the *haham bashı* as the securer of Jewish privilege continued throughout the late Ottoman period, persisting beyond the Young Turk Revolution. As communal leaders acknowledged in 1912, as they were debating replacing Joseph Bensenyor:

> In saying "chief rabbi," many imagine a leader concerned only with the preservation of the Jewish religion. This is a big mistake. A chief rabbi in Turkey has an entirely different importance than that which he has in other countries. There is a multitude of civil and political privileges that non-Muslims enjoy in Turkey, an essentially religious country. The Turkish government accords us these privileges only through the vehicle of a chief rabbi of any constituted community. This chief rabbi is therefore the only one invested with the power of using these privileges in front of the community he heads and the government he faces.[114]

The Rabbinate as Progress

Given the public function of the chief rabbi, the rabbinate also became a symbol and metric of the community's "progress." The ongoing efforts to draft and implement organic statutes enjoyed marked rabbinic support, leading *La Buena Esperanza* to note how "lucky our community is to have such enlightened rabbis who think only about instruction, prosperity, and the progress of our compatriots."[115] When Haim Polako and Alexander Sidi later resigned from the Communal Council upon the defeat of the statutes in 1884, it was Chief Rabbi Abraham Palacci who urged them to reconsider, assuring them that their drive to "do good in the community would always enjoy his support."[116] Even when some among the rabbinic establishment feared the encroachment of statutes on their authority, Palacci's support was never in question, as members of the Communal Council told him: "with you at our head, we do not fear anything."[117] Again in 1896, Palacci pressed the need for rationalizing statutes, arguing that without them, "there can be no peace in the community."[118]

FIGURE 14. Chief Rabbi, Abraham Palacci, Izmir, 1896.
Source: © Beit Hatfustot, The Oster Visual Documentation Center, Tel Aviv, Courtesy of Families Hasson, Izmir/Alexandria/Marseille.

The reconfiguration of the rabbinate as a vehicle for communal progress continued throughout the late Ottoman era. Just as the 1908 nomination of Rabbi Haim Nahum to the post of chief rabbi of the empire was celebrated as "a very great success for the new spirit,"[119] similar hopes surrounded the search for a replacement for Rabbi Joseph Bensenyor in 1912. Beseeching the community for donations to underwrite the search process, the Communal Council declared that "no one denies the need to have a chief rabbi of modern culture at our head." Reflecting the rabbi's role in disseminating this "modern culture," lay notables described their ideal candidate as one who would help "develop the instruction of our children" and advocate for their entrance into the "establishments of higher learning of the imperial government."[120] Once appointed in 1913, Rabbi Nissim Danon spoke of his responsibility to "walk at the head of the holy army of those who strive to serve the progress of humanity."[121]

Perhaps the most salient expression of the evolution of Izmir's chief rabbinate into a vehicle for social advancement was its steadfast support of the activities of the *Alliance Israélite Universelle*. From its earliest days in Izmir in the 1870s, *Alliance* administrators found in the local rabbinate an unflagging ally. At the opening of its first school in town in 1873, Rabbi Abraham Palacci delivered a speech invoking Talmudic passages demonstrating that "instruction was not only tolerated but mandated by the ancient rabbis."[122] This support continued throughout his tenure, even when the lay council was at odds with the *Alliance* over certain aspects of its curriculum.[123] When the community gathered to celebrate the schooling network's twenty-fifth anniversary in Izmir in 1898, Palacci highlighted how "the moral and material progress" of the *Alliance* had been realized without "weakening the religious sentiments" of the community, and even pledged a personal subscription.[124] The significance of Palacci's continued commitment to the *Alliance* was not lost on its administrators. As Gabriel Arié noted, while the *Alliance* had encountered obstacles in its dealings with rabbis in many other communities, "it will be an eternal honor for the Community of Izmir to have had at its head an enlightened and dignified leader such as his Eminence the Chief Rabbi Abraham Palacci, who encouraged with all of his strength the new establishment [the *Alliance*], served as an example for all of the rabbis and councils that have run the community up until this day, and in whom we have always found the most sincere and devoted support."[125] When Palacci died, just a year later, the Ladino press lamented the loss not only of a distinguished scholar but of a leader who helped the community make "enormous steps towards progress"[126] and who was always "the first to applaud every new endeavor in instruction, progress, and civilization."[127]

Rabbinic support for the *Alliance* persisted in Izmir beyond Palacci's time. Celebrating the fiftieth anniversary of the *Alliance* in 1910, a Rabbi Abulafia composed a prayer on the institution's behalf, honoring those French Jews who had "devoted themselves to removing our shame" by establishing *batei haskalah*, or "houses of enlightenment."[128] Accepting his nomination to the post of chief rabbi three years later, Rabbi Nissim Danon, who was himself an *Alliance* alumnus, publicly thanked the institution and promised "to work for the civilizing and humanitarian work of the *Alliance* with self-sacrifice for [his] whole life."[129]

Distinguishing it from many other Ottoman Sephardi communities where a "mutually suspicious and antagonistic"[130] relationship abided between the *Alliance* and local rabbinates, the unflinching support of Izmir's rabbinate for the French-Jewish educational network must be read against the backdrop of the community's struggle with its intense poverty. As scholars such as Matthias Lehmann have shown, Ladino *musar* literature reflects the fact that early modern Ottoman Jewish society was characterized by "an alliance, both ideological and practical, between the learned elite of the *talmidei hahamim* and the wealthy of the community."[131] Yet the view from late Ottoman Izmir suggests that in the modern period, this alliance seems not only to have crumbled but even to have been completely reversed. In the conflict surrounding the nomination of a successor to Rabbi Haim Palacci in 1869, it was reportedly Izmir's Jewish poor and working classes who rallied to his son Abraham's side, appealing to the Ottoman state as well as foreign consuls to allow him to replace Rabbi Joseph Hakim, an avowed critic of secular education who had been designated locum tenens by the chief rabbi of the Empire.[132] Somewhat paradoxically, in 1893 Chief Rabbi Abraham Palacci argued forcefully against refounding *Ozer Dalim*.[133] Perhaps evincing frustration with the association's inability to fund its activities without recourse to controversial *gabela* taxes, Palacci claimed that "it is clear that it favors the rich while causing *sa'akat ani'im* [the cry of the poor]." He rejected outright the proposal to earmark revenue from *ketubbot* and the *gabela* on matza, arguing that the Communal Council could not even cover its own expenses related to the upcoming Passover holiday, and further expressed surprise and dismay at the priorities of the Communal Council. "I do not understand in what conscience the *Kolel* could diminish money for the poor to ensure that *ba'alei batim* [heads of household] are not bothered," Palacci wrote, adding that levying a *gabela* on meat would almost certainly cause many people to violate the dietary laws.[134]

Similarly, in the troubled transfer of power in 1899, Izmir's Jewish poor demonstrated a significant interest in keeping the seat within the Palacci family dynasty. As Gabriel Arié observed in the days after Abraham Palacci died, "small corporations of workers, butchers, day laborers, grocers, etc. have free rein: guided by leaders who are paid underhandedly by interested parties, they clamor for Palacci [to be] at the head of the community."[135] Their favored candidate for the post, Solomon Palacci, made the plight of Izmir's Jewish poor central to his campaign for the rabbinate, calling for the lifting of the despised *gabela* tax on meat and establishing an independent butchery to that end. As Palacci reportedly explained to Arié, "in a community where there is no direct personal tax, the poor man has more of a right to the management of communal affairs than the rich."[136] Furthermore, Palacci promised that as chief rabbi he would protect communal subsidies to the *Alliance* and expressed his "favorable sentiments, along with those of the poor, toward the *Alliance*."[137]

While Solomon Palacci ultimately did not become Izmir's chief rabbi, the discourse employed by those who preceded him demonstrates how the traditional alliance between the rabbinical establishment and the wealthy had been upended. In December 1900, *El Meseret* reported that upon hearing the remarks delivered by the new *haham bashi*, Rabbi Joseph Bensenyor, "the hearts of all of our poor beat with joy" as they "learned that the first words our chief rabbi uttered in front of the governor's residence were that he [would serve] as the father of the poor and would take care of them, and all of us, as though we were his own children."[138] Communal leaders sought to formally institutionalize this new alliance between the rabbinate and the poor in their creation of an official oath to be taken by the chief rabbi upon his nomination. In addition to swearing to "safeguard the prestige of our religion, show loyalty to the country, respect the statutes of the community, and always work for the progress, prestige, and dignity of the community," a new chief rabbi would be required to swear that his acts would always be "inspired by the principles of justice and impartiality without making distinctions between the poor and the rich."[139] In the remarks he delivered after taking this oath in 1913, Rabbi Nissim Danon sketched what he called "the portrait of a chief rabbi," highlighting the qualities he deemed essential in the figure. Among the numerous roles a chief rabbi must play, he argued, was that of a "natural intermediary between the fortunate and the disinherited of the earth." He continued, "the rabbi must strive to garner the support of the first to lessen the suffering of the latter." Charged no longer with sustaining a traditional social hierarchy but rather with upending it, by 1912 Izmir's chief rabbi had new responsibilities. As Rabbi Danon argued, "instruction, work, the institutions that improve the social status of the people, the alleviation of suffering—none have a better supporter."[140]

While across the Jewish world Jewish self-government was typically dismissed as unsuitable for the modern age, in the Ottoman context, the *kehillah* was regarded as essential to it. Far from dismissing it as a relic of an outdated past or an impediment to Jewish integration, the modern Ottoman state not only tolerated the *kehillah* structure but demanded its preservation. Yet, as this chapter has shown, the undisturbed legitimacy of the *kehillah* by no means suggests that it was static, as both the lay and rabbinical leadership structures saw profound transformation during the late Ottoman period. Through countless debates, drafts, meetings, and arguments spanning more than three decades, Izmir's Jews overturned the traditional flow of authority in their *millet*, vesting it not at the top but at the bottom, in *el puevlo*. They drew on a range of modern tools, such as codes, ballots, elections, and assemblies, to accomplish this. The rabbinate saw a similar reconfiguration, as its traditional religious authority was overshadowed by its personification of the community's state-sanctioned privilege as well as its new mandate to ease social strife and protect the interests of the poor. Animating efforts to transform both of these communal institutions was not only a commitment to "progress" but an understanding that it demanded a reversal of prevailing social hierarchies.

CONCLUSION

Many questions preoccupied the Jews of Ottoman Izmir in the modern period. The "scandal of begging"[1] haunted the community for decades, as elites campaigned to remove the Jewish poor from city streets. Once this "scandal" was controlled, the very legitimacy of poverty itself was questioned, as the poor learned to demonstrate their "authenticity" while traditional institutions such as the *Talmud Tora* were reimagined to solve *la kuestion de los ofisios*, or "the question of trades."[2] Alongside these questions created by shifting attitudes to poverty were ones emerging from its replacement with middle-class values, as Izmir's Jews endeavored to master a subtle set of behaviors "not acquired in books."[3]

More questions emerged within the structure of the *kehillah* itself. The desire for *el buen rijo*, good administration,[4] led to protracted debates about how to serve an increasingly self-confident *puevlo*, while journalists and lay leaders alike spoke of a *kuestion rabinika* and a *kuestion de eleksiones*[5] as they reenvisioned the structures undergirding lay and rabbinic authority. And, of course, the most persistent, controversial, and divisive questions throughout the late Ottoman period remained those surrounding the kosher meat industry. Vexing rabbis, lay oligarchs, suppliers, sellers, and consumers alike, *la kuestion de los shohatim*, *la kuestion de la gabela*, *la kuestion de la karne*, and even *la kuestion del dia*[6] reflect not merely the exploitation entrenched in a frequently corrupt monopoly but a protracted struggle to reconcile the longstanding taxation system with the ongoing need for a self-sufficient *kehillah* that might remain sensitive to the needs of the impoverished.

What unites these many questions are their socioeconomic dimensions and implications. As this book has demonstrated, the modern age demanded that the Jews of Ottoman Izmir reconsider their relationship to poverty—its public visibility, causes, remedies, and even its very legitimacy. This changed relationship reverberated across many communal structures and settings, as communal leaders debated how it should impact the domains of charity, governance, and finances. Alongside this changed position of poverty was the evolution of a new set of attitudes to socioeconomic difference and stratification in general, as the discourses and practices of a Westernized middle class were ascendant. As this transformed landscape demonstrates, what is far more revealing than sorting Izmir's Jews into discrete and non-overlapping categories such as bourgeois, petty bourgeois, working class, and poor, among others, is examining instead their negotiation of the boundaries between them, reinforcing the utility of conceiving of class not as "faction" but as "relationship."[7] These shifting boundaries were constantly debated in an evolving and vibrant Ladino public sphere that was deeply invested in "progress" and its demands.

Crucially, this sustained engagement with the demands of modernity unfolded in the absence of a "Jewish question." The challenge as Izmir's Jews understood it was not how to minimize their religious distinctiveness or harmonize it with that of a majority, but instead how to mobilize it in service of new social hierarchies. Thus the festival of Purim preoccupied them not because of its public declaration of Jewish "nationality" but because of its annual unveiling of the poverty the community had worked so hard to hide. The *Talmud Tora* became the object of intense reform efforts due not to a critique of Jewish tradition but to the school's failure to foster upward social mobility for its hundreds of students. Those who sought such upward social mobility through the cultivation of new residential patterns, associational life, and philanthropic activities displayed no anxiety about marking themselves openly as Jews, nor was their access to the city's broader bourgeois culture stalled because of it. It was, notably, the semiautonomous *kehillah* that remained both a primary venue and a vehicle for these transformations. The copious and ever-escalating attention directed at the kosher meat industry involved no controversy over Jewish ritual as a marker of difference,[8] nor did protracted efforts to reform rabbinical and lay structures reflect a struggle to negotiate dueling allegiances or loyalties. The *kehillah* in late Ottoman Izmir remained relevant and significant and ultimately became an instrumental bearer of a modern agenda.

In addition to cautioning against a presumed universality of the "Jewish question" and its various formulations across the Jewish world, this case study invites a reappraisal even of how social class has been studied in Jewish history. The Sephardi Jews of Ottoman Izmir were certainly not the only heavily impoverished Jewish community to confront the modern age, nor were they alone in striving for upward social mobility. Yet existing paradigms of class in the Jewish world still assume its interaction with a navigation of Jewish difference that typically intensified in contexts of deepening politicization. In the Russian Pale of Settlement, for example, an unrelenting and increasingly violent "Jewish question" led Jews to debate the elaboration of a new and just social order as they cultivated diverse ideological commitments to socialism, nationalism, or some combination thereof.[9] Such class awareness intensified in locales like New York City, where Jews participated heavily in a rapidly industrializing economy.[10] Even in contexts where social class has been treated apart from its relationship to politicization, such as in relatively tolerant England, socioeconomic transformation is still measured in terms of the European metrics of acculturation and assimilation, as the weakening of corporate Jewish identity and the retreat of religious tradition provide a corrective to the assumption that Jewish modernity emerged from ideological change alone.[11]

The case study of Izmir, then, suggests new directions in the study of Sephardi Jewish modernity. Nearly all accounts of the Sephardi world of the modern Mediterranean take its endemic poverty and polarization as a given, leaving them as an un-interrogated part of the scenery and a reflection of larger decline. However, as this book has demonstrated, it is precisely within this social landscape and its nineteenth-century reconfiguration that we find profound adjustment, experimentation, and negotiation among the Jews of Izmir. This analysis thus invites immediate comparison with other Sephardi communities across the Ottoman world. Istanbul, for example, saw numerous conflicts in its kosher meat industry over the course of the nineteenth century, culminating in a massive strike of butchers in 1908, while Salonica too saw periodic friction around the levy of the *gabela* tax.[12] Approaching the Sephardi diaspora through the prism of class relationships might also put other conflicts, such as those that roiled Istanbul Jewry over educational reform in the 1850s and 1860s, in a new light. Situating the socioeconomic transformations of Izmir within a regional context thus points to the potential of mapping a broader Ottoman Sephardi paradigm of modernity that merits further study.

At the same time, a focus on social class will undoubtedly reveal the diversity that characterized the Ottoman Sephardi world as well. Just across the Aegean in Salonica, a very different set of circumstances shaped the experience of the Jewish community there. By the 1880s, the city had seen significant industrialization, with the establishment of more than thirty factories and mills, and given their demographic majority, Jews were heavily represented among an increasingly self-aware working class. In 1909, Jews were instrumental in establishing the Workers Socialist Federation of Salonica, which counted thousands of Jews among its membership and published numerous Ladino newspapers and pamphlets.[13] Their activities in those few, but consequential, years until Salonica's exit from Ottoman rule in 1912 both reinforce and complicate the crucial function of social class in Ottoman lands. Like their Sephardi coreligionists in Izmir, Salonican Jewish socialists found in their socioeconomic status a modern category of belonging that demanded sustained attention. On the other hand, the industrialization and politicization that marked that belonging for Salonica's Jews suggests a variegated engagement with social class that was heavily contingent on local factors.

Furthermore, the interpretive gains offered by a social prism in studying Ottoman Sephardi Jewry are not restricted to the confines of Jewish history alone. As a category of analysis, socioeconomic class has the potential to illuminate important parallels between the experiences of Jews and their Muslim neighbors that is obscured by the standard and often uninterrogated "Muslim/dhimmi (or ex-dhimmi)" social taxonomy. Prioritizing the socioeconomic status of Jewish stevedores and shoe shiners thus unsettles the category of "Ottoman non-Muslim" in productive ways, given that the category is so often used as a shorthand for the empire's commercial bourgeoisie.

Moreover, a focus on social class and the spheres in which it is most visible, such as work, the family, the neighborhood, and the street, provides much-needed tools with which to test, refine, and reassess categories that are often taken for granted, such as "coexistence." The approach taken in this book suggests that it is not only possible but perhaps likely that the vision of progress held by a Jewish *hamal* in Izmir was much more similar to that of his Muslim fellow dockworkers than to that of a Greek or Armenian merchant on Frank Street. This is a mutuality worthy of further research and interrogation.

Ultimately, this book has sought to tell the story of a neglected community and, through that story, to enrich our understanding of both Ottoman and Jewish modernity and the place of the eastern Sephardi world within it. In so doing, I hope not only to have claimed a voice for Izmir's Jews and the world they inhabited but to argue that their experiences as beggars and rabbis, housewives and peddlers is of profound historical significance.

NOTES

Introduction

1. "Un poko de aktualidad—siempre los shohatim," *La Buena Esperanza*, May 5, 1899, 1.

2. Cazès, October 26, 1873, AAIU I C I-7.

3. Aron Rodrigue, "Difference and Tolerance in the Ottoman Empire," interview with Nancy Reynolds, *Stanford Humanities Review* 5 (Fall 1995): 81–92; Karen Barkey, *Empire of Difference: The Ottomans in Comparative Perspective* (Cambridge: Cambridge University Press, 2008), especially 109–53.

4. The complex mutuality between ethnoreligious belonging and ideologies such as Ottomanism has received significant attention recently. For a study of this relationship through the prism of Palestine, see Michelle Campos, *Ottoman Brothers: Muslims, Christians, and Jews in Early Twentieth-Century Palestine* (Stanford: Stanford University Press, 2011). For a case study of Ottoman Sephardi Jews, see Julia Phillips Cohen, *Becoming Ottomans: Sephardi Jews and Imperial Citizenship in the Modern Era* (Oxford: Oxford University Press, 2014). For a comparative treatment of Ottoman Armenians, Arabs, and Jews, see Bedross Der Matossian, *Shattered Dreams of Revolution: From Liberty to Violence in the Late Ottoman Empire* (Stanford: Stanford University Press, 2014).

5. Esther Benbassa, "Associational Strategies in Ottoman Jewish Society in the Nineteenth and Twentieth Centuries," in *The Jews of the Ottoman Empire*, ed. Avigdor Levy (Princeton: Darwin Press, 1994), 457–84; Esther Benbassa and Aron Rodrigue, *Sephardi Jewry: A History of the Judeo-Spanish Community, 14th–20th Centuries* (Berkeley: University of California Press, 2000), 121–29.

6. See Daniel Goffman, *Izmir and the Levantine World: 1550–1650* (Seattle: University of Washington Press, 1990), especially 1–76; and Daniel Goffman, "Izmir: From

Village to Colonial Port City," in *The Ottoman City Between East and West: Aleppo, Izmir, and Istanbul*, eds. Edhem Eldem, Daniel Goffman, and Bruce Masters (Cambridge: Cambridge University Press), 87–90.

7. Abraham Galante, *Les Juifs d'Anatolie: Les Juifs d'Izmir* (Istanbul: Imprimerie Babok, 1937), 12. For more on Jewish settlement in western Anatolia, see Feridun Emecen, *Unutulmuş Bir Cemaat: Manisa Yahudileri* (Istanbul: Eren, 1997), 1–42.

8. Jacob Barnai, "The Origins of the Jewish Community in Izmir in the Ottoman Period," *Peamim: Studies in Oriental Jewry* 12 (1982): 51 (in Hebrew).

9. Goffman, *Izmir and the Levantine World*, 83.

10. Ibid., 80–83, 88.

11. Barnai, "The Origins of the Jewish Community," 51–57.

12. Jacob Barnai, "Organization and Leadership in the Jewish Community of Izmir in the Seventeenth Century," in *The Jews of the Ottoman Empire*, ed. Avigdor Levy (Princeton: Darwin Press, 1994), 279.

13. For example, Seduta no. 47, 24 Nisan [5]645, Prochesos verbales, CAHJP, Tr/Iz. 28 *(soletreo)*.

14. Salomon Rosanes, *Korot ha-Yehudim be-Turkiyah ve'Artzot ha-Kedem* (Sofia: Defus ha-Mishpat, 1934–35), 5:127.

15. Elena Frangakis, "The Ottoman Port of Izmir in the Eighteenth and Early Nineteenth Centuries, 1695–1820," *Revue de l'Occident musulman et de la Méditerranée* 39 (1985): 149–62. For more on the port's commercial activities during this period, see Elena Frangakis-Syrett, *The Commerce of Smyrna in the Eighteenth Century (1700–1820)* (Athens: Centre for Asia Minor Studies, 1992).

16. Reşat Kasaba, *The Ottoman Empire and the World Economy: The Nineteenth Century* (Albany: State University of New York Press, 1988), 61.

17. Ibid., 97.

18. Frangakis, "The Ottoman Port of Izmir," 149.

19. Reşat Kasaba, "İzmir," *Review* XVI, 4 (Fall 1993): 396.

20. Ibid., 398.

21. Traian Stoianovich, "The Conquering Balkan Orthodox Merchant," *The Journal of Economic History* 20, no. 2 (1960): 234–313.

22. Goffman, "Izmir: From Village to Colonial Port City," 121.

23. Kasaba, *The Ottoman Empire and the World Economy*, 97.

24. Ibid., 70.

25. Vangelis Kechriotis, "La Smyrne Grecque: Des communautés au Panthéon de l'Histoire," in *Smyrne, la ville oubliée? Mémoires d'un grand port ottoman, 1830–1930*, ed. Marie-Carmen Smyrnelis (Paris: Editions Autrement, 2006), 64–65. Kechriotis cites the work of the French geographer Vital Cuinet.

26. Elena Frangakis-Syrett, "The Economic Activities of the Greek Community of Izmir in the Second Half of the Nineteenth and Early Twentieth Centuries," in

Ottoman Greeks in the Age of Nationalism: Politics, Economy, and Society in the Nineteenth Century, eds. Dimitri Gondicas and Charles Issawi (Princeton: Darwin Press, 1999), 17–44.

27. Galante, *Les Juifs d'Anatolie*, 15. Galante relies on the *Izmir Vilayeti Salnamesi*, the city's provincial yearbook, for the year 1307 (1891).

28. For more on the division of taxpayers, see Kemal Karpat, *Ottoman Population, 1830–1914: Demographic and Social Characteristics* (Madison: University of Wisconsin Press, 1985), 19.

29. CAHJP, Tr/Iz. 731 (*soletreo*).

30. CAHJP, Tr/Iz. 715 (*soletreo*).

31. Ibid.

32. CAHJP, Tr/Iz. 118 (*soletreo*).

33. "Un ermozo proyekto," *El Comercial*, June 27, 1907, 200.

34. Defter del bedel, CAHJP, Tr/Iz. 113 (*soletreo*).

35. For example, "Novedades lokales," *La Buena Esperanza*, July 6, 1876, 4; "El bedelat askieri," *El Meseret*, January 4, 190, 4.

36. CAHJP, Tr/Iz. 114 (*soletreo*).

37. See for example Prochesos verbales, 5652–1891, 20 Iyar [5]656 (*soletreo*) CAHJP, Tr/Iz. 30; 20 Av Iyar [5]653 (*soletreo*) CAHJP, Tr/Iz. 30; "El konsilio komunal," *La Buena Esperanza*, January 16, 1891, 1.

38. Arié, December 20, 1900, AAIU, Turquie LXXII E 899.

39. "Siempre la alila de sangre," *La Esperanza*, July 16, 1875, 1.

40. "Novedades lokales—ayinda la alila de sangre," *La Esperanza*, March 15, 1877, 4.

41. Pariente, June 14, 1891, AAIU, Turquie II C 8–14. For more on blood libels in western Anatolia, see Leon Kontente, *L'Antisémitisme Grec en Asie Mineure* (Istanbul: Libra Kitap, 2015).

42. Such was the case in 1872 and 1901. See Rabbi Abraham Palacci and telegram, May 3, 1872, AAIU, Turquie II C 8–14; Esther Benbassa, "Le procès des sonneurs de tocsin: Une accusation calomnieuse de meurtre rituel à Izmir en 1901." Reprint from Abraham Haim, ed., *Society and Community: Proceedings of the Second International Congress for Research of the Sephardi and Oriental Jewish Heritage 1984* (Jerusalem: Institute for Research of the Sephardi and Oriental Jewish Heritage, 1991), 35–53.

43. Arié, May 11, 1897, AAIU, Turquie LXXV E 911.05.

44. Ibid., and May 12, 1897.

45. Arié, AAIU, Turquie LXXIV E 911.03 (excerpt from *Alliance Bulletin* as reprinted in *Le Courrier de Smyrne*, February 3, 1894); Communal Council, September 3, 1911, AAIU, Turquie LXXIII E 886.5.

46. Pariente, December 1, 1889, AAIU, Turquie LXXXVII E 1015.8.

47. Arié, May 30, 1900, AAIU, Turquie LXXVI E 911.07.

48. Ibid.

49. "Un poko de aktualidad—siempre los shohatim," *La Buena Esperanza*, May 5, 1899, 1.

50. Matthias Lehmann, *Ladino Rabbinic Literature and Ottoman Sephardic Culture* (Bloomington: Indiana University Press, 2005), 97–99.

51. Yaron Ben-Naeh, "Poverty, Paupers and Poor Relief in Ottoman Jewish Society," *Revue des Études Juives* 163, nos. 1–2 (January–June 2004): 171.

52. Éric Chaumont, "Pauvreté et richesse dans le Coran et dans les sciences religieuses musulmanes," in *Pauvreté et richesse dans le monde méditerranéen*, ed. Jean-Paul Pascual (Paris: Maisonneuve et Larose, 2003), 17–25.

53. Amy Singer, *Charity in Islamic Societies* (Cambridge: Cambridge University Press, 2008), 154.

54. Abraham Marcus, *The Middle East on the Eve of Modernity: Aleppo in the Eighteenth Century* (New York: Columbia University Press, 1989), 214–15.

55. Bronislaw Geremek, *Poverty: A History* (Oxford: Basil Blackwell, 1994), 102.

56. Robert Jütte, *Poverty and Deviance in Early Modern Europe* (Cambridge: Cambridge University Press, 1994), 158–77.

57. Thomas McStay Adams, *Bureaucrats and Beggars: French Social Policy in the Age of Enlightenment* (New York: Oxford University Press, 1990), 33–36.

58. Geremek, *Poverty*, 231.

59. Deniz T. Kilinçoğlu, *Economics and Capitalism in the Ottoman Empire* (Abingdon: Routledge, 2015), 3–4, 85–126.

60. See, for example, Stéphane Yerasmos, "A propos des réformes urbaines des Tanzimat," in *Villes ottomanes à la fin de l'Empire*, eds. Paul Dumont and François Georgeron (Paris: L'Harmattan, 1992), 17–32; Zeynep Çelik, *The Remaking of Istanbul: Portrait of an Ottoman City in the Nineteenth Century* (Seattle: University of Washington Press, 1986).

61. Nadir Özbek, *Osmanlı İmparatorluğu'nda Sosyal Devlet: Siyaset, İktidar ve Meşrutiyet 1876–1914* (Istanbul: İletşim Yayınları, 2002), esp. 65–116.

62. Ferdan Ergut, "Policing the Poor in the Late Ottoman Empire," *Middle Eastern Studies* 38, no. 2 (April 2002): 151–54.

63. Ibid., 153.

64. Sibel Zandi-Sayek, *Ottoman Izmir: The Rise of a Cosmopolitan Port, 1840–1880* (Minneapolis: University of Minnesota Press, 2012), 87.

65. Ergut, "Policing the Poor," 154–57.

66. Aron Rodrigue, *French Jews, Turkish Jews: The Alliance Israélite Universelle and the Politics of Jewish Schooling in Turkey, 1860–1925* (Bloomington: Indiana University Press, 1990), 100–101.

67. Cazès, October 26, 1873, AAIU, I C I.

68. Aron Rodrigue, *Jews and Muslims: Images of Sephardi and Eastern Jewries in Modern Times* (Seattle: University of Washington Press, 2003), esp. 71–104.

69. Cazès, October 26, 1873, AAIU, I C I.
70. Arié, February 19, 1894, AAIU, LXXIV E 911.03.
71. Arié, January 6, 1895, AAIU, LXXIV E 911.02.
72. Angel, December 20, 1900, AAIU, LXXIII E 899.
73. Reşat Kasaba, Çağlar Keyder, and Faruk Tabak, "Eastern Mediterranean Port Cities and Their Bourgeoisies: Merchants, Political Projects, and Nation-States," *Review* X, no. 1 (Summer 1986): 122, 124. For an influential study of the emergence and function of multiple bourgeoisies in the late Ottoman period, see Fatma Müge Göçek, *Rise of the Bourgeoisie, Demise of Empire: Ottoman Westernization and Social Change* (New York: Oxford University Press, 1996).
74. Çağlar Keyder, Y. Eyüp Özveren, and Donald Quataert, "Port Cities in the Ottoman Empire: Theoretical and Historical Perspectives," *Review* XVI, no. 4 (Fall 1993): 524–25.
75. Kasaba, Keyder, and Tabak, "Eastern Mediterranean Port Cities," 121–35; Reşat Kasaba, "Was There a Compradore Bourgeoisie in Mid-Nineteenth Century Western Anatolia?" *Review* XI, no. 2 (Spring 1988): 215–28; Athanasios (Sakis) Gekas, "Class and Cosmopolitanism: The Historiographical Fortunes of Merchants in Eastern Mediterranean Ports," *Mediterranean Historical Review* 24, no. 2 (December 2009): 95–114.
76. Edhem Eldem, "(A Quest for) the Bourgeoisie of Istanbul: Identities, Roles, and Conflicts," in *Urban Governance Under the Ottomans: Between Cosmopolitanism and Conflict*, eds. Ulrike Freitag and Nora Lafi (Abingdon, Oxon: Routledge, 2014), 161–62.
77. Carol E. Harrison, "The Bourgeois after the Bourgeois Revolution: Recent Approaches to the Middle Class in European Cities," *Journal of Urban History* 31, no. 3 (2005): 386.
78. For an important example of such a paradigm in a Middle Eastern context, see Keith David Watenpaugh, *Being Modern in the Middle East* (Princeton: Princeton University Press, 2006).
79. Haris Exertzoglou, "The Cultural Uses of Consumption: Negotiating Class, Gender, and Nation in the Ottoman Urban Centers During the 19th Century," *International Journal of Middle East Studies* 35, no. 1 (February 2003): 85.
80. Vangelis Kechriotis, "Civilisation and Order: Middle-Class Morality among the Greek Orthodox in Smyrna/Izmir at the End of the Ottoman Empire," in *Social Transformation and Mass Mobilisation in the Balkans and Eastern Mediterranean, 1900–1923*, eds. Andreas Lyberatos and Christos Chatziosif (Rethymnon: Crete University Press, 2013), 137–53.
81. Cem Emrence, *Remapping the Ottoman Middle East: Modernity, Imperial Bureaucracy and the Islamic State* (London: I. B. Tauris, 2012), 41–46.
82. Vangelis Kechriotis, "The Greeks of Izmir at the End of the Empire: A Non-Muslim Community Between Autonomy and Patriotism" (PhD diss., Leiden University, 2005), 57.

83. Vangelis Kechriotis, "La Smyrne grecque: Des communautés au panthéon de l'histoire," in *Smyrne, la ville oubliée? Mémoires d'un grand port ottoman, 1830–1930*, ed. Marie-Carmen Smyrnelis (Paris: Editions Autrement, 2006), 70.

84. Anahide Ter Minassian, "Les Arméniens: Le dynamisme d'une petite communauté," in *Smyrne, la ville oubliée? Mémoires d'un grand port ottoman, 1830–1930*, ed. Marie-Carmen Smyrnelis (Paris: Editions Autrement, 2006), 87–90.

85. Marie-Carmen Smyrnelis, *Une société hors de soi: Identités et relations sociales à Smyrne aux XVIIIe et XIXe siècles*, Collection Turcica 10 (Paris: Peeters, 2005), 222.

86. Ibid., 222–28.

87. Zandi-Sayek, *Ottoman Izmir*, 27–28; 128–30.

88. Ibid.

89. Smyrnelis, *Une société hors de soi*, 271.

90. See, for example, Jacob Barnai, "The Origins of the Jewish Community in Izmir in the Ottoman Period," *Peamim: Studies in Oriental Jewry* 12 (1982), 47–58 (in Hebrew); Jacob Barnai, "Congregations in Smyrna in the Seventeenth Century," *Peamim: Studies in Oriental Jewry* 48 (1991): 66–84 (in Hebrew); Jacob Barnai, "Organization and Leadership in the Jewish Community of Izmir in the Seventeenth Century," in *The Jews of the Ottoman Empire*, ed. Avigdor Levy (Princeton: Darwin Press, 1994), 275–83; Jacob Barnai, "The Development of Community Organizational Structures: The Case of Izmir," in *Jews, Turks, Ottomans: A Shared History, Fifteenth Through the Twentieth Century*, ed. Avigdor Levy (Syracuse: Syracuse University Press, 2002), 35–51; Eliezer Bashan, "A Jewish Guild in Izmir at the Beginning of the Eighteenth Century," *Mi-mizrah umi-ma'arav* 5, ed. Ariel Toaff (Ramat Gan: Bar Ilan University Press, 1986), 155–72 (in Hebrew); Eliezer Bashan, "Contacts between Jews in Smyrna and the Levant Company of London in the Seventeenth and Eighteenth Centuries," *Transactions of the Jewish Historical Society of England* 29 (1988): 53–73; Nechama Grunhaus, "The Taxation System of the Jewish Community of Izmir in the Seventeenth through the Nineteenth Centuries," (PhD diss., New York University, 1995); Nechama Grunhaus, *Ha-Misui ba-Kehilah ha-Yehudit be-Izmir ba-me'ot ha'sheva 'esreh veha-shemonah esreh: al pi sefer Avodat Masa le-R. Yehoshu'a Avraham Yehuda* (Tel Aviv: ha-Makhon le-heker ha-Tefutsot, Tel Aviv University, 1997).

91. Since Abraham Galante's 1937 *Les Juifs d'Anatolie: Les Juifs d'Izmir*, which catalogued the community over the course of multiple centuries, very few other works have studied Izmir's Jews diachronically. For a study of Izmir's Jews in the last fifteen years of the Ottoman Empire, see Siren Bora, *Izmir Yahudileri 1908–1923* (Istanbul: Gözlem Gazetecilik, 1995). For another synthetic treatment that focuses on the World War I period and the emergence of the Turkish Republic, see Henri Nahum, *Juifs de Smyrne: XIXe–XX siècle* (Paris: Aubier, 1997). For other work treating specific moments in the community, see Avner Levi, "Ha'Itonut Ha'Yehudit Be'Izmir," *Peamim: Studies in Oriental Jewry* 12 (1982): 86–104; Olga Borovaya, "The

Emergence of the Ladino Press: The First Attempt at Westernization of Ottoman Jews (1842–6), *European Judaism* 43, no. 2 (Autumn 2010): 63–75; Amelia Barquín López, "Un periódico sefardí: 'El Meseret' de Alexandr Ben Guiat," *Sefarad* 57, no. 1 (1997): 3–31. For a translation of forty-five Ottoman-language legal documents into Hebrew, spanning the years 1847 to 1866, see Haim Gerber and Jacob Barnai, *Yehude Izmir ba-me'ah ha-tesha'esreh: Te'udot Turkiyot me-Arhkiyon bet-ha-Din ha-Shar'i* (Jerusalem: Misgav Yerushalayim, 1984). See also Avner Levi, "Ha-Tmurot ba-Manhigut ha-Kehilot ha-Sefardiyot ha-Merkaziyot ba-Imperiyah ha'Otomanit be-Meah ha-Tsha Esre," in *Yemei ha-Sahar: Prakim be-Toldot ha-Yehudim ba-Imperiyah ha-Otomanit*, ed. Minna Rozen (Tel Aviv: Tel Aviv University, 1996) 245–54, (in Hebrew); Avner Levi, "*Shavat Aniim*: Social Cleavage, Class War, and Leadership in the Sephardi Community—The Case of Izmir 1847," in *Ottoman and Turkish Jewry: Community and Leadership*, ed. Aron Rodrigue, Indiana University Turkish Studies 12 (Bloomington: Indiana University Turkish Studies, 1992), 183–202; Benbassa, "Le procès des sonneurs de tocsin; Eliezer Bashan, "Fires and Earthquakes in Izmir in the Seventeenth through the Nineteenth Centuries and a Document on the Accusation Directed against the Jews of Lighting the Fires," *Miqqedem Umiyyam* 2 (1986): 13–27.

92. See, for example, Will Hanley, "Grieving Cosmopolitanism in Middle East Studies," *History Compass* 6/5 (2008): 1346–67; Malte Furhmann, "Cosmopolitan Imperialists and the Ottoman Port Cities: Conflicting Logics in the Urban Social Fabric," *Cahiers de la Méditerranée* 67 (2003): 149–63; Henk Driessen, "Mediterranean Port Cities: Cosmopolitanism Reconsidered," *History and Anthropology* 16, no. 1 (2005): 129–41.

93. Maureen Jackson, "Cosmopolitan Smyrna: Illuminating or Obscuring Cultural Histories?" *The Geographical Review* 102, no. 3: 337–49.

94. Maria Illiou, dir., *Smyrna: The Destruction of a Cosmopolitan Port, 1900–1922* (2012; Proteus Films), DVD.

95. For a classic overview of these questions, see Michael A. Meyer, "Where Does the Modern Period of Jewish History Begin?" *Judaism* 24 (1975): 329–38.

96. See, for example, Jacob Katz, *Out of the Ghetto: The Social Background of Jewish Emancipation, 1770–1870* (New York: Schocken Books, 1973); David Sorkin, *The Transformation of German Jewry, 1740–1840* (New York: Oxford University Press, 1987).

97. Ronald O. Schechter, *Obstinate Hebrews: Representations of Jews in France 1715–1815* (Berkeley: University of California Press, 2003), 35–109.

98. For more on the Russian case, see Jonathan Frankel, *Prophecy and Politics: Socialism, Nationalism, and the Russian Jews, 1862–1917* (Cambridge: Cambridge University Press, 1981); Eli Lederhandler, *The Road to Modern Jewish Politics: Political Tradition and Political Reconstruction in the Jewish Community of Tsarist Russia* (New York: Oxford University Press, 1989); Michael Stanislawski, "Russian Jewry, the Russian State, and the Dynamics of Jewish Emancipation," in *Paths of Emancipation: Jews, States, and*

Citizenship, eds. Pierre Birnbaum and Ira Katznelson, (Princeton: Princeton University Press, 1995), 262–83.

99. Benjamin Nathans, *Beyond the Pale: The Jewish Encounter with Late Imperial Russia* (Berkeley: University of California Press, 2002), 377.

100. David Sorkin, "The Port Jew: Notes Toward a Social Type," *Journal of Jewish Studies* L, no. 1 (Spring 1999): 87–97. For an influential case study of port Jewry, see Lois Dubin, *The Port Jews of Habsburg Trieste: Absolutist Politics and Enlightenment Culture* (Stanford: Stanford University Press, 1999).

101. Steven J. Zipperstein, *The Jews of Odessa: A Cultural History, 1794–1881* (Stanford: Stanford University Press, 1985); Todd M. Endelman, *The Jews of Georgian England, 1714–1830, Tradition and Change in a Liberal Society* (1979; repr., Ann Arbor: University of Michigan Press, 1999).

102. Yosef Kaplan, *An Alternative Path to Modernity: The Sephardi Diaspora in Western Europe* (Leiden: Brill, 2000), 17.

103. For more on "the nation," see Miriam Bodian, *Hebrew of the Portuguese Nation: Conversos and Community in Early Modern Amsterdam* (Bloomington: Indiana University Press, 1997).

104. Yirmiyahu Yovel, *The Other Within: The Marranos* (Princeton: Princeton University Press, 2009).

105. Mitchell B. Hart and Tony Michels, "Introduction," *Cambridge History of Judaism, The Modern World 1815–2000*, eds. Mitchell B. Hart and Tony Michels (Cambridge: Cambridge University Press, 2017), 4.

106. Sarah Abrevaya Stein makes this point with respect to the term "acculturation" in her *Making Jews Modern: The Yiddish and Ladino Press in the Russian and Ottoman Empires* (Bloomington: Indiana University Press, 2004).

107. See the work of Dipesh Chakrabarty, *Provincializing Europe: Postcolonial Thought and Historical Difference* (Princeton: Princeton University Press, 2008).

108. For classic work on the world-systems perspective, see Huri Islamoğlu-İnan, ed., *The Ottoman Empire and the World-Economy* (Cambridge: Cambridge University Press, 1987), especially Immanuel Wallerstein, Hale Decdeli, and Reşat Kasaba, "The Incorporation of the Ottoman Empire into the World Economy," 88–97. For work challenging periodizations of modernity in the Ottoman context, see Butrus Abu-Manneh, "The Islamic Roots of the Gülhane Rescript," *Die Welt des Islams* 34, no. 2 (1994): 173–203; Huri Islamoğlu, "Modernities Compared: State Transformations and Constitutions of Property in the Qing and Ottoman Empires," in *Shared Histories of Modernity: China, India, and the Ottoman Empire*, eds. Huri Islamoğlu and Peter C. Perdue (London: Routledge, 2009), 109–46.

109. For recent examples of such an approach in the study of Ottoman lands, see Kent Schull, *Prisons in the Late Ottoman Empire: Microcosms of Modernity* (Edinburgh: Edinburgh University Press, 2014); Avner Wishnitzer, *Reading Clocks, Alla*

Turca: Time and Society in the Late Ottoman Empire (Chicago: University of Chicago Press, 2015).

110. Timothy Mitchell, "The Stage of Modernity," in *Questions of Modernity*, ed. Timothy Mitchell (Minneapolis: University of Minnesota Press, 2000), 2.

111. Frederick Cooper, *Colonialism in Question: Theory, Knowledge, History* (Berkeley: University of California Press, 2005), 113–49. More recently, Isa Blumi has made this point by drawing on "peripheral" areas of the Ottoman Empire: Isa Blumi, *Foundations of Modernity: Human Agency and the Imperial State* (New York: Routledge, 2012); Isa Blumi, *Reinstating the Ottomans: Alternative Balkan Modernities, 1800–1912* (New York: Palgrave Macmillan, 2011).

112. Watenpaugh, *Being Modern in the Middle East*, 14.

113. Carol Gluck, "The End of Elsewhere: Writing Modernity Now," *The American Historical Review* 116, no. 3 (June 2011): 678.

114. Harry Harootunian, *History's Disquiet: Modernity, Cultural Practice, and the Question of Everyday Life* (New York: Columbia University Press, 2000), 55. This kind of approach has begun to make inroads in Ottoman studies. See Avi Rubin, *Ottoman Nizamiye Courts: Law and Modernity* (New York: Palgrave Macmillan, 2011).

115. Joshua Lewis Goldstein, "Introduction," in *Everyday Modernity in China*, eds. Madeleine Yue Dong and Joshua Lewis Goldstein (Seattle: University of Washington Press, 2006), 6.

116. For an overview of *Tanzimat* reforms, see Roderic Davison, *Reform in the Ottoman Empire, 1856–1876* (Reprint. New York: Gordian Press, 1973); Carter Findley, *Bureaucratic Reform in the Ottoman Empire: The Sublime Porte, 1789–1922* (Princeton: Princeton University Press, 1980); M. Şükrü Hanioğlu, *A Brief History of the Late Ottoman Empire* (Princeton: Princeton University Press, 2008), 55–108. For an early treatment of the reforms and their particular social impact, see Halil İnalcik, "Application of the Tanzimat and Its Social Effects," *Archivum Ottomanicum* 5 (1973): 97–127.

117. Nazan Maksudyan, *Orphans and Destitute Children in the Late Ottoman Empire* (Syracuse: Syracuse University Press, 2014), 78–115; Nazan Maksudyan, "Orphans, Cities, and the State: Vocational Orphanages (*Islahhanes*) and Reform in the Late Ottoman Urban Space," *International Journal of Middle Eastern Studies* 43 (2011): 493–511; Schull, *Prisons in the Late Ottoman Empire*, 111–41, especially 132; Omri Paz, "Civil-Servant Aspirants: Ottoman Social Mobility in the Second Half of the Nineteenth Century," *Journal of the Economic and Social History of the Orient* 60 (2017): 381–419.

118. E. Attile Aytekin, "Peasant Protest in the Late Ottoman Empire: Moral Economy, Revolt, and the *Tanzimat* Reforms," *IRSH* 57 (2012): 191–227; Masayuki Ueno, "For the Fatherland and the State: Armenians Negotiate the Tanzimat Reforms," *International Journal of Middle East Studies* 45 (2013): 93–109; Milen V. Petrov, "Everyday Forms of Compliance: Subaltern Commentaries on Ottoman Reform, 1864–1868," *Comparative Studies in Society and History* 46, no. 4 (October 2004): 730–59.

119. Maurus Reinkowski, "The State's Security and the Subjects' Prosperity: Notions of Order in Ottoman Bureaucratic Correspondence (19th Century)," in *Legitimizing the Order: The Ottoman Rhetoric of State Power*, eds. Hakan Karateke and Maurus Reinkowski (Leiden: Brill, 2005), 200.

120. M. Alper Yalcınkaya, *Learned Patriots: Debating Science, State, and Society in the Nineteenth Century Ottoman Empire* (Chicago: University of Chicago Press, 2015), 219–20.

121. Kilinçoğlu, *Economics and Capitalism*, 72.

122. Ibid., 194, 85–126.

123. M. Şükrü Hanioğlu, *The Young Turks in Opposition* (New York: Oxford University Press, 1995), 214.

124. Y. Doğan Çetinkaya, *The Young Turks and the Boycott Movement: Nationalism, Protest, and the Working Classes in the Formation of Modern Turkey* (London: I. B. Tauris, 2014), 208.

125. Yavuz Selim Karakışla, "The 1908 Strike Wave in the Ottoman Empire," *Turkish Studies Association Bulletin* 16, no. 2 (September 1992), 153–77, especially 156–61.

126. Palmira Brummet, *Image and Imperialism in the Ottoman Revolutionary Press 1908–1911* (Albany: State University Press of New York, 2000), 181–83.

127. M. Şükrü Hanioğlu, "The Second Constitutional Period, 1908–1918," in *Cambridge History of Turkey*, Vol. 4, *Turkey in the Modern World*, ed. Reşat Kasaba (Cambridge: Cambridge University Press, 2008), 82, 109–10.

128. Cohen, *Becoming Ottomans*.

129. For a case study of Ottoman Greeks, see the work of Vangelis Kechriotis, "Greek-Orthodox, Ottoman Greeks, or Just Greeks? Theories of Coexistence in the Aftermath of the Young Turk Revolution," *Études balkaniques* 41, no. 1 (2005): 51–72. For a case study of Ottoman Palestine, see Campos, *Ottoman Brothers*.

130. Der Matossian, *Shattered Dreams*, 7.

131. For more on the Armenian case, see Der Matossian, *Shattered Dreams*, 53–56, 64–66, 74–78, 102–104; for the Greek case, see Vangelis Kechriotis, "The Greeks of Izmir at the End of the Empire: A Non-Muslim Ottoman Community Between Autonomy and Patriotism" (PhD diss., Leiden University, 2005), esp. 134–67.

132. While Der Matossian's argument regarding the insecurity experienced by "nondominant" Ottoman communities does draw on the Jewish case study, it relies heavily on the activities of isolated Zionists, many of whom were European Ashkenazi Jews who failed to attract significant local support.

Chapter 1

This chapter is an adapted version of "Mobilizing the Judería in Service of the City: Shifting Perspectives on Poverty Among the Jews of Late Ottoman Izmir," *International Journal of Turkish Studies* (21:2015), 35–54.

1. "Manifesto ofisial al onorado publiko" (Izmir: La Munisipalidad de Izmirna, n.d., approx. 1910).
2. Ibid.
3. Ibid.
4. For literature exploring this trend across the Ottoman world, see Jens Hanssen, "Public Morality and Marginality in Fin de Siècle Beirut," in *Outside In: On the Margins of the Modern Middle East*, ed. Eugene Rogan (London: I. B. Tauris, 2002), 183–211; Ferdan Ergut, "Policing the Poor in the Late Ottoman Empire," *Middle Eastern Studies* 38, no. 2 (April 2002): 149–64; Nadir Özbek, "'Beggars' and 'Vagrants' in Ottoman State Policy and Public Discourse, 1876–1914," *Middle Eastern Studies* 45, no. 5 (September 2009): 783–801.
5. Roderic Davison, *Reform in the Ottoman Empire, 1856–1876* (1963; Reprint, New York: Goridan Press, 1973), 160.
6. Cânâ Bilsel, "Vers une métropole moderne de la Mediterranée," in *Smyrne, la ville oubliée? Mémoires d'un grand port ottoman, 1830–1930*, ed. Marie-Carmen Smyrnelis (Paris: Editions Autrement, 2006), 128. For more on the early years of Izmir's municipality, see Erkan Serçe, *Tanzimat'tan Cumhuriyet'e Izmir'de Belediye* (Izmir: Dokuz Eylül Yayinlari, 1998), 21–87.
7. Reşat Kasaba, *The Ottoman Empire and the World Economy: The Nineteenth Century* (Albany: State University of New York Press, 1988), 73.
8. Sibel Zandi-Sayek, *Ottoman Izmir: The Rise of a Cosmopolitan Port, 1840–1880* (Minneapolis: University of Minnesota Press, 2012), 115–49.
9. Ibid., 132–37.
10. Baron du Gabé, *Impressions d'un français: échelles du Levant* (Paris: Librairie Th. J. Plange, 1902), 229.
11. François-René Chateaubriand, *Itinéraire de Paris à Jérusalem* (Paris: Garnier Frères, 1872), 182-3.
12. Marcel Monmarché, *De Paris à Constantinople* (Paris: Hachette, 1912), 404.
13. Firmin Rougon, *Smyrne: Situation commerciale et économique des pays compris dans la circonscription du consulat général de France*, (Paris: Berger-Levrault et Compagnie, 1892), 448.
14. CAHJP, Tr/Iz. 723 (*soletreo*).
15. CAHJP, Tr/Iz. 117 (*soletreo*). For a useful survey of various historical maps of Ottoman Izmir, including the 1876 Lamec Saad map, see Çınar Atay, *Osmanlı'dan Cumhuriyet'e Izmir Planları* (Ankara: Ajans Türk, 1998), 2–121.
16. "Novedades lokales," *La Esperanza*, March 18, 1875, 2.
17. "Novedades lokales," *La Esperanza*, March 4, 1875, 4.
18. "Hefzi Pasha," *La Buena Esperanza*, October 12, 1893, 3.
19. Ibid.
20. "La polisia de Izmirna," *El Novelista*, May 4, 1906, 232.
21. "El repozo publiko," *El Novelista*, June 4, 1907, 200.
22. Ibid.

23. "Las kuarentinas," *La Buena Esperanza*, October 26, 1893, 1.

24. Arié, October 20, 1896, AAIU, Turquie LXXIV E 911.01.

25. "Dipteria & mizuras sanitarias," *El Comersial*, October 24, 1907, 3.

26. Arié, June 22, 1900, AAIU, Turquie LXXVI E 911.07.

27. "La landre," *El Meseret*, June 22, 1900, 7.

28. Procheso verbal 77, 25 Heshvan 5671, CAHJP, Tr/Iz. 37 (*soletreo*).

29. "El djudería," *El Meseret*, March 18, 1898, 80.

30. Yaron Ben-Naeh, "Poverty, Paupers and Poor Relief in Ottoman Jewish Society," *Revue des études juives* 163, nos. 1–2 (January–June 2004): 175.

31. CAHJP Tr/Iz. 713 (*soletreo*).

32. Robert Jütte, *Poverty and Deviance in Early Modern Europe* (Cambridge: Cambridge University Press, 1994), 143–46.

33. Ibid., 158–77.

34. Robert Schwartz, *Policing the Poor in Eighteenth-Century France* (Chapel Hill: University of North Carolina Press, 1988), 162.

35. Thomas McStay Adams, *Bureaucrats and Beggars: French Social Policy in the Age of Enlightenment* (New York: Oxford University Press, 1990), 71–90.

36. Stuart Woolf, *The Poor in Western Europe in the Eighteenth and Nineteenth Centuries* (London: Methuen, 1986), 119.

37. Amy Singer, *Charity in Islamic Societies* (Cambridge: Cambridge University Press, 2008), 198–99.

38. "Los limozneros en Izmir," *La Esperanza*, December 31, 1874, 1.

39. "A nuestros meldadores," *La Esperanza*, March 23, 1875, 1.

40. "La kupa Gabbaé Sedaka," *La Buena Esperanza*, June 21, 1888.

41. "Ad matai?" *La Buena Esperanza*, July 13, 1893, 2.

42. "Novedades lokales," *La Esperanza*, August 9, 1878, 2.

43. "Una buena notisia," *La Esperanza*, August 1, 1878, 4.

44. Ibid.

45. Ibid.

46. Abraham Galante, *Les Juifs d'Anatolie: Les Juifs d'Izmir* (Istanbul: Imprimerie Babok, 1937), 89.

47. Procès-verbal de la séance tenue à l'occasion de la présence à Smyrne de M. le Chevalier Veneziani, October 20, 1879, AAIU, Turquie LXXXV E 1015.2.

48. Pariente, August 9, 1878, AAIU, Turquie LXXXV E 1015.2.

49. "Una buena notisia," *La Buena Esperanza*, August 1, 1878, 4.

50. Procès-verbal, October 20, 1879, AAIU, Turquie LXXXV E 1015.2.

51. Pariente, August 9, 1879, AAIU, Turquie LXXXV E 1015.2.

52. Pariente, February 7, 1879, AAIU, Turquie LXXXV E 1015.2.

53. "La kupa Gabbaé Sedaka," *La Buena Esperanza*, October 21, 1880, 1.

54. Procheso verbal, 27 Nisan [5]643, CAHJP, Tr/Iz. 853 (*soletreo*).
55. "La kupa Ozer Dalim," *La Buena Esperanza*, February 2, 1883, 1.
56. "La kupa Gabbaé Sedaka," *La Buena Esperanza*, October 21, 1880, 1; "La kupa Gabbaé Sedaka," *La Buena Esperanza*, January 18, 1883, 3.
57. "La kupa Ozer Dalim," *La Buena Esperanza*, December 21, 1885, 3.
58. "Ozer Dalim a refundar," *El Meseret*, July 11, 1902, 5.
59. "Ozer Dalim," *El Novelista*, May 25, 1906, 301; "Ozer Dalim," *El Novelista*, February 15, 1907, 66.
60. Vangelis Kechriotis, "The Greeks of Izmir at the End of the Empire: A Non-Muslim Community Between Autonomy and Patriotism" (PhD diss., Leiden University, 2005), 64–65.
61. Vangelis Constantinos Kechriotis, "Protecting the City's Interest: The Greek Orthodox and the Conflict between Municipal and *Vilayet* Authorities in Izmir (Smyrna) in the Second Constitutional Period," *Mediterranean Historical Review* 24, no. 2 (December 2009): 214–18.
62. BOA. DH.MKT. 1982/84 10 M 1310; BOA. DH.MKT. 1982/118 11 M 1310.
63. "Las barakas del viejo semeterio," *La Buena Esperanza*, June 1, 1893, 2–3.
64. Arié, January 17, 1894, AAIU, Turquie II C.
65. Prochesos verbales, seduta no. 20, 26 Tammuz [5]642, CAHJP, Tr/Iz. 28 (*soletreo*).
66. Secours distribué aux réfugiés Israélites de Chio, June 5, 1881, AAIU, Turquie LXXIII E 887.3.
67. "Los emigrados rusos," *La Buena Esperanza*, February 2, 1893, 2.
68. One *okka* was equivalent to 1282 grams.
69. "Los emigrados rusos," *La Buena Esperanza*, March 23, 1893, 2.
70. "Los emigrados rusos," *La Buena Esperanza*, April 27, 1893, 2.
71. "Los rusos," *La Buena Esperanza*, May 25, 1893, 2.
72. Ibid.
73. *Journal de Smyrne*, May 11, 1894, AAIU, Turquie LXXIV E 911.03.
74. Ibid.; *Courrier de Smyrne*, May 9, 1894, AAIU, Turquie LXXIV E 911.03.
75. Arié, June 4, 1893, AAIU, Turquie LXXIV E 911.03.
76. "Los rusos," *La Buena Esperanza*, May 25, 1893, 2.
77. "Las barakas del viejo semeterio," *La Buena Esperanza*, June 1, 1893, 2.
78. Bilsel, "Vers une métropole moderne," 134.
79. "Ozer Dalim—las barakas," *La Buena Esperanza*, July 20, 1893, 1.
80. Prochesos verbales, seduta no. 16, 29 Heshvan [5]654, CAHJP, Tr/Iz. 30 (*soletreo*).
81. Galante, *Les Juifs d'Anatolie*, 78; *Ahenk*, January 9, 1915, 3; *Ahenk*, Jan. 18, 1915, 3.
82. Benveniste, May 4, 1891, AAIU, Turquie I C 1.6.

83. Cem Emrence, *Remapping the Ottoman Middle East: Modernity, Imperial Bureaucracy and the Islamic State* (London: I. B. Tauris, 2012), 43.
84. Abraham Benveniste, May 4, 1891, AAIU, I C 1.6.
85. "Novedades lokales," *La Buena Esperanza*, March 4, 1880, 4.
86. Kopia del papel ke se meldo en las kehilot por las kupot i el karnval, [5]645, Prochesos verbales, CAHJP, Tr/Iz. 28 (*soletreo*).
87. Ibid.
88. Ibid.
89. Ibid.
90. "Purim," *La Buena Esperanza*, March 14, 1889, 3.
91. Ibid.
92. See for example "El karnaval defendido," *La Buena Esperanza*, March 14, 1900, 3; "El karnaval," *La Buena Esperanza*, March 4, 1901, 2.
93. "En Purim," *La Buena Esperanza*, March 21, 1889, 2–3.
94. "Novedades lokales," *La Buena Esperanza*, March 11, 1890, 3.
95. "Los karnavales," *La Buena Esperanza*, March 17, 1892, 2.
96. Zandi-Sayek, *Ottoman Izmir*, 159.
97. "Novedades lokales," *La Buena Esperanza*, March 3, 1902, 3.
98. "El Karnaval," *La Buena Esperanza*, February 26, 1903.
99. Zandi-Sayek, *Ottoman Izmir*, 160–70.
100. Vangelis Kechriotis, "Allons, Enfants de la . . . Ville: National Celebrations, Political Mobilisation and Urban Space in Izmir at the Turn of the 20th Century," in *Ottoman Izmir: Studies in Honour of Alexander H. de Groot*, ed. Maurits H. van den Boogert (Leiden: Nederlands Instituut voor het Nabije Oosten, 2007), 133–34.
101. Benveniste, May 4, 1891, AAIU, Turquie I C 1.6.
102. Ibid.
103. "Buen Purim," *La Buena Esperanza*, March 6, 1896, 4.
104. "Los anuyos de Purim," *La Buena Esperanza*, March 23, 1902, 1.
105. Ibid.
106. Ibid.
107. "Avizo de los senyores memunim ve-parnasim al onorado publiko," *La Buena Esperanza*, March 9, 1884, 3.
108. "Prochesos verbales, kopia del papel ke se meldo en las kehilot por las kupot i el karnaval," [5]645, CAHJP, Tr/Iz. 28 (*soletreo*).
109. See, for example: "Las kojitas de Purim," *La Buena Esperanza*, February 28, 1890, 3; Seduta no. 15, 12 Adar Bet 5651, Prochesos verbales, CAHJP, Tr/Iz. 29 (*soletreo*).
110. "Purim: nochada de bayle," *El Meseret*, March 18, 1898, 83.
111. Ibid.
112. Ibid.

113. Ibid.
114. "Reprezentasion teatrala," *La Buena Esperanza*, March 21, 1889, 2.
115. Ibid.
116. "La reprezentasion teatrala," *La Buena Esperanza*, March 17, 1892, 2.
117. Ibid.
118. "Ozer Dalim," *El Novelista*, February 15, 1907, 66.
119. "Ozer Dalim—la reprezentasion teatral de noche de Purim," *El Novelista*, March 16, 1906, 163.
120. *Istoria del ospital Rotshild de Izmir* (Izmir: Rosh Hodesh Tammuz, 5635 [1875]), 1–2. For a recent overview of Izmir's Jewish Hospital, see Siren Bora, *Bir Semt, Bir Bina: Karataş Hastahanesi ve Cevresinde Yahudi Izleri* (Izmir: Izmir Büyükşehir Belediyesi, 2015).
121. "Veinte i sinko anyos de vida de la komunidad israelit de Izmirna," *Edision espesial de La Buena Esperanza*, January 1896, 11.
122. Yom-Tov Assis, "Welfare and Mutual Aid in the Spanish Jewish Communities," in *The Sephardi Legacy*, vol. 1, ed. Haim Beinart (Jerusalem: Magnes Press, 1992), 330–33; Singer, *Charity in Islamic Societies*, 86.
123. Miri Shefer, "Charity and Hospitality: Hospitals in the Ottoman Empire in the Early Modern Period," in *Poverty and Charity in Middle Eastern Contexts*, ed. Michael Bonner, Mine Ener, and Amy Singer (Albany: State University of New York Press, 2003), 137.
124. *Istoria del ospital Rotshild*, 1–2.
125. Ibid., 31.
126. "Veinte i sinko anyos de vida," 10.
127. Galante, *Les Juifs d'Anatolie*, 94.
128. Pariente, October 18, 1878, AAIU, Turquie LXXXV E 1015.2.
129. "Notas sovre el ospidal," *El Novelista*, May 30, 1902, 4.
130. *Istoria del Ospital Rotshild*, 3.
131. Ibid., 5.
132. Ibid., 25–26.
133. Ibid., 57.
134. "El ospidal," *La Buena Esperanza*, September 20, 1894, 1.
135. Ibid.
136. "El ospidal," *La Buena Esperanza*, January 22, 1903, 1.
137. "La fiesta del Ospidal," *La Buena Esperanza*, February 5, 1903.
138. BOA. BEO. 2861/214514 7 Ca 1324; "El ospital israelit," *El Novelista*, May 18, 1905, 284; "Por el bien de la komunidad," *El Novelista*, January 18, 1907, 41.
139. "La fiesta del ospital," *El Comersial*, May 2, 1907, 7.
140. "Izmir ermozeado," *El Soytari*, August 25, 1910, 1–2.
141. Once on the outskirts of Izmir, by the early twentieth century the "Punta"

was deeply integrated into the larger city, connected to the center by train, tramway, and the extended quays. See Bilsel, "Vers une métropole moderne," 126–34.

142. "Izmir ermozeado," *El Soytari*, August 25, 1910, 1–2. The "spear of Pinhas" is a biblical reference, to an episode in the Book of Numbers during which Pinhas zealously kills sinners with his spear to rid the Israelites of idolatry and lewdness.

Chapter 2

1. Albasha Accounts, 1859, CAHJP, Tr/Iz. 821(*soletreo*).
2. "Novedades israelitas," *La Esperanza*, March 4, 1875, 4.
3. Derek Penslar, *Shylock's Children: Economics and Jewish Identity in Modern Europe* (Berkeley: University of California Press, 2001), 95–96.
4. Amy Singer, *Charity in Islamic Societies* (Cambridge: Cambridge University Press, 2008), 186.
5. Ibid., 188.
6. Nadir Özbek, "The Politics of Poor Relief in the Late Ottoman Empire, 1876–1914," *New Perspectives on Turkey* 21 (Fall 1999): 18.
7. Ibid., 21–25.
8. Pariente, August 9, 1879, AAIU, Turquie LXXXV E 1015.2.
9. "Una buena notisia," *La Esperanza*, August 1, 1878, 4.
10. "Procès-verbal de la troisième et dernière séance, tenue à l'occasion de la présence à Smyrne de M. le Chevalier Veneziani, délégué de l'Alliance Israélite Universelle," October 30, 1879, AAIU, Turquie LXXXV E 1015.2.
11. See for example Michel Mollat, *The Poor in the Middle Ages*, trans. Arthur Goldhammer (New Haven: Yale University Press, 1986).
12. Mark Cohen, *Poverty and Charity in the Jewish Community of Medieval Egypt* (Princeton: Princeton University Press, 2005), 48–53.
13. Ibid., 53–71.
14. Defter de reklamos de Gabbaé Sedaka, CAHJP, Tr/Iz. 851 (*soletreo*).
15. Ibid.
16. October 20, 1879, AAIU, Turquie LXXXV E 1015.2.
17. Defter de reklamos de Gabbaé Sedaka, CAHJP, Tr/Iz. 851 (*soletreo*).
18. Ibid.
19. Ibid.
20. Ibid.
21. Ibid.
22. Cohen, *Poverty and Charity*, 88–104.
23. *Regulamentos de la kupa ve-Aavtem et a-Ger* (Izmir: 27 Tishrei, 5649 [October 2, 1888]).
24. Letter from *ve-Aavtem et a-Ger*, 11 Nisan 5651, CAHJP, Tr/Iz. 578 (*soletreo*).
25. Defter de reklamos de Gabbaé Sedaka, CAHJP, Tr/Iz. 851 (*soletreo*).

26. Ibid.
27. Ibid.
28. Ibid.
29. Ibid.
30. Ibid.
31. Ibid.
32. Ibid.
33. Ibid.
34. "Novedades lokales," *La Buena Esperanza*, August 9, 1878, 4.
35. Defter de reklamos de Gabbaé Sedaka, CAHJP, Tr/Iz. 851 (*soletreo*).
36. Ibid.
37. Ibid.
38. Ibid.
39. Ibid. For more on the currency of the Ottoman Empire in this period, see Şevket Pamuk, *A Monetary History of the Ottoman Empire* (Cambridge: Cambridge University Press, 2000), 205–23.
40. Ibid.
41. Ibid.
42. Ibid.
43. *Sirkular de Ozer Dalim* (Izmir: Kislev 5659).
44. Arié, May 31, 1898, AAIU, Turquie LXXV E 911.04.
45. "Konsilio komunal, Ismirna—regulamiento por la ariha del bedelat-i askieri por el anyo 1317–1318 a la era turka," *El Meseret*, August 2, 1901, 4.
46. *Kuento de la kupa Gabbaé Sedaka* (Izmir: Estamperia La Esperanza, Rosh Hodesh Kislev [5]642).
47. Seduta no. 9, 28 Iyar [5]642, Prochesos verbales, CAHJP, Tr/Iz. 28 (*soletreo*).
48. Seduta no. 11, Avizo al onorado publiko, 10 Sivan [5]642, Prochesos verbales, CAHJP Tr/Iz. 28 (*soletreo*).
49. "La kupa Ozer Dalim—una albrisiya," *La Buena Esperanza*, February 8, 1883, citing Psalm 128:2.
50. "La kupa Ozer Dalim—una albrisiya," *La Buena Esperanza*, February 8, 1883.
51. *Sirkular de Ozer Dalim*, 6.
52. "Kualo es la vera karidad," *La Buena Esperanza*, March 5, 1903.
53. "Ozer Dalim refundido!" *La Buena Esperanza*, April 30, 1903.
54. "A la atansion publika," *El Pregonero*, February 28, 1913, 3.
55. "Ozer Dalim," *La Buena Esperanza*, May 7, 1903, 1.
56. "La kupa Ozer Dalim kayida," *La Buena Esperanza*, June 14, 1888, 4.
57. "Ozer Dalim," *La Buena Esperanza*, May 21, 1903, 1.
58. *Sirkular de Ozer Dalim*, 1.
59. "Los eskandalos de los povres," *La Buena Esperanza*, June 28, 1888, 4.

60. "La kupa Ozer Dalim," *La Buena Esperanza*, December 20, 1888, 3.

61. Seduta no. 12, 17 Menahem [5]653, Prochesos Verbales, CAHJP, Tr/Iz. 30 (*soletreo*).

62. "La kupa Ozer Dalim—una albrisiya," *La Buena Esperanza*, February 8, 1883, 3; *Sirkular de Ozer Dalim*, 2.

63. "La kupa Ozer Dalim—una albrisiya," *La Buena Esperanza*, February 8, 1883, 3.

64. *Sirkular de Ozer Dalim*, 1.

65. Procheso verbal de la asamblia jeneral de alhad 8 Tammuz, raporto del sekretario, *Reuniones del meclis umumi en el 2 Shvat 5672 i en el 8 Tammuz 5672* (Izmir: Imprimido en El Novelista, n.d.), 24.

66. "Las kojitas," *La Buena Esperanza*, June 5, 1884, 3; "Las kojitas," *La Buena Esperanza*, February 10, 1891, 2.

67. "Kopia del papel ke se melda en las kehilot por las kupot i el karnaval," 2 Adar [5]645, CAHJP, Tr/Iz. 28 (*soletreo*).

68. "Las kojitas," *La Buena Esperanza*, March 9, 1893.

69. *Procheto de estatuto*, Article 53, 1884; *Regulamento de administrasion de la komunidad israelit de Izmir*, Art. 55, CAHJP, Tr/Iz. 17 and 31.

70. Regulamento de la komision de karidad, *Kolel Izmir kuento rendido de la anyada 5658*, 45–48, CAHJP, Tr/Iz. 9.

71. "Letra de la sivdad," *El Comercial*, March 26, 1908, 3.

72. "Letra de la sivdad," *El Comercial*, April 2, 1908, 3.

73. "Kozas de la komunidad—las kojitas," *El Novelista*, May 5, 1908.

74. "Komunikado," *El Novelista*, July 28, 1905, 182.

75. "Ozer Dalim," *El Novelista*, August 8, 1905, 348.

76. "Sosiedad Ozer Dalim," *La Buena Esperanza*, April 26, 1907, 6; "Entrada i salida de la kupa Ozer Dalim," *El Comercial*, May 2, 1907, 7.

77. "Por el bien de la komunidad," *El Novelista*, January 18, 1907, 41–42.

78. Ibid.

79. "Porke no progresa Ozer Dalim," *El Novelista*, May 15, 1908, 1.

80. "El kolel no va dar masa," *El Soytari*, January 28, 1910, 3–4.

81. Derek Penslar, *Shylock's Children*, 107–8; Derek Penslar, "The Origins of Modern Jewish Philanthropy," in *Philanthropy in the World's Traditions*, eds. Warren F. Ilchman, Stanley N. Katz, and Edward L. Queen II (Bloomington: Indiana University Press, 1988), 206.

82. Penslar, *Shylock's Children*, 108–23.

83. Lee Shai Weissbach, "The Nature of Philanthropy in Nineteenth-Century France and the *mentalité* of the Jewish Elite," *Jewish History* 8, no. 1/2 (1994): 197–98; Phyllis Cohen Albert, *The Modernization of French Jewry: Consistory and Community in the Nineteenth Century* (Hanover: Brandeis University Press, 1977), 136–40.

84. Aron Rodrigue, *French Jews, Turkish Jews: The Alliance Israélite Universelle and the Politics of Jewish Schooling in Turkey, 1860–1925* (Bloomington: Indiana University Press, 1990), 100.

85. Ibid., 100–109.

86. Nazan Maksudyan, "Orphans, Cities, and the State: Vocational Orphanages (Islahhanes) and Reform in the Late Ottoman Urban Space," *International Journal of Middle Eastern Studies* 43 (2011): 493–511; Nazan Maksudyan, *Orphans and Destitute Children in the Late Ottoman Empire* (Syracuse: Syracuse University Press, 2014), 78–115.

87. "Nuestros uerfanikos," *El Novelista*, March 15, 1907, 124.

88. Rapport sur les écoles israélites, October 10, 1874, AAIU, Turquie LXXX E 944.

89. Ibid.

90. Mémoire sur la réforme du Talmud Thora de Smyrne, September 24, 1886, AAIU, Turquie LXXXVI E 1015.4.

91. Amado, November 20, 1890, AAIU, Turquie LXXIII E 897.

92. Cazès, rec'd October 26, 1873, AAIU, Turquie I C 1.6.

93. Amado, November 20, 1890, AAIU, Turquie LXXIII E 897.

94. "Talmud Tora," *El Novelista*, June 26, 1906, 357.

95. Cazès 1873, AAIU, Turquie I C 1.6.

96. "Novedades diversas," *La Esperanza*, March 11, 1875.

97. Rodrigue, *French Jews, Turkish Jews*, 100–101.

98. AAIU Cazès, June 18, 1875, Turquie II C 9.1.

99. Assael, December 25, 1874, AAIU, Turquie LXXIII E 904.

100. "Diskorso de los guerfanos de Talmud Tora (suplimiento al numero 39,)" *La Esperanza*, July 8, 1875, 5.

101. Ibid.

102. Ibid.

103. Ibid.

104. Ibid.

105. "La presa por todos," *La Buena Esperanza*, February 17, 1876, 3. The article cites Ethics of the Fathers 2:2 and 3:17.

106. "Novedades diversas," *La Buena Esperanza*, March 9, 1876, 3. The article cites Ethics of the Fathers 2:2.

107. "Novedades lokales," *La Esperanza*, August 9, 1877, 4.

108. "Gemilut hasadim," *La Buena Esperanza*, February 18, 1892, 2.

109. Arié, February 5, 1895, AAIU, Turquie LXXIV E 911.02.

110. Arié, July 15, 1895, AAIU, Turquie LXXIV E 911.02.

111. Arié, June 24, 1898, AAIU, Turquie LXXV E 911.04.

112. Arié, June 10, 1901, AAIU, Turquie LXXVI E 911.06.

113. Ibid.

114. Seduta 26, Iyar [5]669, CAHJP, Tr/Iz. 773 (*soletreo*).

115. Letters to *Haham Bashı*, 25 Tammuz 5669, CAHJP (*soletreo*).
116. "Piedad!!!" *El Novelista*, July 5, 1905, 265.
117. Arié, November 27, 1898, AAIU, Turquie LXXV E 911.04.
118. March 8, 1878, AAIU, Turquie LXXIII E 887.9.
119. Arié, November 27, 1898, AAIU, Turquie LXXV E 911.04.
120. *El Guiyon*, April 1910.
121. Arié, January 6, 1895, AAIU, Turquie LXXIV E 911.02.
122. Ibid.
123. Arié, June 16, 1897, AAIU, Turquie LXXV E 911.05.
124. Ibid.
125. Ibid.
126. Ibid.
127. Rodrigue, *French Jews, Turkish Jews*, 107–8; Esther Benbassa and Aron Rodrigue, "L'Artisanat juif en Turquie à la fin du XIXe siècle: L'Alliance israélite universelle et ses oeuvres d'apprentissage," *Turcica* 17 (1985): 113–26.
128. Rodrigue, *French Jews, Turkish Jews*, 107–8.
129. Ibid.
130. Elena Frangakis-Syrett, "Commercial Growth and Economic Development in the Middle East: Izmir from the Early 18th to the Early 20th Centuries," in *Ottoman Izmir: Studies in Honour of Alexander H. de Groot*, ed. Maurits H. van den Boogert (Leiden: Nederlands Instituut voor het Nabije Oosten, 2007), 14.
131. "El hal de los esnafikos," *El Meseret*, November 20, 1914, 1.
132. "Una ovra de utilidad publika," *La Buena Esperanza*, May 24, 1907, 4.
133. Angel, April 2, 1903, AAIU, Turquie LXXIII E 899.
134. "La konferensia," *La Buena Esperanza*, March 26, 1903, 3.
135. Albert Tarica, *El Komersio* (Izmir: Imprimeria Frankos, 1904). For a discussion of Izmir's stock market, see 72; for the city's quays, see 199–201.
136. Tarica, *El Komersio*, 228.
137. "El proyekto grandeozo," *El Comercial*, June 6, 1907, 5.
138. "Un ermozo proyekto," *El Novelista*, June 27, 1907, 249–51.
139. 1 *metalika* is approximately 1/4 of a *kuruş*.
140. "Un ermozo proyekto," *El Novelista*, June 27, 1907, 249–51.
141. Ibid.
142. Ibid.
143. "Dos emprezas," *El Comercial*, March 28, 1907, 1.
144. "Sirkulario," *El Comercial*, July 11, 1907, 3.
145. "Sirkularios," *El Comercial*, January 1, 1908, 2.
146. "Sosieta en komandita internasional," *El Meseret*, August 18, 1908, 4.
147. "Kualo es la vera karidad?" *La Buena Esperanza*, February 19, 1903, 2.
148. Ibid.

Chapter 3

1. "Nuestro konkurso—los djudios de Izmirna," *La Buena Esperanza*, December 22, 1905, 3.

2. Elena Frangakis-Syrett, "The Economic Activities of the Greek Community of Izmir in the Second Half of the Nineteenth and Early Twentieth Centuries," in *Ottoman Greeks in the Age of Nationalism: Politics, Economy, and Society in the Nineteenth Century*, eds. Dimitri Gondicas and Charles Issawi (Princeton: Darwin Press, 1999), 17–44.

3. Jürgen Kocka, "The Middle Classes in Europe," *The Journal of Modern History* 67, no. 4 (December 1995): 787.

4. Pierre Bourdieu, *Distinction: A Social Critique of the Judgment of Taste* (London: Routledge, 2010), 50.

5. Ibid., 53.

6. Ibid., 50.

7. Scholars have noticed a similar disjuncture among some German Jews. For more on this "strained relationship between class and status," through the prism of Breslau, see the work of Till van Rahden, *Jews and Other Germans: Civil Society, Religious Diversity, and Urban Politics in Breslau, 1860–1925* (Madison: University of Wisconsin Press, 2008), 24.

8. Alan Duben and Cem Behar, *Istanbul Households: Marriage, Family, and Fertility, 1880–1940* (Cambridge: Cambridge University Press, 1991), 203–4.

9. "Uzos negros," *El Comercial*, August 1, 1907, 11–12.

10. Marie-Carmen Smyrnelis, ed., *Une Société hors de soi: Identités et relations sociales à Smyrne aux XVIIIe et XIXe siècles*. Collection Turcica 10 (Paris: Peeters, 2005), 263.

11. Abraham Galante, *Les Juifs d'Anatolie: Les Juifs d'Izmir* (Istanbul: Imprimerie Babok, 1937), 77.

12. Ibid.

13. CAHJP, Tr/Iz. 117 (*soletreo*).

14. Arié, June 22, 1900, AAIU, Turquie LXXVI E 911.07.

15. Seduta no. 9, 29 Heshvan [5]655, Prochesos verbales, CAHJP, Tr/Iz. 30 (*soletreo*).

16. BOA. BEO. 2497/187265.

17. BOA. DH.MKT. 930/83.

18. *Reuniones del meclis umumi en el 2 Shvat 5672 i en el 8 Tammuz 5672* (Izmir: Imprimido en El Novelista), 25–26; Letter from Nissim Levi to Communal Council, 6 Tevet [5]672, CAHJP, Tr/Iz. 885 (*soletreo*).

19. Kuento rendido de la entrada i salida (5662–5663), CAHJP, Tr/Iz. 108.

20. See, for example, "Ozer Dalim," *La Buena Esperanza*, May 21, 1903, 1.

21. See, for example, "La ovra de la komida del Talmud Tora," *El Meseret*, July 25, 1902, 3; "Komitado de damas del Talmud Tora–yamada," *El Novelista*, March 23, 1906, 179.

22. Arié, March 9, 1896, AAIU, Turquie LXXIV E 911.01.
23. Arié, June 22, 1900, AAIU, Turquie LXXVI E 911.07.
24. Arié, November 30, 1900, AAIU, Turquie LXXVI E 911.07.
25. Arié, March 9, 1896, AAIU, Turquie LXXIV E 911.01.
26. "Café L'Abri—Karataş," *El Comercial*, June 3, 1908, 1.
27. "Karataş—grandes fasilidades," *La Boz de Izmir*, June 26, 1912, 1–2.
28. "El asansor de Karataş," *El Comercial*, June 18, 1908, 4 [translation of an article from *Hizmet*].
29. "Notas de la semana," *El Novelista*, July 14, 1908.
30. Ibid.
31. Ibid.
32. "El estrenamiento del Asansor," *El Comercial*, July 10, 1908, 3.
33. Arié, June 22, 1900, AAIU, Turquie LXXVI E 911.07.
34. Arié, November 30, 1900, AAIU, Turquie LXXVI E 911.07.
35. Ibid.
36. "El gevirombre en Karataş," *El Pregonero*, September 19, 1913, 1.
37. "Novedades lokales," *La Esperanza*, February 17, 1876, 4.
38. "La suare," *La Buena Esperanza*, January 9, 1889, 1.
39. "Un banketo en onor del Senyor Pariente," *El Novelista*, November 23, 1893, 288–91.
40. "La fiesta de la Aliansa," *La Buena Esperanza*, May 16, 1907, 4.
41. "Novedades lokales—el balo," *La Buena Esperanza*, February 8, 1883, 4.
42. "La segunda suare Ozer Dalim," *La Buena Esperanza*, March 17, 1887, 3.
43. "La reprezentasion teatrala," *La Buena Esperanza*, March 17, 1892, 2–3.
44. "La fiesta de la Aliansa," *La Buena Esperanza*, May 16, 1907, 4.
45. "La suare de Ozer Dalim," *La Buena Esperanza*, January 9, 1889, 1.
46. "El bedelat askieri," *El Meseret*, January 4, 1901, 4.
47. "Balos de bienfazensia," *La Esperanza*, March 7, 1878, 4.
48. "Novedades lokales—el balo," *La Buena Esperanza*, February 8, 1883, 4.
49. "La segunda suare Ozer Dalim," *La Buena Esperanza*, March 17, 1887, 3.
50. "El Talmud Tora," *El Novelista*, May 7, 1908, 187.
51. "La segunda suare Ozer Dalim," *La Buena Esperanza*, March 17, 1887, 3.
52. "La reprezentasion teatrala," *La Buena Esperanza*, March 17, 1892, 2–3.
53. Ibid.
54. "Nashim Sadkaniot," *El Novelista*, February 20, 1906, 115.
55. "Ozer Dalim," *El Novelista*, February 15, 1907.
56. Thomas Adam, *Buying Respectability: Philanthropy and Urban Society in Transnational Perspective, 1840s to 1930s* (Bloomington: Indiana University Press, 2009), 8.

57. Seduta no. 35, 8 Tevet [5]643, Prochesos verbales, CAHJP, Tr/Iz. 28 (*soletreo*).
58. "Suare nasional al profeto de Keter Tora," *La Buena Esperanza*, January 15, 1889, 2.
59. "La suare Ozer Dalim," *La Buena Esperanza*, January 17, 1889, 1.
60. Seduta no. 19, 19 Adar [5]670, CAHJP, Tr/Iz. 773 (*soletreo*).
61. "Reprezentasion teatrala," *La Buena Esperanza*, March 21, 1889, 2.
62. Arié, December 20, 1893, AAIU, Turquie LXXIV E 911.03.
63. Arié, January 29, 1894, AAIU, Turquie LXXIV E 911.03.
64. Ibid.
65. Galante, *Les Juifs d'Anatolie*, 123.
66. "La suare de Mahzikei Ani'im," *La Buena Esperanza*, January 6, 1902, 2.
67. Hervé Georgelin, *La fin de Smyrne: Du cosmopolitisme aux nationalismes* (Paris: CNRS Éditions, 2005), 136–37.
68. Ibid.
69. "Téâtre [sic] Sporting-Club," *El Novelista*, December 6, 1907, 509.
70. Georgelin, *La fin de Smyrne*, 137.
71. "Kozas de la sivdad," *El Meseret*, March 17, 1905, 6; "Ozer Dalim," *El Novelista*, February 15, 1907, 66.
72. "Programa," *El Novelista*, October 3, 1906, 548.
73. "Nochada dramatika i muzikal," *El Novelista*, March 28, 1907, 148.
74. *Ahenk*, May 31, 1908, 2.
75. "Inaugurasion del grande otel Kramer Palas," *El Comercial*, [nd] Anyo 3, No. 7.
76. Ibid.
77. Galante, *Les Juifs d'Anatolie*, 90.
78. "Nashim Sadkaniot," *El Novelista*, February 20, 1906, 115.
79. "Novedades lokales," *La Esperanza*, February 17, 1876, 4.
80. AIU Local Committee, January 25, 1883, AAIU, Turquie LXXIII E 887.3.
81. "Novedades lokales—el balo," *La Buena Esperanza*, February 8, 1883, 4.
82. Ibid.
83. Habif, January 25, 1883, AAIU, Turquie LXXIII E 887.3.
84. Ibid.
85. "La reprezentasion teatrala," *La Buena Esperanza*, March 17, 1892, 2–3.
86. For more on Jewish patriotism in the late Ottoman Empire, see Julia Phillips Cohen, *Becoming Ottomans: Sephardi Jews and Imperial Citizenship in the Modern Era* (Oxford: Oxford University Press, 2014).
87. "El balo," *La Buena Esperanza*, January 31, 1884, 2.
88. Arié, February 4, 1894, AAIU, Turquie LXXIV E 911.03.
89. Ibid.
90. Sibel Zandi-Sayek, *Ottoman Izmir: The Rise of a Cosmopolitan Port, 1840–1880* (Minneapolis: University of Minnesota Press, 2012), 129.

91. "Portrait d'une communauté méconnue: Les Musulmans: Entretien avec Fikret Yilmaz," in *Smyrne, la ville oubliée? Mémoires d'un grand port ottoman, 1830–1930*, ed. Marie-Carmen Smyrnelis (Paris: Éditions Autrement, 2006), 60.

92. "Novedades lokales—el balo," *La Buena Esperanza*, February 8, 1883, 4.

93. "El balo," *La Buena Esperanza*, January 31, 1884, 2.

94. Ibid.

95. "La segunda suare Ozer Dalim," *La Buena Esperanza*, March 17, 1887, 3.

96. "Novedades lokales—Talmud Tora," *El Comercial*, March 21, 1907, 3.

97. Nabon, April 6, 1907, AAIU, Turquie LXXXIII E 1007.2.

98. See, for example, "Novedades lokales," *La Esperanza*, February 24, 1876, 4.

99. Ibid.

100. "Balos de bienfazensia," *La Esperanza*, March 7, 1878, 4 (1 lira apiece).

101. "Una fiesta de karidad—el komitado de damas del Talmud Tora," *El Novelista*, March 21, 1906, 171.

102. "Novedades lokales," *La Buena Esperanza*, January 15, 1903, 4.

103. Ibid.

104. Marion Kaplan, *The Making of the Jewish Middle Class: Women, Family and Identity in Imperial Germany* (Oxford: Oxford University Press, 1991), 31.

105. Todd Endelman, *Broadening Jewish History: Towards a Social History of Ordinary Jews* (Oxford: Littman Library of Jewish Civilization, 2011), 36.

106. For a fuller discussion of bourgeois womanhood, see Bonnie G. Smith, *Ladies of the Leisure Class: The Bourgeoises of Northern France in the Nineteenth Century* (Princeton: Princeton University Press, 1981); Karin Hausen, "Family and Role-Division: The Polarisation of Sexual Stereotypes in the Nineteenth Century—An Aspect of the Dissociation of Work and Family," in *The German Family: Essays on the Social History of the Family in Nineteenth and Twentieth Century Germany*, eds. Richard Evans and W. R. Lee (London: Croom Helm, 1981), 51–83; Leonore Davidoff and Catherine Hall, *Family Fortunes: Men and Women of the English Middle Class, 1780–1850* (London: Hutchinson, 1987), 149–92.

107. Aron Rodrigue, *Jews and Muslims: Images of Sephardi and Eastern Jewries in Transition* (Seattle: University of Washington Press, 2003), 80–82.

108. "La intelijensia de la mujer," *El Comercial*, March 28, 1907, 12.

109. "Respektamos la mujer," *El Comercial*, April 25, 1907, 9–10.

110. "La mujer djudia," *El Novelista*, March 28, 1907, 151–52.

111. Graziella Benghiat, "Le Féminisme," *Le Trait de l'Union* 3, no. 4 (April 1913): 4–6 and 3, no. 6 (June 1913): 2–3; 6, in *Sephardi Lives: A Documentary History, 1700–1950*, eds. Julia Phillips Cohen and Sarah Abrevaya Stein (Stanford: Stanford University Press, 2014), 231–35.

112. Ibid.

113. Ibid.

114. "El rolo de una mujer—la sosiedad Bikkur Holim Shel Nashim," *El Novelista*, November 30, 1906, 648.
115. "Novedades diversas," *La Esperanza*, December 17, 1874, 2–3.
116. Ibid.
117. Galante, *Les Juifs d'Anatolie*, 90–91.
118. "Karidad djudia," *La Buena Esperanza*, January 6, 1902, 2.
119. "Una tokante seremonia," *El Novelista*, February 20, 1907, 74.
120. "Nuestros uerfanikos," *El Novelista*, March 15, 1907, 124.
121. "El rolo de una mujer—La Sosiedad Bikkur Holim Shel Nashim," *El Novelista*, November 30, 1906, 648.
122. "God's Will," *El Novelista*, March 28, 1907, 148.
123. Ibid.
124. "Diskorso de los guerfanos de Talmud Tora," *La Esperanza*, July 8, 1875, 5 (Suplimiento al numero 39).
125. "Novedades lokales," *La Esperanza*, February 17, 1876, 4.
126. "El balo," *La Buena Esperanza*, January 31, 1884, 2.
127. "La segunda suare Ozer Dalim," *La Buena Esperanza*, March 17, 1887, 3.
128. "Repuesta," *El Comercial*, July 11, 1907, 4.
129. "El teatro i las ovras de bienfazensia," *El Comercial*, May 2, 1907, 3–4.
130. Ibid.
131. "Nuestras ijas i las ovras de bienfazensia," *El Comercial*, May 9, 1907, 9.
132. "Un poko de todo—nuestras ijas i el teatro," *El Comercial*, May 23, 1907, 3.
133. Ibid.
134. "Baylar a la franka," *El Meseret*, January 11, 1901, 6.
135. Ibid.
136. Sarah Abrevaya Stein, *Making Jews Modern: The Yiddish and Ladino Press in the Russian and Ottoman Empires* (Bloomington: Indiana University Press, 2004), 177–87.
137. CAHJP, Tr/Iz. 713 (*soletreo*); CAHJP, Tr/Iz. 715 (*soletreo*).
138. CAHJP, Tr/Iz. 117 (*soletreo*).
139. "El estrenamiento de nuestras eskolas i el balo," *La Buena Esperanza*, January 18, 1883, 2–3.
140. Ibid.
141. Ibid.
142. "La soirée nasionala," *La Buena Esperanza*, February 25, 1892, 2–3.
143. "En los balos," *El Meseret*, November 22, 1901, 4.
144. Ibid.
145. Angel, June 9, 1902, AAIU, Turquie LXXIII E 899.
146. "Un remedio por nuestra avenir," *El Novelista*, February 27, 1906, 133.
147. Ibid.
148. "El dover de los padres de familya," *El Novelista*, February 23, 1906, 121.

149. "El pie en el lodo," *El Novelista*, March 2, 1906, 137.

150. "Novedades lokales," *La Buena Esperanza*, January 18, 1877, 4. The phrase "long winter nights" referred to an emerging concept of "leisure time" in the Sephardi world. For example, Matthias Lehmann, *Ladino Rabbinic Literature and Ottoman Sephardic Culture* (Bloomington: Indiana University Press, 2005), 67–68, has shown that Sephardi rabbis encouraged the reading of Ladino *musar* literature on "long winter nights." Olga Borovaya, *Modern Ladino Culture: Press, Belles Lettres, and Theater in the Late Ottoman Empire* (Bloomington: Indiana University Press, 2012), 48 has argued that such reading practices continued with the Ladino press in the late nineteenth and early twentieth centuries.

151. "Novedades lokales," *La Buena Esperanza*, January 18, 1877, 4.

152. "Un remedio por nuestra avenir," *El Novelista*, February 27, 1906, 133.

153. Ibid.

154. "El kabineto de lektura," *La Buena Esperanza*, January 25, 1884, 3.

155. Ibid.

156. "El kabineto de lektura, *La Buena Esperanza*, January 31, 1884, 2.

157. Liste des livres offerts au cabinet de lecture "La Jeunesse Israélite" de Smyrne par Monsieur S.H. Goldschmidt, May 26, 1884, AAIU, Turquie LXXXV E 1015.1.

158. Arié, November 20, 1896, AAIU, Turquie LXXIV E 911.01.

159. Ibid.

160. This is likely the same as the *kabineto de lektura*, but I cannot confirm a date for the name change.

161. "La konferensia de alhad," *La Buena Esperanza*, January 27, 1905, 1.

162. Ibid.

163. Angel, June 9, 1902, AAIU, Turquie LXXIII E 899.

164. Ibid.

165. "El Fut-bol," *El Comercial*, May 2, 1907.

166. "Sala de Lektura—grande eksursion a Tiria," *El Novelista*, May 11, 1906, 272.

167. Ibid.

168. "Una briyante ekskursion," *El Comercial*, June 6, 1907, 3.

169. "La fiesta de alhad ultimo—el pik-nik," *El Meseret*, May 6, 1898, 129.

170. Arié, December 1, 1899, AAIU, Turquie LXXVI E 911.08.

171. "El orden i la ermozura en la familya," *El Comercial*, October 17, 1907, 4.

172. *Los doveres entre los ermanos de la Liga de Pas i Solidaridad i mujeres* (Izmir: Imprimeria Frankos, 1914).

173. Ibid.

174. Haris Exertzoglou, "The Cultural Uses of Consumption: Negotiating Class, Gender, and Nation in the Ottoman Urban Centers During the 19th Century," *International Journal of Middle East Studies* 35, no. 1 (February 2003): 81–83.

175. "Los vestimientos de las mujeres en Izmirna," *La Buena Esperanza*, September 21, 1883, 2. *Tokadiko* is a diminutive of *tokado*.
176. "Programa," *El Novelista*, October 3, 1906. 548.
177. "El chapeo en el teatro," *El Comercial*, May 2, 1907, 9–10.
178. Ibid.
179. "La ekskorsion: la ijas i el lukso," *El Comercial*, May 23, 1907, 4.
180. Ibid.
181. "El lukso," *El Comercial*, May 16, 1907, 10–11.
182. "Las devdas," *El Meseret*, May 18, 1900, 10.
183. "La ekonomia," *El Meseret*, June 8, 1900, 7.
184. "Las sosiedades de esparanyo," El *Novelista*, June 19, 1908, 261.
185. "Ekonomia i lavoro," *El Pregonero*, November 27, 1908, 8.
186. Attias, June 16, 1904, AAIU, Turquie LXXIII E 909.
187. Carol E. Harrison, *The Bourgeois Citizen in Nineteenth-Century France: Gender, Sociability, and the Uses of Emulation* (Oxford: Oxford University Press, 1999), 2.

Chapter 4

1. "Agada de la karne," *El Soytari*, April 5, 1909, 3.
2. Minna Rozen, "A Pound of Flesh: The Meat Trade and Social Struggle in Jewish Istanbul, 1700–1923," in *Crafts and Craftsmen of the Middle East: Fashioning the Individual in the Muslim Mediterranean*, eds. Suraiya Faroqhi and Randi Deguilhem (London: I. B. Tauris, 2005), 207–24.
3. Aron Rodrigue and Sarah Abrevaya Stein, eds., *A Jewish Voice from Ottoman Salonica: The Ladino Memoir of Sa'adi Besalel a-Levi*, trans. Isaac Jerushalmi (Stanford: Stanford University Press, 2011), 56–58.
4. Phyllis Cohen Albert, *The Modernization of French Jewry: Consistory and Communityin the Nineteenth Century* (Hanover: Brandeis University Press, 1977), 227–30.
5. Natan M. Meir, *Kiev, Jewish Metropolis: A History, 1859–1914* (Bloomington: Indiana University Press, 2010), 72–73.
6. Paula E. Hyman, "Immigrant Women and Consumer Protest: The New York City Kosher Meat Boycott of 1902," *American Jewish History* 70, no. 1 (September 1980): 91–105.
7. Benjamin Nathans, *Beyond the Pale: The Jewish Encounter with Late Imperial Russia* (Berkeley: University of California Press, 2003), 142.
8. Nechama Grunhaus, "The Procedure and the Halakhic Basis for the Purchase Tax in the Community of Izmir," *Peamim: Studies in Oriental Jewry* 116 (Summer 2008): 79–116 (in Hebrew).
9. Eliezer Bashan, "The Freedom of Trade and the Imposition of Taxes and Customs Duties on Foreign Jewish Traders in the Ottoman Empire," in *Mi-mizrah umi-ma'arav*,

Vol. 1, ed. Haim Zeev Hirschberg, (Ramat Gan: Bar-Ilan University Press, 1974), 130 (in Hebrew).

10. See for example the 1692 issue mentioned in Yaron Ben-Naeh, *Jews in the Realm of the Sultans: Ottoman Jewish Society in the Seventeenth Century* (Tübingen: Mohr Siebeck, 2008), 26.

11. Nechama Grunhaus, "The Taxation System of the Jewish Community of Izmir in the Seventeenth through the Nineteenth Centuries" (PhD diss., New York University, 1995), 345–431.

12. Abraham Galante, *Histoire des Juifs de Turquie*, 9 vols. (Istanbul: Isis Press, 1985), 1:278.

13. See, for example, "Kuento de entrada i salida de 10 semanas del Konsilio Komunal," *El Meseret*, February 7, 1901, 4; "El Konsilio Komunal, entrada i salida del 1 Tevet 5666," *La Buena Esperanza*, January 12, 1906, 6; "Konsilio Komunal, kuento de entrada i salida de la komunidad de seis semanadas sea del 5 Heshvan asta el 16 Kislev 5668," *El Novelista*, December 4, 1907, 505.

14. Stanford J. Shaw, *History of the Ottoman Empire and Modern Turkey*, Vol. 1, *Empire of the Gazis: The Rise and Decline of the Ottoman Empire, 1280–1808* (Cambridge: Cambridge University Press, 1976), 120–21.

15. For more on the figure of the *kahya*, see Ben-Naeh, *Jews in the Realm of the Sultans*, 203–5.

16. Seduta no. 51, 14 Kislev 5651, Prochesos verbales, CAHJP, Tr/Iz. 29 (*soletreo*).

17. Seduta no. 50, 11 Kislev 5651, Prochesos verbales, CAHJP, Tr/Iz. 29 (*soletreo*).

18. CAHJP, Tr/Iz. 538 (*soletreo*).

19. See, for example, the 1879 pamphlet war with *Gabbaé Sedaka* mentioned below and the 1891 implementation of *kuchiyo atado*, Avizo al onorado publiko, Kolel Izmir, 7 Adar A 5651, Prochesos verbales, CAHJP, Tr/Iz. 29 (*soletreo*).

20. Abraham Galante, *Les Juifs d'Anatolie: Les Juifs d'Izmir* (Istanbul: Imprimerie Babok, 1937), 29.

21. Pariente, February 25, 1887, AAIU, Turquie LXXXVI E 1015.4.

22. Kolel Izmir kuento rendido de la anyada 5658, 4, CAHJP, Tr/Iz. 9.

23. "Kualo es hahamhane," *El Pregonero*, May 7, 1909, 3.

24. Pariente, April 6, 1888, AAIU, Turquie LXXXVI E 1015.3.

25. Ibid.

26. Pariente, Rescrit publié dans les synagogues de Smyrne le 9 Avril, 1888, traduction, AAIU, Turquie LXXXVI E 1015.3.

27. Pariente, May 4, 1888, AAIU, Turquie LXXXVI E 1015.3.

28. Pariente, July 6, 1888, AAIU, Turquie LXXXVI E 1015.3.

29. "La pas," *La Buena Esperanza*, November 22, 1888, 1.

30. "Nuestra komunidad," *La Buena Esperanza*, February 7, 1889.

31. Pariente, July 6, 1888, AAIU, Turquie LXXXVI E 1015.3.

32. Arié, February 9, 1897, AAIU, Turquie LXXV E 911.05.
33. Seduta no. 36, 5 Elul 5658, Prochesos verbales, CAHJP, Tr/Iz. 32 (*soletreo*).
34. Arié, July 22, 1898, AAIU, LXXV E 911.04.
35. BOA. ŞD 2544–23, 27–10.1306 (26 June 1889).
36. See, for example, Seduta no. 36, 5 Elul [5]658, Prochesos verbales, CAHJP, Tr/Iz. 32 (*soletreo*); 12 Elul [5]658, Prochesos verbales, CAHJP, Tr/Iz. 32 (*soletreo*).
37. *Reuniones del meclis umumi en el 2 Shvat 5672 i en el 8 Tammuz 5672*, (Izmir: El Novelista, n.d.), 17.
38. Ibid., 37.
39. *Procheso verbal de las reuniones del meclis umumi de las sedutas tenidas en el 19 Elul, en el 10 Kislev 5672 [i] en el 12 Tevet en el 8 Tammuz 5673* (Izmir: Estamperia el Novelista), 12.
40. Ibid., 50.
41. CAHJP, Tr/Iz. 118 (*soletreo*).
42. For example, in September of 1915, the Communal Council laid out a detailed plan for the *derito komunal*, establishing seven categories of taxpayers, identifying those who would be exempt, and ordering the nomination of commissions to classify eligible taxpayers according to their wealth (Procheso verbal no. 7, 11 Tishrei [5]676, Prochesos verbales, CAHJP, Tr/Iz. 42 [*soletreo*]). Yet only a few weeks later, the Communal Council revisited this plan, as some in the community complained that their economic situation had worsened as a result of the war and they were embarrassed to see themselves "taxed in a category inferior to their rank." Interestingly, it was instead decided to base the classification for the tax on each person's "consumption of meat and financial position." (Procheso verbal no. 9, 19 Tishrei [5]676, Prochesos verbales, CAHJP, Tr/Iz. 42, [*soletreo*]). Yet "financial crises" continued to make such assessments both "uncertain" and even "impossible" (Procheso verbal no. 13, 2 Heshvan [5]676 ([*soletreo*]).
43. Procheso verbal no. 27, 26 Tevet [5]676, Prochesos verbales, CAHJP, Tr/Iz. 42 (*soletreo*).
44. Ibid., Procheso verbal no. 28, 4 Shvat [5]676 (*soletreo*).
45. *Reuniones del meclis umumi en el 2 Shvat 5672 i en el 8 Tammuz 5672*, 18. The *derito komunal* remained a priority for the community beyond the dissolution of the empire. In a 1921 report on the state of the community, the Communal Council discussed the virtue of a *derito nasional* that might yield a "reserve fund [comprised] of a fixed source of revenue that would at the same time alleviate the [burden of] *gabela* taxes (Raporto meldado en la asamblia nasional por el prezidente del konsilio komunal, 17 Av 5681, 6, CAHJP, Tr/Iz. 10).
46. Jürgen Habermas, *The Structural Transformation of the Public Sphere: An Inquiry into a Category of Bourgeois Society*, trans. Thomas Burger (Cambridge: MIT Press, 1989), 27.

47. See Jeffrey Veidlinger, *Jewish Public Culture in the Late Russian Empire* (Bloomington: Indiana University Press, 2009).

48. See, for example, Scott Ury, *Barricades and Banners: The Revolution of 1905 and the Transformation of Warsaw Jewry* (Stanford: Stanford University Press, 2012); Ela Bauer, "From the Salons to the Street: The Development of a Jewish Public Sphere in Warsaw at the End of the 19th Century," *Simon Dubnow Institute Yearbook* 7 (2008): 143–59.

49. See, for example, Nadir Özbek, "Philanthropic Activity, Ottoman Patriotism and the Hamidian Regime, 1876–1909," *International Journal of Middle Eastern Studies* 37, no. 1 (2005): 59–81.

50. Nadir Özbek, "Defining the Public Sphere During the Late Ottoman Empire: War, Mass Mobilization, and the Young Turk Regime, 1908–1918," *Middle Eastern Studies* 43, no. 5 (2007): 807.

51. Reşat Kasaba, "Economic Foundations of a Civil Society: Greeks in the Trade of Western Anatolia, 1840–1876," in *Ottoman Greeks in the Age of Nationalism: Politics, Economy, and Society in the Nineteenth Century*, ed. Dimitri Gondicas and Charles Issawi, 77–87 (Princeton: The Darwin Press, 1999).

52. See the discussion in Avner Levi, "Shavat Aniim: Social Cleavage, Class War, and Leadership in the Sephardi Community--The Case of Izmir 1847," in *Ottoman and Turkish Jewry: Community and Leadership*, edited by Aron Rodrigue, 183–202, Indiana University Turkish Studies 12 (Bloomington: Indiana University Turkish Studies, 1992); Grunhaus, "The Taxation System," 350–91.

53. *Shavat Ani'im*, 24 Shvat 5607.

54. Ibid.

55. Ibid.

56. Ibid.

57. Ibid.

58. *Kra ve-garon al tahshokh ka-shofar harem kolekha* (Izmir: La kupa Gabbaé Sedaka, 8 Iyar [5]639 [May 1, 1879]). From Isaiah 58:1, "Cry with full throat, without restraint; Raise your voice like a ram's horn!"

59. Ibid.

60. *La salvasion: va-ye'anhu vnei Yisrael min-ha'avoda* (Izmir: La kupa Gabbaé Sedaka, 20 Nisan [5]639 [April 13, 1879]). From Exodus 2:23, "The Israelites were groaning under the bondage."

61. Ibid.

62. *Kol ha-shofar holekh ve-hazek me'od* (Izmir: La kupa Gabbaé Sedaka, 11 Iyar [5]639 [May 4, 1879]). From Exodus 19:19, "The blare of the horn grew louder and louder."

63. Ibid.

64. *Kinso nes harim ti'ru ve-hbitho'a shofar tishme'u* (Izmir: 13 Iyar [5]639 [May 6,

1879]). From Isaiah 18:3, "When a flag is raised in the hills, take note! When a ram's horn is blown, give heed!"
    65. *Kol ha-shofar holekh ve-hazek me'od.*
    66. AAIU, Turquie LXXXV E 1015.2 Pariente, May 16, 1879.
    67. Sarah Abrevaya Stein, *Making Jews Modern: The Yiddish and Ladino Press in the Russian and Ottoman Empires* (Bloomington: Indiana University Press, 2004), 55–82, 123–49, 175–201.
    68. "A los lektores," *Edision espesial de La Buena Esperanza*, (1896).
    69. "A los lektores," *El Meseret*, January 15, 1897, 1.
    70. Ibid.
    71. "Introduksion," *La Verdad*, June 15, 1884.
    72. "Letra al editor," *El Pregonero*, December 11, 1908, 1.
    73. Veinte i sinko anyos de vida de la komunidad israelit de Izmirna," *Edision espesial de La Buena Esperanza* (1896).
    74. "El estado de nuestra komunita," *La Buena Esperanza*, December 19, 1879, 2.
    75. "El bilanso del Kolel," *La Buena Esperanza*, July 8, 1886, 3.
    76. "Una kesha," *El Novelista*, May 11, 1906, 269.
    77. "La karne," *El Novelista*, June 19, 1908, 260.
    78. "De la komunidad," *El Comersial*, July 31, 1908, 2.
    79. "El kuchiyo atado," *El Pregonero*, May 3, 1912, 2.
    80. Arié, March 9, 1896, AAIU, Turquie LXXIV E 911.01.
    81. Arié, February 10, 1896, AAIU, Turquie LXXIV E 911.01.
    82. Ibid.
    83. Arié, February 14, 1896, AAIU, Turquie LXXIV E 911.01.
    84. Seduta no. 14, 25 Shvat [5]656, Prochesos verbales, CAHJP, Tr/Iz. 30 (*soletreo*).
    85. Kontinuasion de seduta no. 14, 6 Heshvan [5]657, Prochesos verbales, CAHJP, Tr/Iz. 31 (*soletreo*).
    86. Ibid.
    87. BOA DH.MKT 1163/33,(H) 18.03.1325 (1 May 1907).
    88. Procès-verbal de la séance tenue à l'occasion de la présence à Smyrne de M. le Chevalier Veneziani délégué de l'Alliance Israélite Universelle, October 20, 1879, AAIU, Turquie LXXXV E 1015.2.
    89. Ibid.
    90. Ibid.
    91. Pariente, July 2, 1888, AAIU, Turquie LXXXVI E 1015.3.
    92. "Avizo," *La Buena Esperanza*, July 19, 1888, 4.
    93. "Komunikasion," *La Buena Esperanza*, October 4, 1888, 1.
    94. "Letra al redaktor," *La Buena Esperanza*, July 8, 1880, 3.
    95. "Avizo," *La Buena Esperanza*, July 19, 1880, 4.
    96. "Komunikasion," *La Buena Esperanza*, October 4, 1888, 1.

97. "Va-yamat Avraham be-seva tova zaken ve-save'a va-ye'asef el-amav, ve-ata tavo el avotekha be-shalom tekaver be-seva tova," *La Buena Esperanza*, January 20, 1899, 1. Part of the title is based on Genesis 25:8, "And Abraham breathed his last, dying at a good ripe age, old and contented; and he was gathered to his kin."

98. "Biografia de su eminensia nuestro gran rabino Avraham Palacci," *El Meseret*, January 13, 1899, 9–11.

99. See, for example, *Ahenk*, January 6, 1899, 2; "Va-yamat Avraham be-seva tova zaken ve-save'a va-ye'asef el-amav, ve-ata tavo el avotekha be-shalom tekaver be-seva tova," *La Buena Esperanza*, January 20, 1899, 1.

100. Arié, January 13, 1899, AAIU, Turquie LXXVI E 911.08.

101. Ibid.

102. April 4, 1899, AAIU, Turquie LXXVI E 911.08.

103. Ibid.

104. Letter to the *Haham Bashi*, 29 Nisan 5659, CAHJP, HM28638 (*soletreo*).

105. Arié, April 6, 1899, AAIU, Turquie LXXVI E 911.08.

106. Ibid.

107. Ibid.

108. Letter to the *Haham Bashi* from Communal Council, 26 Nisan 5659, CAHJP, HM28638 (*soletreo*).

109. Ibid.

110. Arié, April 6, 1899, AAIU, Turquie LXXVI E 911.08.

111. "Echos de la komunidad," *El Meseret*, April 14, 1899, 1.

112. "Los shohatim," *La Buena Esperanza*, April 21, 1899, 2.

113. "Echos de la komunidad—nuestra opinion," *El Meseret*, June 23, 1899, 182.

114. Arié, September 28, 1899, AAIU, Turquie LXXVI E 911.08.

115. "Pesah," *La Buena Esperanza*, February 16, 1900, 1. Emphasis in original.

116. "Pesah," *La Buena Esperanza*, February 23, 1900, 1.

117. "Echos de la komunidad," *El Meseret*, April 14, 1899, 1.

118. "Las eksantrisidades de la kestion," *El Meseret*, July 14, 1899, 210.

119. Letter to the *Haham Bashi* 1 Shvat 5660, CAHJP, HM28638 (*soletreo*).

120. Ibid.

121. Ibid.

122. Letter to the *Haham Bashi* from Communal Council, 26 Nisan 5659, CAHJP, HM28638 (*soletreo*).

123. Appel à la jeunesse et aux personnes éclaireés de notre communauté, 27 Nisan 5659, AAIU, Turquie LXXXVI E 911.08.

124. "Las firmas," *El Meseret*, April 14, 1899, 113.

125. Ibid.

126. Arié, June 9, 1899, AAIU, Turquie LXXVI E 911.08.

127. "La kuestion del dia," *La Buena Esperanza*, February 23, 1899, 1.

128. "Los dezmodramientos del karnaval," *La Buena Esperanza*, March 3, 1900, 3.

129. Ad for Bayrakli, *La Buena Esperanza*, March 14 & 23, 1900.

130. "Por los echos de la komunidad," *La Buena Esperanza*, April 1, 1900, 2.

131. "Echos de la komunidad," *La Buena Esperanza*, May 14, 1900, 1.

132. For a translation of a portion of the text, see "Class Conflict Amidst the Jews of Izmir: A Rebellion of the Jewish Poor (1847)," trans. Dina Danon [Shav'at Aniyim, Izmir, 1847] in *Sephardi Lives: A Documentary History, 1700 – 1950*, eds. Julia Phillips Cohen and Sarah Abrevaya Stein (Stanford University Press, 2014), 43-44.

133. *Shavat Ani'im*.

134. Ibid.

135. Ibid.

136. Avigdor Levy, "Introduction," in Avigdor Levy, ed., *The Jews of the Ottoman Empire* (Princeton: Darwin Press, 1994), 107.

137. Levi, "Shavat Aniim," 184–86.

138. *Shavat Ani'im*.

139. Ibid.

140. Ibid.

141. Ibid.

142. Ibid.

143. Ibid.

144. Ibid.

145. Letter to the editor, 14 Iyar [5]636, *La Buena Esperanza*, May 11, 1876, 3.

146. Eliezer Papo, *And Thou Shalt Jest with Thy Son: Judeo-Spanish Parodies on the Passover Haggadah*, Vol. 1 (Jerusalem: Ben-Zvi Institute, 2012), 86–100 [Hebrew].

147. "Agada de la karne," *El Soytari*, April 5, 1909, 3–4.

148. Yavuz Selim Karakïsla, "The Emergence of the Ottoman Industrial Working Class, 1839–1923," in *Workers and the Working Class in the Ottoman Empire and the Turkish Republic 1839–1950*, eds. Donald Quataert and Erik J. Zürcher (London: I. B. Tauris, 1995), 22.

149. See for example *Kopia de la karta ke se mando a su eminensia morenu a-rav a-kolel* (4 Adar [5]639), in which the *esnaf* of flea marketers and tinsmiths issued a statement celebrating the work of *Gabbaé Sedaka*, and *Kopia de la askama del esnaf de los bakales*, 8 Tammuz 5652, CAHJP, Tr/Iz. 29 (*soletreo*), which reflects agreements regarding sales and price setting for grocers. Evidence of significant activity in the guilds among Izmir's Jews can be attested only starting in the 1800s. See Jacob Barnai, *Smyrna, The Microcosmos of Europe: The Jewish Community of Smyrna in the 17th and 18th Centuries* (Jerusalem: Carmel, 2014), 121 (in Hebrew); Jacob Barnai, "Gildot Yehudiot be-Turkia be-me'ot ha-16-19," in *Yehudim ba-Kalkalah*, ed. Nahum Gross (Jerusalem: Merkaz Zalman Shazar, 1985), 133–47. For a broader discussion of Ottoman guilds and a critique of their supposed decline in the late imperial period, see Donald Quataert, "The Age of Reforms," in *An Economic*

and Social History of the Ottoman Empire, 1300–1914, ed. Halil İnalcik and Donald Quataert (Cambridge: Cambridge University Press, 1994), 890–98.

150. "Los esnafes," *La Boz del Puevlo*, March 16, 1909, 1.

151. Seduta, 27 Tevet 5669, Prochesos verbales, CAHJP, Tr/Iz. 35 *(soletreo)*; Seduta, 3 Adar 5669, CAHJP, Tr/Iz. 35 *(soletreo)*.

152. Procheso verbal no. 8, 29 Nissan 5669, Livro de prochesos verbales del meclis umumi, CAHJP, Tr/Iz. 57 *(soletreo)*.

153. See, for example, Seduta del meclis umumi, 15 Tevet 5671, Livro de prochesos verbales del meclis umumi, CAHJP, Tr/Iz. 57 *(soletreo)* in which administrators seek the participation of the *esnafes* in a commission specifically devoted to studying the taxation of kosher meat; and 5 Kislev [5]672, CAHJP, Tr/Iz. 773 *(soletreo)* in which *Talmud Tora* administrators seek approval from the *esnafes* before raising tuition.

154. "A propozito de konferensias," *El Meseret*, October 21, 1909, 3; "Kontinuasion de la suskripsion echa por el Klub de Esnafes," *La Boz de Izmir*, October 17, 1911, 4.

155. "Agada de la karne," *El Soytari*, April 5, 1909, 3.

156. Ibid.

157. Raporto milrado en la asamblia nasional por el prezidente del Konsilio Komunal, 7, 17 Av 5681, CAHJP, Tr/Iz. 10.

158. Ibid.

159. Ibid.

160. Letter from the chief rabbinate in Istanbul, September 5, 1934, CAHJP, Tr/Iz. 129.

161. "El kuchiyo atado," *El Pregonero*, May 3, 1912, 2.

Chapter 5

1. "La kuestion de las eleksiones," *El Comercial*, August 27, 1908, 2.

2. For example, Letter to the *Haham Bashi*, 27 Heshvan 5673, CAHJP, HM 9070.1 *(soletreo)*; "El meclis umumi," *La Buena Esperanza*, September 17, 1897, 1.

3. For more on *millet* reform, see Roderic Davison, *Reform in the Ottoman Empire, 1856–1876* (1963; repr., New York: Gordian Press, 1973), 114–35.

4. Abraham Galante, *Documents officiels turcs concernant les Juifs de Turquie: recueil de 114 lois, règlements, firmans, bérats, ordres, et décisions de tribunaux* (Istanbul: Haim Rozio, 1931), 7–27.

5. Ibid., 10.

6. "Korespondensia partikular de *La Esperanza*," *La Esperanza*, December 14, 1876, 2; "Novedades israelitas," *La Esperanza*, December 21, 1876, 2; "Avizo ofisial," *La Buena Esperanza*, November 27, 1879, 2.

7. *Procheto de estatuto (regulamiento) organiko por la komunidad israelitika de Izmirna* (Izmir: n.d.), Article 1.

8. Ibid., Article 13.

9. "Avizo ofisial," *La Esperanza*, November 27, 1879, 2.
10. *Procheto de estatuto (regulamiento) organiko por la komunidad israelitika de Izmirna*, Kapitulo 2, Article 4.
11. Ibid., Articles 63–64.
12. Ibid., Article 53.
13. Ibid.
14. "El konsilio komunal," *La Buena Esperanza*, July 4, 1884, 2.
15. Seduta no. 2, 29 Tammuz [5]644, Prochesos verbales, CAHJP, Tr/Iz. 28 (*soletreo*).
16. "El konsilio komunal," *La Buena Esperanza*, July 4, 1884, 2.
17. "El estatuto organiko," *La Buena Esperanza*, August 14, 1884, 2 (letter to the editor).
18. "El estatuto organiko," *La Buena Esperanza*, August 21, 1884, 2 (letter to the editor).
19. "El estatuto organiko," *La Buena Esperanza*, August 14, 1884, 2 (letter to the editor).
20. "El estatuto organiko, o nizamname de la komunidad," *La Buena Esperanza*, August 7, 1884, 2–3 (letter to the editor).
21. Seduta no. 5, 3 Rahamim [5]644, Prochesos verbales, CAHJP, Tr/Iz. 28 (*soletreo*).
22. Ibid.
23. Zafer Toprak, "From Plurality to Unity: Codification and Jurisprudence in the Late Ottoman Empire," in *Ways to Modernity in Greece and Turkey: Encounters with Europe, 1850–1950*, eds. Anna Frangoudaki and Çağlar Keyder (London: I. B. Tauris, 2007), 32.
24. "El estatuto organiko, o nizamname de la komunidad," *La Buena Esperanza*, Letter to editor, August 7, 1884.
25. "El estatuto organiko," *La Buena Esperanza*, August 14, 1884; "El estatuto organiko," *La Buena Esperanza* August 21, 1884.
26. Avi Rubin, "Modernity as a Code: The Ottoman Empire and the Global Movement of Codification," *Journal of the Economic and Social History of the Orient* 59 (2016): 841.
27. "El konsilio komunal," *La Buena Esperanza*, July 4, 1884.
28. Seduta no. 57, 23 Sivan [5]644, CAHJP, Tr/Iz. 28 (*soletreo*).
29. "El konsilio komunal," *La Buena Esperanza*, July 4, 1884, 2.
30. Ibid.
31. Ibid.
32. "El estatuto organiko, o nizamname de la komunidad," *La Buena Esperanza*, Letter to editor, August 7, 1884, 2–3.
33. "El estatuto organiko," *La Buena Esperanza*, August 14, 1884, 2.

34. El estatuto organiko," *La Buena Esperanza*, August 21, 1884, 2.

35. Seduta no. 55, 15 Sivan [5]644, Prochesos verbales, CAHJP, Tr/Iz. 28 (*soletreo*).

36. Seduta no. 5, 3 Rahamim [5]644, Prochesos verbales, CAHJP, Tr/Iz. 28 (*soletreo*).

37. Seduta no. 63, 12 Shvat 5651, Prochesos verbales, CAHJP, Tr/Iz. 29 (*soletreo*).

38. Avizo al onorado publiko, 7 Adar 5651, Prochesos verbales, CAHJP, Tr/Iz. 29.

39. "El meclis umumi," *La Buena Esperanza*, April 3, 1891, 1; Seduta no. 25, Rosh Hodesh Sivan [5]651, Prochesos verbales, CAHJP, Tr/Iz. 29 (*soletreo*).

40. Seduta no. 26, seduta del meclis umumi, Rosh Hodesh Sivan [5]651, Prochesos verbales, CAHJP, Tr/Iz. 29 (*soletreo*).

41. "Avizo del gran rabinato," *La Buena Esperanza*, July 21, 1891, 1.

42. Avizo al onorado publiko, 7 Adar 5651, Prochesos verbales, CAHJP, Tr/Iz. 29.

43. "El meclis umumi," *La Buena Esperanza*, April 3, 1891, 1.

44. "Avizo del gran rabinato," *La Buena Esperanza*, July 21, 1891.

45. Seduta no. 31, 13 Sivan [5]651, Prochesos verbales, CAHJP, Tr/Iz. 29, (*soletreo*).

46. Seduta no. 28, 10 Sivan [5]651, Prochesos verbales, CAHJP, Tr/Iz. 29, (*soletreo*).

47. "El meclis umumi," *La Buena Esperanza*, June 23, 1891, 2–3.

48. Seduta no. 17, 16 Iyar [5]656, Prochesos verbales, CAHJP, Tr/Iz. 30 (*soletreo*).

49. "El meclis umumi," *El Novelista*, June 19, 1896, 153.

50. "El meclis umumi," *La Buena Esperanza*, July 21, 1896, 1.

51. Seduta espesial del meclis umumi, 16 Av 5651, Prochesos verbales, CAHJP, Tr/Iz. 31 (*soletreo*).

52. Seduta no. 1, 3 Elul 5656, Prochesos verbales, CAHJP, Tr/Iz. 31 (*soletreo*).

53. Seduta no. 10, 14 Tishrei [5]657, Prochesos verbales, CAHJP, Tr/Iz. 31 (*soletreo*).

54. *Regulamento de administrasion de la komunidad israelit de Izmir* (Tatikian, 1911), CAHJP, Tr/Iz. 17.

55. Regulamiento de administrasion de la komunidad israelit de Izmir, Article 58, Prochesos verbales, CAHJP, Tr/Iz. 31 (*soletreo*).

56. Ibid., Articles 59 and 60(a), CAHJP, Tr/Iz. 31 (*soletreo*).

57. "El meclis umumi," *El Novelista*, June 19, 1896, 153.

58. "Nuestra komunidad," *El Meseret*, September 17, 1897, 1–2.

59. Seduta regular, no. 42, 27 Tishrei 5658, Prochesos verbales, CAHJP, Tr/Iz. 32 (*soletreo*); Kolel Izmir, 19 Tishrei 5659, Prochesos verbales, CAHJP, Tr/Iz. 9. The *meclis umumi* convened in both 1897 and 1898 to review the lay council's activities and approve its management of the budget.

60. 25 Nisan [5]659, AAIU, Turquie LXXXVI E 911.07.

61. "Rabbi Yosef Eli," *La Buena Esperanza*, July 21, 1899, 1.

62. Arié, December 17, 1900, AAIU, Turquie LXXVI E 911.07.

63. "Su eminensia ma'alat Rabi Yosef Bensenyor," *El Meseret*, December 21, 1900, 4

64. AAIU, Turquie LXXVI E 911.06 part 13, January 29, 1901.
65. "Echos komunales," *La Buena Esperanza*, July 16, 1903, 1.
66. "Por el bien de la komunidad," *El Novelista*, January 18, 1907, 41–42.
67. "Notisia alegre," *El Novelista*, March 15, 1907, 122.
68. "La kuestion de las eleksiones del meclis umumi," *El Comercial*, August 19, 1908, 1.
69. "El meclis umumi," *El Comercial*, August 19, 1908, 2.
70. Ibid.
71. Procheso verbal no. 1, 10 Elul 5668, Livro de prochesos verbales del meclis umumi, CAHJP, Tr/Iz. 57, (*soletreo*).
72. Ibid.
73. Nabon, February 4, 1909, AAIU, Turquie LXXXIII E 1007.1.
74. *Regulamento de administrasion de la komunidad israelit de Izmirna*, 5671 (1911), Articles 116, 117, 118; Articles 122, 123, 125, CAHJP, Tr/Iz. 17.
75. Ibid., Kapitulo 2, CAHJP, Tr/Iz. 17.
76. Ibid., Kapitulo 3.
77. Pinkas protokoles meclis umumi (1908–1913), CAHJP, Tr/Iz. 57, (*soletreo*).
78. Communal Council, Letter to the *Haham Bashi*, 27 Heshvan 5673, CAHJP, HM 9070.1 (*soletreo*).
79. *Procheso verbal de las reuniones del meclis umumi de las sedutas tenidas en el 19 Elul, en el 10 Kislev 5672 [i] en el 12 Tevet en el 8 Tammuz 5673* (Izmir: Imprimeria el Novelista), 18.
80. Ibid.
81. Esther Benbassa, ed., *Haim Nahum: A Sephardic Chief Rabbi in Politics, 1892–1923*, trans. Miriam Kochan (Tuscaloosa: University of Alabama Press, 1995), 13.
82. Rubin, "Modernity as a Code," 829.
83. *Procheso verbal de las reuniones del meclis umumi de las sedutas tenidas en el 19 Elul, en el 10 Kislev 5672 [i] en el 12 Tevet en el 8 Tammuz 5673*(Izmir: Imprimeria el Novelista), 5.
84. Joseph Hacker, "Jewish Autonomy in the Ottoman Empire," in *The Jews of the Ottoman Empire*, ed. Avigdor Levy (Princeton: Darwin Press, 1994), 183.
85. Haim Gerber and Jacob Barnai, *Yehude Izmir ba-me'ah ha-tesha'esreh: Te'udot Turkiyot me'Arhkiyon bet-ha-din ha-shar'i* (Jerusalem: Misgav Yerushalayim, 1984).
86. BOA A.AMD 3/82 1 R 1264; BOA A.DVN 32/86 19 M 1264; BOA A.DVN 33/47 26 S 1264.
87. BOA, ŞD 2544–23.
88. BOA BEO 88/6572 22 Ra 1310.
89. BOA DH.ID 116/76 22 Z 1331.
90. Aron Rodrigue, *French Jews, Turkish Jews: The Alliance Israélite Universelle and*

the Politics of Jewish Schooling in Turkey, 1860–1925 (Bloomington: Indiana University Press, 1990), 32.

91. Davison, *Reform in the Ottoman Empire*, 114–15.

92. *Procheto de estatuto (regulamiento) organiko por la komunidad israelitika de Izmirna*, Artikulos 2, 13–1; *Regulamento de administrasion* 1911 Article 29 A.

93. *Procheto de estatuto (regulamiento) organiko por la komunidad israelitika de Izmirna*, Article 22; *Regulamento de administrasion* Articles 103, 104, 137.

94. Seduta no. 57, 23 Sivan [5]644, Prochesos verbales, CAHJP, Tr/Iz. 28 (*soletreo*).

95. Seduta ekstraordinaria, 15 Elul [5]657, Prochesos verbales, CAHJP, Tr/Iz. 31 (*soletreo*).

96. Seduta ekstraordinaria, 23 Shvat [5]669, Prochesos verbales, CAHJP, Tr/Iz. 773 (*soletreo*).

97. Rescrit publié dans les synagogues de Smyrne le 9 Avril 1888, AAIU, Turquie LXXXVI E 1015.3.

98. Pariente, May 4, 1888, AAIU, Turquie LXXXVI E 1015.3.

99. Pariente, July 6, 1888, AAIU, Turquie LXXXVI E 1015.3.

100. Seduta no. 14, 25 Shvat 5656, Prochesos verbales, CAHJP, Tr/Iz. 30 (*soletreo*).

101. Arié, February 10, 1896, AAIU, Turquie LXXIV E 911.01.

102. Ibid.

103. See for example Moïse Franco, *Essai sur l'histoire des Israélites de l'Empire Ottoman depuis les origines jusqu'à nos jours*, (1897; repr., Paris: Durlacher, 2007), 200.

104. Appendix to Abraham Galante, *Les Juifs d'Anatolie: Les Juifs d'Izmir* (Istanbul: Imprimerie Babok, 1937), 358.

105. Seduta no. 60, 7 Shvat 5651, Prochesos verbales, CAHJP, Tr/Iz. 29 (*soletreo*).

106. Seduta ekstraordinaria, no. 4, 11 Heshvan 5659, Prochesos verbales, CAHJP, Tr/Iz. 33 (*soletreo*).

107. Seduta, 22 Kislev 5670, CAHJP, Tr/Iz. 773 (*soletreo*).

108. *Procheto de estatuto (regulamiento) organiko por la komunidad israelitika de Izmirna*, Article 15.

109. Ibid., Article 18.

110. *Regulamento de administrasion*, 1911, Article 92, CAHJP, Tr/Iz. 17.

111. "Novedades lokales," *La Esperanza*, March 23, 1876, 4.

112. Galante, *Les Juifs d'Anatolie*, Document D, 357.

113. Ibid.

114. *Procheso verbal de las reuniones del meclis umumi de las sedutas tenidas en el 19 Elul, en el 10 Kislev 5672 [i] en el 12 Tevet en el 8 Tammuz 5673* (Izmir: Imprimeria el Novelista), 5–6.

115. "El konsulio komunal," *La Buena Esperanza*, July 4, 1884, 2.

116. "El estatuto organiko," *La Buena Esperanza*, August 28, 1884, 3.

117. Seduta ekstraordinaria, 15 Elul 5657, CAHJP, Tr/Iz. 31 (*soletreo*).
118. "El meclis umumi," *La Buena Esperanza*, July 28, 1896, 1.
119. "Rabbi Haim Nahum," *El Comercial*, August 18, 1908, 1.
120. *Konsulio komunal israelit Ismirna, objeto: dono nasional*, 28 Shvat 5670 [February 7, 1910].

121. *Procheso verbal de las reuniones del meclis umumi de las sedutas tenidas en el 19 Elul, en el 10 Kislev 5672 [i] en el 12 Tevet en el 8 Tammuz 5673* (Izmir: Imprimeria el Novelista), 32.

122. AAIU, Turquie LXXX E 944, August 29, 1873.

123. See, for example, Arié, September 25, 1895, AAIU, Turquie LXXIV E 911.02. Shortly after Arié's arrival in Izmir, the Communal Council tried to set up a local committee to oversee the activities and curriculum of the *Alliance*. A conflict ensued and ultimately the request was denied.

124. Arié, December 2, 1898, AAIU, Turquie LXXV E 911.04.
125. Arié, November 27, 1898, AAIU, Turquie LXXV E 911.04.

126. "Va-yamat Avraham be-seva tova zaken ve-save'a va-ye'asef el-amav, ve-ata tavo el avotekha be-shalom tekaver be-seva tova," *La Buena Esperanza*, January 20, 1899, 1. Part of the title is based on Genesis 25:8, "And Abraham breathed his last, dying at a good ripe age, old and contented; and he was gathered to his kin."

127. "Biografia de su eminensia nuestro gran rabino Avraham Palacci," *El Meseret*, January 13, 1899, 9–11. Other Ottoman rabbis were celebrated for their commitment to progress. See the discussion of Rabbi Jacob Covo of Salonica in Devin E. Naar, *Jewish Salonica: Between the Ottoman Empire and Modern Greece* (Stanford: Stanford University Press, 2016), 93.

128. Prayer composed by Rabbi Abulafia, May 22, 1910, AAIU, Turquie LXXXIV E 1007.6.

129. *Procheso verbal de las reuniones del meclis umumi de las sedutas tenidas en el 19 Elul, en el 10 Kislev 5672 [i] en el 12 Tevet en el 8 Tammuz 5673* (Izmir: Imprimeria el Novelista), 33–34.

130. Rodrigue, *French Jews, Turkish Jews*, 65.

131. Lehmann, *Ladino Rabbinic Literature and Ottoman Sephardic Culture* (Bloomington: Indiana University Press, 2005), 203.

132. Franco, *Essai sur l'histoire des Israélites*, 200.
133. Kontinuasion de seduta, 20 Av [5]653, CAHJP, Tr/Iz. 30 (*soletreo*).
134. Ibid.
135. Arié, February 3, 1899, AAIU, Turquie LXXVI E 911.08.
136. Arié, April 6, 1899, AAIU, Turquie LXXVI E 911.08.
137. Ibid.
138. "Su eminensia ma'alat Rabi Yosef Bensenyor," *El Meseret*, December 21, 1900, 4.

139. *Regulamento de administrasion de la komunidad de Izmirna*, 1911, Article 98.

140. *Procheso verbal de las reuniones del meclis umumi de las sedutas tenidas en el 19 Elul, en el 10 Kislev 5672 [i] en el 12 Tevet en el 8 Tammuz 5673* (Izmir: Imprimeria El Novelista), 32.

Conclusion

1. For example, "Los limozneros en Izmir," *La Esperanza*, December 31, 1874, 1; "Los eskandalos de los povres," *La Buena Esperanza*, June 28, 1888, 2.

2. For example, "Diskorso de los guerfanos de Talmud Tora," *La Esperanza*, July 8, 1875, 5 (suplimiento al numero 39).

3. "Les bonnes manières," *El Novelista*, June 27, 1902.

4. For example, Letter to the *Haham Bashi*, 27 Heshvan 5673, CAHJP, HM 9070.1 (*soletreo*).

5. For example, "Solusion de la kuestion rabinika," *El Comercial*, November 15, 1907, 3–4; "La kuestion de las eleksiones," *El Comercial*, August 27, 1908, 1.

6. For example, "La kuestion de los shohatim," *La Buena Esperanza*, April 28, 1899, 3; "La kuestion de la karne," *La Buena Esperanza*, February 7, 1889, 4; "La kuestion del dia," *El Meseret*, July 7, 1899, 1.

7. William M. Reddy, "The Concept of Class," in *Social Orders and Social Classes in Europe since 1500: Studies in Social Stratification*, ed. M. L. Bush (London and New York: Longman, 1992), 16.

8. For more on debates surrounding the difference marked by the kosher meat industry, see Robin Judd, *Contested Rituals: Circumcision, Kosher Butchering, and Jewish Political Life in Germany 1843–1933* (Ithaca: Cornell University Press, 2007), 154–89; Robin Judd, "The Politics of Beef: Animal Advocacy and the Kosher Butchering Debates in Germany," *Jewish Social Studies* 10, no. 1 (Autumn 2003): 117–50.

9. See, for example Jonathan Frankel, *Prophecy and Politics: Socialism, Nationalism, and the Russian Jews, 1862–1917* (Cambridge: Cambridge University Press, 1981); Ezra Mendelsohn, *On Modern Jewish Politics* (Oxford: Oxford University Press, 1993).

10. Tony Michels, *A Fire in Their Hearts: Yiddish Socialists in New York* (Cambridge: Harvard University Press, 2005).

11. Todd Endelman, *The Jews of Georgian England 1714–1830* (Ann Arbor: University of Michigan Press, 1979); Todd Endelman, "The Englishness of Jewish Modernity in England," in *Toward Modernity: The European Jewish Model*, ed. Jacob Katz (New York: Transaction Books, 1987), 225–46.

12. See, for example, Minna Rozen, "A Pound of Flesh: The Meat Trade and Social Struggle in Jewish Istanbul, 1700–1923," In *Crafts and Craftsmen of the Middle East: Fashioning the Individual in the Muslim Mediterranean*, ed. Suraiya Faroqhi and Randi

Deguilhem (London: I.B. Tauris, 2005); Esther Benbassa, *Une diaspora sépharade en transition: Istanbul XIX–XXe siècles* (Paris: Les Éditions du Cerf, 1993), 38–40; Aron Rodrigue and Sarah Abrevaya Stein, eds., *A Jewish Voice from Ottoman Salonica: The Ladino Memoir of Sa'adi Besalel a-Levi*, trans. Isaac Jerushalmi (Stanford: Stanford University Press, 2011), 57.

13. Donald Quataert, "The Industrial Working Class of Salonica, 1850–1912," in *Jews, Turks, Ottomans: A Shared History, Fifteenth Through the Twentieth Century*, 194–211; Paul Dumont, "A Jewish, Socialist and Ottoman Organization: the Workers Federation of Salonica" in *Socialism and Nationalism in the Ottoman Empire, 1876–1923*, eds. Mete Tuncay and Erik J. Zürcher, (New York: British Academic Press, 1994), 49–75.

BIBLIOGRAPHY

Archives

Archives of Alliance Israélite Universelle (AAIU), Série Turquie

Başbakanlık Osmanlı Arşivi (BOA)
A.AMD
A.DVN
BEO
DH.ID
DH.MKT
ŞD

Central Archives for the History of the Jewish People, Jerusalem (CAHJP), Tr/Iz.
HM28638 Letters to the *Haham Bashı*
HM 9070 Letters to the *Haham Bashı*

Published Primary Sources

Newspapers

Ahenk

La Boz de Izmir

La Boz del Puevlo

La Esperanza / La Buena Esperanza (name change in February, 1880)

El Comercial

El Guiyon

El Meseret

El Novelista

El Pregonero

El Soytari

La Verdad

Books and Pamphlets

Chateaubriand, François-René, *Itinéraire de Paris à Jerusalem*. Paris: Garnier Frères, 1872.

De Saint-Martin, Louis Vivien. *Description historique de l'Asie mineure*. Vol. 2. Paris: Arthus Bertrand, 1852.

Du Gabé, Baron. *Impressions d'un français: échelles du Levant*. Paris: Librairie Th. J. Plange, 1902.

Los doveres entre los ermanos de la Liga de Pas i Solidaridad i sus mujeres. Izmir: Imprimeria Frankos, 1914.

Edision espesial de La Buena Esperanza. Izmir: January 1896.

Estatutos de la Smirna-Loja Nu' 680. Izmir: Imprimido en El Novelista, January 1915.

Istoria del ospital Rotshild de Izmir. Izmir: Rosh Hodesh Tammuz, 5635 (1875).

Kinso nes harim ti'ru ve-khitko'a shofar tishme'u. Izmir: 13 Iyar [5]639 (May 6, 1879).

Kol ha-shofar holekh ve-hazek me'od. Izmir: La kupa Gabbaé Sedaka, 11 Iyar [5]639 (May 4, 1879).

Konsulio komunal israelit Ismirna, objeto: dono nasional, 28 Shvat 5670 [February 7, 1910].

Kopia de la karta ke se mando a su eminensia morenu a-rav a-Kolel. 25 Adar [5]639 (March 20, 1879).

Kra ve-garon al tahshokh ka-shofar harem kolekha. Izmir: La kupa Gabbaé Sedaka, 8 Iyar [5]639 (May 1, 1879).

Kuento de la kupa Gabbaé Sedaka. Izmir: Estamperia la Esperanza, [5]642 (1881–82).
MacFarlane, Charles. *Constantinople et la Turquie en 1828*. Vol. 1. Translated by A. F. Nettement. Paris: Moutardier, 1829.
Manifesto ofisial al onorado publiko. Izmir: La Munisipalidad de Izmirna, [1910?].
Monmarché, Marcel. *De Paris à Constantinople*. Paris: Hachette, 1912.
Procheso verbal de las reuniones del meclis umumi de las sedutas tenidas en el 19 Elul, en el 10 Kislev 5672 [i] en el 12 Tevet en el 8 Tammuz 5673. Izmir: Imprimeria el Novelista, n.d.
Procheto de estatuto (regulamiento) organiko por la komunidad israelitika de Izmirna. Izmir: n.d.
Regulamento de administrasion de la komunidad de Izmirna, 1911.
Regulamentos de la kupa ve-Aavtem et ha-Ger. Izmir: 27 Tishrei 5649 (October 2, 1888).
Reuniones del meclis umumi en el 2 Shvat 5672 i en el 8 Tammuz 5672. Izmir: Imprimido en *El Novelista*, n.d.
Rougon, Firmin. *Smyrne: Situation commerciale et économique des pays compris dans la circonscription du consulat général de France*. Paris: Berger-Levrault et Compagnie, 1892.
La Salvasion: va-ye'anhu vnei Yisrael min-ha'avoda. Izmir: La kupa Gabbaé Sedaka, 20 Nisan [5]639 (April 13, 1879).
Shavat Ani'im. N.p.: 24 Shvat 5607 (February 10, 1847).
Sirkular de Ozer Dalim. Izmir: Kislev 5659 (1898–99).
Tarica, Albert. *El Komersio*. Izmir: Imprimeria Frankos, 1904.
Yamada presante a la karidad. N.p.: Sosiedad Ozer Dalim, Shvat [5]681 (January 1921).

Secondary Sources

Abu-Manneh, Butrus. "The Islamic Roots of the Gülhane Rescript." *Die Welt des Islams* 34, no. 2 (1994): 173–203.
Adam, Thomas. *Buying Respectability: Philanthropy and Urban Society in Transnational Perspective, 1840s to 1930s*. Bloomington: Indiana University Press, 2009.
Adams, Thomas McStay. *Bureaucrats and Beggars: French Social Policy in the Age of the Enlightenment*. New York: Oxford University Press, 1990.
Albert, Phyllis Cohen. *The Modernization of French Jewry: Consistory and Community in the Nineteenth Century*. Hanover: Brandeis University Press, 1977.
Assis, Yom-Tov. "Welfare and Mutual Aid in the Spanish Jewish Communities." In *The Sephardi Legacy*. Vol. 1, edited by Haim Beinart, 318–45. Jerusalem: Magnes Press, 1992.
Atay, Çınar. *Osmanlı'dan Cumhuriyet'e Izmir Planları*. Ankara: Ajans Türk, 1998.
Aytekin, E. Attile. "Peasant Protest in the Late Ottoman Empire: Moral Economy, Revolt, and the *Tanzimat* Reforms." *IRSH* 57 (2012), 191–227.

Barkey, Karen. *Empire of Difference: The Ottomans in Comparative Perspective.* Cambridge: Cambridge University Press, 2008.

Barnai, Jacob. "Christian Messianism and the Portuguese Marranos: The Emergence of Sabbateanism in Smyrna." *Jewish History* 7, no. 2 (1993): 119–24.

———. "Congregations in Smyrna in the Seventeenth Century." *Peamim: Studies in Oriental Jewry* 48 (1991): 66–84 (in Hebrew).

———. "The Development of Community Organizational Structures: The Case of Izmir." In *Jews, Turks, Ottomans: A Shared History, Fifteenth Through the Twentieth Century*, edited by Avigdor Levy, 35–51. Syracuse: Syracuse University Press, 2002.

———. "Gildot Yehudiot be'Turkia be'me'ot ha-16-19." In *Yehudim ba'Kalkalah*, edited by Nahum Gross, 133–47. Jerusalem: Merkaz Zalman Shazar, 1985.

———. "Organization and Leadership in the Jewish Community of Izmir in the Seventeenth Century." In *The Jews of the Ottoman Empire*, edited by Avigdor Levy, 275–83. Princeton: Darwin Press, 1994.

———. "The Origins of the Jewish Community in Izmir in the Ottoman Period." *Peamim: Studies in Oriental Jewry* 12 (1982): 47–58 (in Hebrew).

———. "Prototypes of Leadership in a Sephardic Community." In *Crisis and Continuity in the Sephardic World, 1391–1648*, edited by Benjamin Gampel, 146–63. New York: Columbia University Press, 1997.

———. "Rabbi Yosef Eskapa and the Rabbinate in Izmir." *Sefunot* 18, no. 3 (1985): 53–81 (in Hebrew).

———. "The Sabbatean Movement in Smyrna: The Social Background." In *Jewish Sects, Religious Movements, and Political Parties*, edited by Menachem Mor, 113–22. Omaha, NE: Creighton University Press, 1992.

———. *Smyrna, The Microcosmos of Europe: The Jewish Community of Smyrna in the 17th and 18th Centuries.* Jerusalem: Carmel, 2014 (in Hebrew).

Bashan, Eliezer. "Contacts between Jews in Smyrna and the Levant Company of London in the Seventeenth and Eighteenth Centuries." *Transactions of the Jewish Historical Society of England* 29 (1988): 53–73.

———. "Fires and Earthquakes in Izmir in the Seventeenth through the Nineteenth Centuries and a Document on the Accusation Directed against the Jews of Lighting the Fires." *Miqqedem Umiyyam* 2 (1986): 13–27 (in Hebrew).

———. "The Freedom of Trade and the Imposition of Taxes and Customs Duties on Foreign Jewish Traders in the Ottoman Empire." In *Mi-mizrah umi-ma'arav*. Vol. 1, edited by Haim Zeev Hirschberg, 105 - 166. Ramat Gan: Bar-Ilan University Press, 1974 (in Hebrew).

———. "A Jewish Guild in Izmir at the Beginning of the Eighteenth Century." In *Mi-mizrah umi-ma'arav*. Vol 5, edited by Ariel Toaff, 155–72. Ramat Gan: Bar-Ilan University Press, 1986 (in Hebrew).

Bauer, Ela. "From the Salons to the Street: The Development of a Jewish Public Sphere in Warsaw at the End of the 19th Century." *Simon Dubnow Institute Yearbook* 7 (2008): 143–59.
Benbassa, Esther. "Associational Strategies in Ottoman Jewish Society in the Nineteenth and Twentieth Centuries." In *The Jews of the Ottoman Empire*, edited by Avigdor Levy, 457–84. Princeton: Darwin Press, 1994.
———. *Une diaspora sépharade en transition: Istanbul XIX–XXe siècles*. Paris: Les Éditions du Cerf, 1993.
———., ed. *Haim Nahum: A Sephardic Chief Rabbi in Politics, 1892–1923*. Translated by Miriam Kochan. Tuscaloosa: University of Alabama Press, 1995.
———. "Le procès des sonneurs de tocsin: Une accusation calomnieuse de meurtre rituel à Izmir en 1901." Reprint from Abraham Haim, ed., *Society and Community: Proceedings of the Second International Congress for Research of the Sephardi and Oriental Jewish Heritage 1984*. Jerusalem: Institute for Research of the Sephardi and Oriental Jewish Heritage, 1991, 35–53.
Benbassa, Esther, and Aron Rodrigue. "L'Artisanat juif en Turquie à la fin du XIXe siècle: L'Alliance israélite universelle et ses oeuvres d'apprentissage." *Turcica* 17 (1985): 113–26.
———. *Sephardi Jewry: A History of the Judeo-Spanish Community, 14th–20th Centuries*. Berkeley: University of California Press, 2000.
Ben-Naeh, Yaron. *Jews in the Realm of the Sultans: Ottoman Jewish Society in the Seventeenth Century*. Tübingen: Mohr Siebeck, 2008.
———. "Poverty, Paupers and Poor Relief in Ottoman Jewish Society." *Revue des études juives* 163, nos. 1–2 (January–June 2004): 151–92.
Bilsel, Cânâ. "Vers une métropole moderne de la Mediterranée." In *Smyrne, la ville oubliée? Mémoires d'un grand port ottoman, 1830–1930*, edited by Marie-Carmen Smyrnelis, 122–37. Paris: Editions Autrement, 2006.
Birnbaum, Pierre, and Ira Katznelson. *Paths of Emancipation: Jews, States, and Citizenship*. Princeton: Princeton University Press, 1995.
Blumi, Isa. *Foundations of Modernity: Human Agency and the Imperial State*. New York: Routledge, 2012.
———. *Reinstating the Ottomans: Alternative Balkan Modernities, 1800–1912*. New York: Palgrave Macmillan, 2011.
Bodian, Miriam. *Hebrew of the Portuguese Nation: Conversos and Community in Early Modern Amsterdam*. Bloomington: Indiana University Press, 1997.
Bora, Siren. *Bir Semt, Bir Bina: Karataş Hastahanesi ve Cevresinde Yahudi Izleri*. Izmir: Izmir Büyükşehir Belediyesi, 2015.
———. *Izmir Yahudileri 1908–1923*. Istanbul: Gözlem Gazetecilik, 1995.
Borovaya, Olga. "The Emergence of the Ladino Press: The First Attempt at Westernization of Ottoman Jews (1842–6)," *European Judaism* 43, no. 2 (Autumn 2010): 63–75.

———. *Modern Ladino Culture: Press, Belles Lettres, and Theater in the Late Ottoman Empire*. Bloomington: Indiana University Press, 2012.

Bourdieu, Pierre. *Distinction: A Social Critique of the Judgment of Taste*. London: Routledge, 2010.

Brummet, Palmira. *Image and Imperialism in the Ottoman Revolutionary Press 1908–1911*. Albany: State University Press of New York, 2000.

Bush, M.L., ed. *Social Orders and Social Classes in Europe since 1500: Studies in Social Stratification*. London and New York: Longman, 1992.

Campos, Michelle. *Ottoman Brothers: Muslims, Christians, and Jews in Early Twentieth-Century Palestine*. Stanford: Stanford University Press, 2011.

Çelik, Zeynep. *The Remaking of Istanbul: Portrait of an Ottoman City in the Nineteenth Century*. Seattle: University of Washington Press, 1986.

Çetinkaya, Y. Doğan. *The Young Turks and the Boycott Movement: Nationalism, Protest, and the Working Classes in the Formation of Modern Turkey*. London: I. B. Tauris, 2014.

Chakrabarty, Dipesh. *Provincializing Europe: Postcolonial Thought and Historical Difference*. Princeton: Princeton University Press, 2008.

Chaumont, Éric. "Pauvreté et richesse dans le Coran et dans les sciences religieuses musulmanes." In *Pauvreté et richesse dans le monde méditerranéen*, edited by Jean-Paul Pascual, 17–25. Paris: Maisonneuve et Larose, 2003.

Cohen, Julia Phillips. *Becoming Ottomans: Sephardi Jews and Imperial Citizenship in the Modern Era*. New York: Oxford University Press, 2014.

Cohen, Julia Phillips, and Sarah Abrevaya Stein. *Sephardi Lives: A Documentary History*. Stanford: Stanford University Press, 2014.

Cohen, Mark. *Poverty and Charity in the Jewish Community of Medieval Egypt*. Princeton: Princeton University Press, 2005.

Cooper, Frederick. *Colonialism in Question: Theory, Knowledge, History*. Berkeley: University of California Press, 2005.

Davidoff, Leonore, and Catherine Hall. *Family Fortunes: Men and Women of the English Middle Class, 1780–1850*. London: Hutchinson, 1987.

Davison, Roderic. *Reform in the Ottoman Empire, 1856–1876*. 1963; Reprint, New York: Gordian Press, 1973.

Der Matossian, Bedross. *Shattered Dreams of Revolution: From Liberty to Violence in the Late Ottoman Empire*. Stanford: Stanford University Press, 2014.

Dong, Madeleine Yue, and Joshua Lewis Goldstein, eds. *Everyday Modernity in China*. Seattle: University of Washington Press, 2006.

Driessen, Henk. "Mediterranean Port Cities: Cosmopolitanism Reconsidered." *History and Anthropology* 16, no. 1 (2005): 129–41.

Duben, Alan, and Cem Behar. *Istanbul Households: Marriage, Family, and Fertility, 1880–1940*. Cambridge: Cambridge University Press, 1991.

Dubin, Lois. *The Port Jews of Habsburg Trieste: Absolutist Politics and Enlightenment Culture*. Stanford: Stanford University Press, 1999.
Dumont, Paul. "A Jewish, Socialist and Ottoman Organization: The Workers Federation of Salonica." In *Socialism and Nationalism in the Ottoman Empire, 1876–1923*, edited by Mete Tuncay and Erik J. Zürcher, 49–75. New York: British Academic Press, 1994.
Eldem, Edhem. "(A Quest for) the Bourgeoisie of Istanbul: Identities, Roles, and Conflicts." In *Urban Governance Under the Ottomans: Between Cosmopolitanism and Conflict*, edited by Ulrike Freitag and Nora Lafi, 159–86. Abingdon, Oxon: Routledge, 2014.
Emecen, Feridun. *Unutulmuş Bir Cemaat: Manisa Yahudileri*. Istanbul: Eren, 1997.
Emrence, Cem. *Remapping the Ottoman Middle East: Modernity, Imperial Bureaucracy, and the Islamic State*. London: I. B. Tauris, 2012.
Endelman, Todd. *Broadening Jewish History: Towards a Social History of Ordinary Jews*. Oxford: Littman Library of Jewish Civilization, 2011.
———. "The Englishness of Jewish Modernity in England." In *Toward Modernity: The European Jewish Model*, edited by Jacob Katz, 225–46. New York: Transaction Books, 1987.
———. *The Jews of Georgian England, 1714–1830*. 1979. Reprint, Ann Arbor: University of Michigan Press, 1999.
Ener, Mine. *Managing Egypt's Poor and the Politics of Benevolence, 1800–1952*. Princeton: Princeton University Press, 2003.
Ergut, Ferdan. "Policing the Poor in the Late Ottoman Empire." *Middle Eastern Studies* 38, no. 2 (April 2002): 149–64.
Exertzoglou, Haris. "The Cultural Uses of Consumption: Negotiating Class, Gender, and Nation in the Ottoman Urban Centers During the 19th Century." *International Journal of Middle East Studies* 35, no. 1 (February 2003): 77–101.
Findley, Carter. *Bureaucratic Reform in the Ottoman Empire: The Sublime Porte, 1789–1922*. Princeton: Princeton University Press, 1980.
Franco, Moïse. *Essai sur l'histoire des Israélites de l'Empire Ottoman depuis les origines jusqu'à nos jours*. 1897. Reprint, Paris: Durlacher, 2007.
Frangakis, Elena. "The Ottoman Port of Izmir in the Eighteenth and Early Nineteenth Centuries, 1695–1820." *Revue de l'Occident musulman et de la Méditerranée* 39 (1985): 149–62.
Frangakis-Syrett, Elena. *The Commerce of Smyrna in the Eighteenth Century (1700–1820)*. Bibliotheca Asiae Minoris Historica, 2. Athens: Centre for Asia Minor Studies, 1992.
———. "Commercial Growth and Economic Development in the Middle East: Izmir from the Early 18th to the Early 20th Centuries." In *Ottoman Izmir:*

Studies in Honour of Alexander H. de Groot, edited by Maurits H. van den Boogert, 1–38. Leiden: Nederlands Instituut voor het Nabije Oosten, 2007.

———. "The Economic Activities of the Greek Community of Izmir in the Second Half of the Nineteenth and Early Twentieth Centuries." In *Ottoman Greeks in the Age of Nationalism: Politics, Economy, and Society in the Nineteenth Century*, edited by Dimitri Gondicas and Charles Issawi, 17–44. Princeton: Darwin Press, 1999.

Frankel, Jonathan. *Prophecy and Politics: Socialism, Nationalism, and the Russian Jews, 1862–1917.* Cambridge: Cambridge University Press, 1981.

Furhmann, Malte. "Cosmopolitan Imperialists and the Ottoman Port Cities: Conflicting Logics in the Urban Social Fabric," *Cahiers de la Méditerranée* 67 (2003): 149–63.

Galante, Abraham. *Documents officiels turcs concernant les Juifs de Turquie: Recueil de 114 lois, règlements, firmans, bérats, ordres, et décisions de tribunaux.* Istanbul: Haim Rozio, 1931.

———. *Histoire des Juifs de Turquie*, 9 vols. Istanbul: Isis Press, 1985.

———. *Les Juifs d'Anatolie: Les Juifs d'Izmir.* Istanbul: Imprimerie Babok, 1937.

Gekas, Athanasios (Sakis). "Class and Cosmopolitanism: The Historiographical Fortunes of Merchants in Eastern Mediterranean Ports." *Mediterranean Historical Review* 24, no. 2 (December 2009): 95–114.

Georgelin, Hervé. *La fin de Smyrne: Du cosmopolitisme aux nationalismes.* Paris: CNRS Éditions, 2005.

Gerber, Haim, and Jacob Barnai. *Yehude Izmir ba-me'ah ha-tesha'esreh: Te'udot Turkiyot me'Arhkiyon bet-ha-din ha-shar'i.* Jerusalem: Misgav Yerushalayim, 1984.

Geremek, Bronislaw. *Poverty: A History.* Oxford: Basil Blackwell, 1994.

Gluck, Carol. "The End of Elsewhere: Writing Modernity Now." *The American Historical Review* 116, no. 3 (June 2011): 676–87.

Goçek, Fatma Müge. *Rise of the Bourgeoisie, Demise of Empire: Ottoman Westernization and Social Change.* New York: Oxford University Press, 1996.

Goffman, Daniel. "Izmir: From Village to Colonial Port City." In *The Ottoman City between East and West: Aleppo, Izmir, and Istanbul*, edited by Edhem Eldem, Daniel Goffman, and Bruce Masters, 79–134. Cambridge: Cambridge University Press, 1999.

———. *Izmir and the Levantine World, 1550–1650.* Seattle: University of Washington Press, 1990.

Goldstein, Joshua Lewis. "Introduction." In *Everyday Modernity in China*, edited by Madeleine Yue Dong and Joshua Lewis Goldstein, 3–21. Seattle: University of Washington Press, 2006.

Grunhaus, Nechama. *Ha-Misui ba-Kehilah ha-Yehudit be-Izmir ba-me'ot ha-sheva 'esreh veha-shemonah esreh: al pi sefer Avodat Masa le-R. Yehoshu'a Avraham Yehuda.* Tel Aviv: ha-Makhon le-heker ha-Tefutsot, Tel Aviv University, 1997.

———. "The Procedure and the Halakhic Basis for the Purchase Tax in the Community of Izmir." *Peamim: Studies in Oriental Jewry* 116 (Summer 2008): 79–116 (in Hebrew).

———. "The Taxation System of the Jewish Community of Izmir in the Seventeenth through the Nineteenth Centuries." PhD diss., New York University, 1995.

Habermas, Jürgen. *The Structural Transformation of the Public Sphere: An Inquiry into a Category of Bourgeois Society*. Translated by Thomas Burger. Cambridge: MIT Press, 1989.

Hacker, Joseph. "Jewish Autonomy in the Ottoman Empire." In *The Jews of the Ottoman Empire*, edited by Avigdor Levy, 153–202. Princeton: Darwin Press, 1994.

Hanioğlu, M. Şükrü. *A Brief History of the Late Ottoman Empire*. Princeton: Princeton University Press, 2008.

———. "The Second Constitutional Period, 1908–1918." In *Cambridge History of Turkey*. Vol. 4, *Turkey in the Modern World*, edited by Reşat Kasaba, 62–111. Cambridge: Cambridge University Press, 2008.

———. *The Young Turks in Opposition*. New York: Oxford University Press, 1995.

Hanley, Will. "Grieving Cosmopolitanism in Middle East Studies." *History Compass* 6/5 (2008): 1346–67.

Hanssen, Jens. "Public Morality and Marginality in Fin de Siècle Beirut." In *Outside In: On the Margins of the Modern Middle East*, edited by Eugene Rogan, 183–211. London: I. B. Tauris, 2002.

Harootunian, Harry. *History's Disquiet: Modernity, Cultural Practice, and the Question of Everyday Life*. New York: Columbia University Press, 2000.

Harrison, Carol E. "The Bourgeois after the Bourgeois Revolution: Recent Approaches to the Middle Class in European Cities." *Journal of Urban History* 31, no. 3 (2005): 382–92.

———. *The Bourgeois Citizen in Nineteenth-Century France: Gender, Sociability, and the Uses of Emulation*. Oxford: Oxford University Press, 1999.

Hart, Mitchell B., and Tony Michels. "Introduction." In *Cambridge History of Judaism*. Volume 8, *The Modern World 1815–2000*, edited by Mitchell B. Hart and Tony Michels, 1–8. Cambridge: Cambridge University Press, 2017.

Hausen, Karin. "Family and Role-Division: The Polarisation of Sexual Stereotypes in the Nineteenth Century—An Aspect of the Dissociation of Work and Family." In *The German Family: Essays on the Social History of the Family in Nineteenth and Twentieth Century Germany*, edited by Richard Evans and W. R. Lee, 51–83. London: Croom Helm, 1981.

Hyman, Paula E. "Immigrant Women and Consumer Protest: The New York City Kosher Meat Boycott of 1902." *American Jewish History* 70, no. 1 (September 1980): 91–105.

Illiou, Maria, dir. *Smyrna: The Destruction of a Cosmopolitan Port, 1900–1922*. Proteus Films, 2012. DVD.

İnalcik, Halil. "Application of the Tanzimat and Its Social Effects." *Archivum Ottomanicum* 5 (1973): 97–127.

İnalcik, Halil, and Donald Quataert. *A Social and Economic History of the Ottoman Empire 1300–1914*. Cambridge: Cambridge University Press, 1994.

Islamoğlu, Huri. "Modernities Compared: State Transformations and Constitutions of Property in the Qing and Ottoman Empires." In *Shared Histories of Modernity: China, India, and the Ottoman Empire*, edited by Huri Islamoğlu and Peter C. Perdue, 109–46. London: Routledge, 2009.

Islamoğlu, Huri, and Peter C. Perdue. *Shared Histories of Modernity: China, India, and the Ottoman Empire*. London: Routledge, 2009.

Islamoğlu-İnan, Huri. *The Ottoman Empire and the World-Economy*. Cambridge: Cambridge University Press, 1987.

Issawi, Charles. *Economic History of Turkey 1800–1914*. Chicago: University of Chicago Press, 1980.

Jackson, Maureen. "Cosmopolitan Smyrna: Illuminating or Obscuring Cultural Histories?" *The Geographical Review* 102, no. 3: 337–49.

Judd, Robin. *Contested Rituals: Circumcision, Kosher Butchering, and Jewish Political Life in Germany 1843–1933*. Ithaca: Cornell University Press, 2007.

———. "The Politics of Beef: Animal Advocacy and the Kosher Butchering Debates in Germany." *Jewish Social Studies* 10, no. 1 (Autumn 2003): 117–50.

Jütte, Robert. *Poverty and Deviance in Early Modern Europe*. Cambridge: Cambridge University Press, 1994.

Kaplan, Marion. *The Making of the Jewish Middle Class: Women, Family and Identity in Imperial Germany*. Oxford: Oxford University Press, 1991.

Kaplan, Yosef. *An Alternative Path to Modernity: The Sephardi Diaspora in Western Europe*. Leiden: Brill, 2000.

Karakışla, Yavuz Selim. "The 1908 Strike Wave in the Ottoman Empire." *Turkish Studies Association Bulletin* 16, no. 2 (September 1992): 153–77.

———. "The Emergence of the Ottoman Industrial Working Class, 1839–1923." In *Workers and the Working Class in the Ottoman Empire and the Turkish Republic 1839–1950*, edited by Donald Quataert and Erik J. Zürcher. London: I. B. Tauris, 1995.

Karpat, Kemal. *Ottoman Population, 1830–1914: Demographic and Social Characteristics*. Madison: University of Wisconsin Press, 1985.

Kasaba, Reşat, ed. *Cambridge History of Turkey*. Vol. 4: *Turkey in the Modern World*. Cambridge: Cambridge University Press, 2008.

———. "Economic Foundations of a Civil Society: Greeks in the Trade of Western Anatolia, 1840–1876." In *Ottoman Greeks in the Age of Nationalism: Politics,*

Economy, and Society in the Nineteenth Century, edited by Dimitri Gondicas and Charles Issawi, 77–87. Princeton: The Darwin Press, 1999.

———. "İzmir." *Review* XVI, 4 (Fall 1993): 387–410.

———. *The Ottoman Empire and the World Economy: The Nineteenth Century*. Albany: State University of New York Press, 1988.

———. "Was There a Compradore Bourgeoisie in Mid-Nineteenth Century Western Anatolia?" *Review* XI, no. 2 (Spring 1988): 215–28.

Kasaba, Reşat, Çağlar Keyder, and Faruk Tabak. "Eastern Mediterranean Port Cities and Their Bourgeoisies: Merchants, Political Projects, and Nation-States." *Review* X, no. 1 (Summer 1986): 121–35.

Katz, Jacob. *Out of the Ghetto: The Social Background of Jewish Emancipation, 1770–1870*. New York: Schocken Books, 1973.

Kechriotis, Vangelis. "Allons, Enfants de la . . . Ville: National Celebrations, Political Mobilisation and Urban Space in Izmir at the Turn of the 20th Century." In *Ottoman Izmir: Studies in Honour of Alexander de Groot*, edited by Maurits H. van den Boogert, 123–37. Leiden: Nederlands Instituut voor het Nabije Oosten, 2007.

———. "Civilisation and Order: Middle-Class Morality among the Greek Orthodox in Smyrna/Izmir at the End of the Ottoman Empire." In *Social Transformation and Mass Mobilisation in the Balkans and Eastern Mediterranean, 1900–1923*, edited by Andreas Lyberatos and Christos Chatziosif, 137–53. Rethymnon: Crete University Press, 2013.

———. "Greek-Orthodox, Ottoman Greeks, or Just Greeks? Theories of Coexistence in the Aftermath of the Young Turk Revolution." *Etudes balkaniques* 41, no. 1 (2005): 51–72.

———. "The Greeks of Izmir at the End of the Empire: A Non-Muslim Ottoman Community Between Autonomy and Patriotism." PhD. diss, Leiden University, 2005.

———. "Protecting the City's Interest: The Greek Orthodox and the Conflict between Municipal and *Vilayet* Authorities in Izmir (Smyrna) in the Second Constitutional Period." *Mediterranean Historical Review* 24, no. 2 (December 2009): 207–21.

———. "La Smyrne grecque: Des communautés au panthéon de l'histoire." In *Smyrne, la ville oubliée? Mémoires d'un grand port ottoman, 1830–1930*, edited by Marie-Carmen Smyrnelis, 63–77. Paris: Editions Autrement, 2006.

Keyder, Çağlar, Y. Eyüp Özveren, and Donald Quataert. "Port Cities in the Ottoman Empire: Theoretical and Historical Perspectives." *Review* XVI, no. 4 (Fall 1993): 519–58.

Kilinçoğlu, Deniz T. *Economics and Capitalism in the Ottoman Empire*. Abingdon: Routledge: 2015.

Kocka, Jürgen. "The Middle Classes in Europe." *The Journal of Modern History* 67, no. 4 (December 1995): 783–806.
Kontente, Leon. *L'Antisémitisme Grec en Asie Mineure*. Istanbul: Libra Kitap, 2015.
Lederhandler, Eli. *The Road to Modern Jewish Politics: Political Tradition and Political Reconstruction in the Jewish Community of Tsarist Russia*. New York: Oxford University Press, 1989.
Lehmann, Matthias. *Ladino Rabbinic Literature and Ottoman Sephardic Culture*. Bloomington: Indiana University Press, 2005.
Levi, Avner. "Ha-Itonut ha-Yehudit be'Izmir." *Peamim: Studies in Oriental Jewry* 12 (1982): 87–104.
———. "Ha-Tmurot ba-Manhigut ha-Kehilot ha-Sefardiyot ha-Merkaziyot ba-Imperiyah ha-Otomanit be-Meah ha-Tsha Esre." In *Yemei ha-Sahar: Prakim be-Toldot ha-Yehudim ba-Imperiyah ha-Otomanit*, edited by Minna Rozen, 237–71. Tel Aviv: Tel Aviv University, 1996.
———. "Shavat Aniim: Social Cleavage, Class War, and Leadership in the Sephardi Community—The Case of Izmir 1847." In *Ottoman and Turkish Jewry: Community and Leadership*, edited by Aron Rodrigue, 183–202. Indiana University Turkish Studies 12. Bloomington: Indiana University Turkish Studies, 1992.
Levy, Avigdor. "Introduction." In *The Jews of the Ottoman Empire*, edited by Avigdor Levy, 1–150. Princeton: Darwin Press, 1994.
———., ed. *The Jews of the Ottoman Empire*. Princeton: Darwin Press, 1994.
———., ed. *Jews, Turks, Ottomans: A Shared History, Fifteenth Through the Twentieth Century*. Syracuse: Syracuse University Press, 2002.
López, Amelia Barquín. "Un periódico sefardí: 'El Meseret' de Alexandr Ben Guiat." *Sefarad* 57, no. 1 (1997): 3–31.
Maksudyan, Nazan. "Orphans, Cities, and the State: Vocational Orphanages (*Islahhanes*) and Reform in the Late Ottoman Urban Space." *International Journal of Middle Eastern Studies* 43 (2011): 493–511.
———. *Orphans and Destitute Children in the Late Ottoman Empire*. Syracuse: Syracuse University Press, 2014.
Marcus, Abraham. *The Middle East on the Eve of Modernity: Aleppo in the Eighteenth Century*. New York: Columbia University Press, 1989.
Meir, Natan M. *Kiev, Jewish Metropolis: A History, 1859–1914*. Bloomington: Indiana University Press, 2010.
Mendelsohn, Ezra. *On Modern Jewish Politics*. Oxford: Oxford University Press, 1993.
Meyer, Michael A. "Where Does the Modern Period of Jewish History Begin?" *Judaism* 24 (1975): 329–38.
Michels, Tony. *A Fire in Their Hearts: Yiddish Socialists in New York*. Cambridge: Harvard University Press, 2005.

Mitchell, Timothy, ed. *Questions of Modernity*. Minneapolis: University of Minnesota Press, 2000.

———. "The Stage of Modernity." In *Questions of Modernity*, edited by Timothy Mitchell, 1–34. Minneapolis: University of Minnesota Press, 2000.

Mollat, Michel. *The Poor in the Middle Ages*. Translated by Arthur Goldhammer. New Haven: Yale University Press, 1986.

Naar, Devin E. *Jewish Salonica: Between the Ottoman Empire and Modern Greece*. Stanford: Stanford University Press, 2016.

Nahum, Henri. "En regardant une photographie: Une famille juive de Smyrne en 1900." In *Smyrne, la ville oubliée? Mémoires d'un grand port ottoman, 1830–1930*, edited by Marie-Carmen Smyrnelis, 93–105. Paris: Editions Autrement, 2006.

———. *Juifs de Smyrne: XIXe–XXe siècle*. Paris: Aubier, 1997.

Nathans, Benjamin. *Beyond the Pale: The Jewish Encounter with Late Imperial Russia*. Berkeley: University of California Press, 2002.

Özbek, Nadir. "'Beggars' and 'Vagrants' in Ottoman State Policy and Public Discourse, 1876–1914." *Middle Eastern Studies* 45, no. 5 (September 2009): 783–801.

———. "Defining the Public Sphere during the Late Ottoman Empire: War, Mass Mobilization, and the Young Turk Regime, 1908–1918." *Middle Eastern Studies* 43, no. 5 (2007): 795–809.

———. *Osmanlı İmparatorluğu'nda Sosyal Devlet: Siyaset, İktidar ve Meşrutiyet 1876–1914*. Istanbul: İletşim Yayınları, 2002.

———. "Philanthropic Activity, Ottoman Patriotism and the Hamidian Regime, 1876–1909." *International Journal of Middle Eastern Studies* 37, no. 1 (2005): 59–81.

———. "The Politics of Poor Relief in the Late Ottoman Empire, 1876–1914." *New Perspectives on Turkey* 21 (Fall 1999): 1–33.

Pamuk, Şevket. *A Monetary History of the Ottoman Empire*. Cambridge: Cambridge University Press, 2000.

———. "Prices in the Ottoman Empire, 1469–1914." *International Journal of Middle Eastern Studies* 36 (2004): 452–54.

Papo, Eliezer. *And Thou Shalt Jest with Thy Son: Judeo-Spanish Parodies on the Passover Haggadah*. Vol. 1. Jerusalem: Ben-Zvi Institute, 2012 (in Hebrew).

Paz, Omri. "Civil-Servant Aspirants: Ottoman Social Mobility in the Second Half of the Nineteenth Century." *Journal of the Economic and Social History of the Orient* 60 (2017): 381–419.

Penslar, Derek. "The Origins of Modern Jewish Philanthropy." In *Philanthropy in the World's Traditions*, edited by Warren F. Ilchman, Stanley N. Katz, and Edward L. Queen II, 197–214. Bloomington: Indiana University Press, 1998.

———. *Shylock's Children: Economics and Jewish Identity in Modern Europe.* Berkeley: University of California Press, 2001.

Petrov, Milen V. "Everyday Forms of Compliance: Subaltern Commentaries on Ottoman Reform, 1864–1868." *Comparative Studies in Society and History* 46, no. 4 (October 2004): 730–59.

"Portrait d'une communauté méconnue: Les Musulmans—entretien avec Fikret Yilmaz." In *Smyrne, la ville oubliée? Mémoires d'un grand port ottoman, 1830–1930,* edited by Marie-Carmen Smyrnelis, 52–62. Paris: Éditions Autrement, 2006.

Quataert, Donald. "The Age of Reforms." In *An Economic and Social History of the Ottoman Empire, 1300–1914,* edited by Halil İnalcık and Donald Quataert, 759–933. Cambridge: Cambridge University Press, 1994.

———. "The Industrial Working Class of Salonica, 1850–1912." In *Jews, Turks, Ottomans: A Shared History, Fifteenth Through the Twentieth Century,* edited by Avigdor Levy, 194–211. Syracuse: Syracuse University Press, 2002.

Reddy, William M. "The Concept of Class." In *Social Orders and Social Classes in Europe since 1500: Studies in Social Stratification,* edited by M. L. Bush, 13–25. London and New York: Longman, 1992.

Reinkowski, Maurus. "The State's Security and the Subjects' Prosperity: Notions of Order in Ottoman Bureaucratic Correspondence (19th Century)." In *Legitimizing the Order: The Ottoman Rhetoric of State Power,* edited by Hakan Karateke and Maurus Reinkowski, 195–212. Leiden: Brill, 2005.

Rodrigue, Aron. "Difference and Tolerance in the Ottoman Empire." Interview with Nancy Reynolds. *Stanford Humanities Review* 5 (Fall 1995): 81–92.

———. *French Jews, Turkish Jews: The Alliance Israélite Universelle and the Politics of Jewish Schooling in Turkey, 1860–1925.* Bloomington: Indiana University Press, 1990.

———. "From *Millet* to Minority: Turkish Jewry." In *Paths of Emancipation: Jews, States, and Citizenship,* edited by Pierre Birnbaum and Ira Katznelson, 238–61. Princeton: Princeton University Press, 1995.

———. *Jews and Muslims: Images of Sephardi and Eastern Jewries in Modern Times.* Seattle: University of Washington Press, 2003.

Rodrigue, Aron, and Sarah Abrevaya Stein, eds. *A Jewish Voice from Ottoman Salonica: The Ladino Memoir of Sa'adi Besalel a-Levi.* Translated by Isaac Jerushalmi. Stanford: Stanford University Press, 2011.

Rogan, Eugene, ed. *Outside In: On the Margins of the Modern Middle East.* London: I. B. Tauris, 2002.

Rosanes, Salomon. *Korot ha-Yehudim be-Turkiyah ve-Artzot ha-Kedem.* Sofia: Defus ha-Mishpat, 1934.

Rozen, Minna. "A Pound of Flesh: The Meat Trade and Social Struggle in Jewish Istanbul, 1700–1923." In *Crafts and Craftsmen of the Middle East: Fashioning the*

Individual in the Muslim Mediterranean, edited by Suraiya Faroqhi and Randi Deguilhem, 195–234. London: I. B. Tauris, 2005.

Rubin, Avi. "Modernity as a Code: The Ottoman Empire and the Global Movement of Codification." *Journal of the Economic and Social History of the Orient* 59 (2016): 828–56.

———. *Ottoman Nizamiye Courts: Law and Modernity*. New York: Palgrave Macmillan, 2011.

Schechter, Ronald O. *Obstinate Hebrews: Representations of Jews in France 1715–1815*. Berkeley: University of California Press, 2003.

Schull, Kent F. *Prisons in the Late Ottoman Empire: Microcosms of Modernity*. Edinburgh: Edinburgh University Press, 2014.

Schwartz, Robert. *Policing the Poor in Eighteenth-Century France*. Chapel Hill: University of North Carolina Press, 1988.

Serçe, Erkan. *Tanzimat'tan Cumhuriyet'e Izmir'de Belediye*. Izmir: Dokuz Eylül Yayinlari, 1998.

Shaw, Stanford J. *History of the Ottoman Empire and Modern Turkey*. Vol. 1, *Empire of the Gazis: The Rise and Decline of the Ottoman Empire, 1280–1808*. Cambridge: Cambridge University Press, 1976.

Shaw, Stanford J., and Ezel Kural Shaw. *History of the Ottoman Empire and Modern Turkey*. Vol. 2, *Reform, Revolution, and Republic: The Rise of Modern Turkey*. Cambridge: Cambridge University Press, 1977.

Shefer, Miri. "Charity and Hospitality: Hospitals in the Ottoman Empire in the Early Modern Period." In *Poverty and Charity in Middle Eastern Contexts*, edited by Michael Bonner, Mine Ener, and Amy Singer, 121–43. Albany: State University of New York Press, 2003.

Singer, Amy. *Charity in Islamic Societies*. Cambridge: Cambridge University Press, 2008.

Smith, Bonnie G. *Ladies of the Leisure Class: The Bourgeoises of Northern France in the Nineteenth Century*. Princeton: Princeton University Press, 1981.

Smyrnelis, Marie-Carmen. "Prologue: Une ville à la recherche de son histoire." In *Smyrne, la ville oubliée? Mémoires d'un grand port ottoman, 1830–1930*, edited by Marie-Carmen Smyrnelis, 7–18. Paris: Éditions Autrement, 2006.

———, ed. *Smyrne, la ville oubliée? Mémoires d'un grand port ottoman, 1830–1930*. Paris: Éditions Autrement, 2006.

———. *Une Société hors de soi: Identités et relations sociales à Smyrne aux XVIIIe et XIXe siècles*. Collection Turcica 10. Paris: Peeters, 2005.

Sorkin, David. "The Port Jew: Notes Toward a Social Type." *Journal of Jewish Studies* L, no. 1 (Spring 1999): 87–97.

———. *The Transformation of German Jewry, 1740–1840*. New York: Oxford University Press, 1987.

Stanislawski, Michael. "Russian Jewry, the Russian State, and the Dynamics of Jewish Emancipation." In *Paths of Emancipation: Jews, States, and Citizenship*, edited by Pierre Birnbaum and Ira Katznelson, 262–83. Princeton: Princeton University Press, 1995.

Stein, Sarah Abrevaya. "Creating a Taste for News: Historicizing Judeo-Spanish Periodicals of the Ottoman Empire." *Jewish History* 14 (2000): 9–28.

———. *Making Jews Modern: The Yiddish and Ladino Press in the Russian and Ottoman Empires*. Bloomington: Indiana University Press, 2004.

Stoianovich, Traian. "The Conquering Balkan Orthodox Merchant." *The Journal of Economic History* 20, no. 2 (1960): 234–313.

Ter Minassian, Anahide. "Les Arméniens: Le Dynamisme d'une petite communauté." In *Smyrne, la ville oubliée? Mémoires d'un grand port ottoman, 1830–1930*, edited by Marie-Carmen Smyrnelis, 79–92. Paris: Editions Autrement, 2006.

Toprak, Zafer. "From Plurality to Unity: Codification and Jurisprudence in the Late Ottoman Empire." In *Ways to Modernity in Greece and Turkey: Encounters with Europe, 1850–1950*, edited by Anna Frangoudaki and Çağlar Keyder, 26–39. London: I. B. Tauris, 2007.

Ueno, Masayuki. "For the Fatherland and the State: Armenians Negotiate the Tanzimat Reforms." *International Journal of Middle East Studies* 45 (2013): 93–109.

Ury, Scott. *Barricades and Banners: The Revolution of 1905 and the Transformation of Warsaw Jewry*. Stanford: Stanford University Press, 2012.

van den Boogert, Maurits H. *Ottoman Izmir: Studies in Honour of Alexander H. de Groot*. Leiden: Nederlands Instituut Voor Het Nabije Oosten, 2007.

van Rahden, Till. *Jews and Other Germans: Civil Society, Religious Diversity, and Urban Politics in Breslau, 1860–1925*. Madison: University of Wisconsin Press, 2008.

Veidlinger, Jeffrey. *Jewish Public Culture in the Late Russian Empire*. Bloomington: Indiana University Press, 2009.

Wallerstein, Immanuel, Hale Decdeli, and Reşat Kasaba. "The Incorporation of the Ottoman Empire into the World Economy." In *The Ottoman Empire and the World-Economy*, edited by Huri Islamoğlu-İnan, 88–97. Cambridge: Cambridge University Press, 1987.

Watenpaugh, Keith David. *Being Modern in the Middle East*. Princeton: Princeton University Press, 2006.

Weissbach, Lee Shai. "The Nature of Philanthropy in Nineteenth-Century France and the *mentalité* of the Jewish Elite." *Jewish History* 8, no. 1/2 (1994): 191–204.

Wishnitzer, Avner. *Reading Clocks, Alla Turca: Time and Society in the Late Ottoman Empire*. Chicago: University of Chicago Press, 2015.

Woolf, Stuart. *The Poor in Western Europe in the Eighteenth and Nineteenth Centuries.* London: Methuen, 1986.

Yalcınkaya, M. Alper. *Learned Patriots: Debating Science, State, and Society in the Nineteenth Century Ottoman Empire.* Chicago: University of Chicago Press, 2015.

Yerasmos, Stéphane. "A propos des réformes urbaines des Tanzimat." In *Villes ottomanes à la fin de l'Empire,* edited by Paul Dumont and François Georgeron, 17–33. Paris: L'Harmattan, 1992.

Yovel, Yirmiyahu. *The Other Within: The Marranos.* Princeton: Princeton University Press, 2009.

Zandi-Sayek, Sibel. *Ottoman Izmir: The Rise of a Cosmopolitan Port, 1840–1880.* Minneapolis: University of Minnesota Press, 2012.

Zipperstein, Steven J. *The Jews of Odessa: A Cultural History, 1794–1881.* Stanford: Stanford University Press, 1985.

INDEX

Note: Page numbers followed by "*f*" and "*t*" refer to figures and tables, respectively.

Abdülhamid II, Sultan, 62–63, 145
Abdülmecid, Sultan, 27, 145
Abulafia, Rabbi, 172
Ades, Isaac, 159
Agada de la karne ("Meat Haggadah"; *El Soytari*), 123–124, 146–149
Agudat a-Perahim, 55
Ahdut ("Unity"), 136
Akohen, Abraham, 67
Algazi, Moses, 64
Algranati, Shlomo, and family, 106*f*
Algrante, Jacob, 107, 135–136
Algrante, Jak, 89
Alhad Literario (Literary Sunday), 116
Alliance Israélite Universelle (Alliance):
  apprenticeships and workshops, 76–77, 81, 82–84, 83*f*; charity events for, 99, 111–112; disparagement of begging by, 43; formation of, 17; on *Gabbaé Sedaka*, 63, 68–69; on *Gemilut Hasadim* Society, 81; girls' education at, 76, 83, 105, 107*f*; on importance of commerce, 85; in meat industry scandal, 135–136; on public health, 39–40; public lecture series, 115–116; Purim plays at, 55, 98; on Russian refugees, 46–47; school in Karataş, 93–96; support by chief rabbinate, 97, 171–174; on *Talmud Tora*, 77, 79, 81; upward social mobility from, 32, 91–92, 102–103, 121–122; vocational training in, 17, 77, 81, 83–84, 83*f*, 154
Amado, Haim, 77
Amado, Senyor Behor, 67
Amsterdam, Jewish community in, 24, 62
Angel, Daniel, 18, 113, 116
anusim of Spain, 144
apprenticeship programs, 5, 17, 76–77, 81, 82–84, 83*f*
Arditi, Moses, 65
Arié, Gabriel: on Algrante scandal, 135; on *Alliance* facilities as venues, 99; on begging by Russian girls, 47; on chief rabbinate support, 171–172; on Christian schools in upward mobility, 96; on citywide philanthropic events, 103; on excommunication of

journalist, 167; on *Gemilut Hasadim* Society, 81; on habits of economy in women, 117; on Karataş, 94–95; on poverty in Jews of Izmir, 17–18; on public health, 39–40; on public lecture series, 115–116; on Solomon Palacci as chief rabbi, 138–139; on vocational training, 83–84

ariha (income tax), 124, 134

Armenians: in Izmir, 7, 10, 20, 100, 103; in Ottoman Empire, 28–29, 30–31, 152

art shows, 114

Asansör (public elevator), 95–96

Attias, J., 121

Bahri Baba (old Jewish cemetery), 47–48, 56, 93

banking and financial services: bankers as elites, 102–103, 153; buying shares, 89; ethnic groups involved in, 10, 92; importance of commercial education, 85

basket dealer of Smyrna, Jewish, 13*f*

batei haskalah (houses of enlightenment), 172

baylar a la franka (European-style dancing), 111–112

Bayrakli Store, 143*f*

bedel-i askeri (military exemption) tax: financial strain from, 12, 14; outstanding debts from, 14, 157–158; strategies for equitable assessment of, 14, 69, 137, 147; submitting registers for, 168

beggars: begging networks and brokerages, 43–44; children as, 43–44, 47, 53; classification of need of, 66–67, 70; dangers to girls as, 46–47; discouraging public from giving to, 44, 70–71; in Enlightenment Europe, 16, 42; foreign, 39, 66; in the Islamic world, 15–17; proposal to house in "old" Jewish cemetery, 47–48; Purim procession of, 52–54, 59, 73; regeneration discourse on, 17–18, 32; removing from public view, 5, 36, 46, 54; Russian refugees as, 46–48, 51; shame from preponderance of, 31, 43, 45, 63, 70; as threat to public order, 31, 42. *See also* charity; poverty

Benghiat, Alexander, 45, 53, 111–113, 134, 146. *See also El Meseret*

Benghiat, Graziella, 107–108

Bensenyor, Chief Rabbi Joseph, 97, 161, 163–164, 171, 173–174

Benveniste, Abraham, 49–50, 52

berat, 144–145, 167–168

Bernhardt, Sarah, 120

Bey, Enver, 146

Bey, Mahzar, 39

Bey, Niyazi, 47, 146

Bigde Kodesh society, 61

Bikkur Holim society, 61, 101, 109–110, 167

bill of exchange, education on, 86

"The Blare of the Horn Grew Louder and Louder" (*Gabbaé Sedaka* pamphlet, 1879), 133

blood libels, 14

Bordeaux, Jewish community in, 23, 62

Bourdieu, Pierre, 92

bourgeoisie. *See* embourgeoisement

"*Buen Purim*" (poem), 53

Bulgarian Christians, 28

Café l'Abri, 95

cafés, socializing in, 20, 46, 49, 95, 113–114

Calev, Gabriel, 152–154, 156

capitalism, poverty and, 16, 27

Catholics, 23–24, 52, 102

Cazès, David, 17, 77, 79

celali revolts (seventeenth century), 7

census, 129–130

Cercle de Smyrne, 20

Cercle Européen, 20, 105
Cercle Israélite, 99
charitable associations: collecting on Purim, 54; examples of, 61; finding work for the able-bodied, 67; Jewish beggars as motivation for, 63; poverty classifications by, 63–66, 70; rationalization by, 73–75; Rothschild Hospital, 56–59; satire of matza distribution, 75; verifying poverty by, 66–67, 70; women's, 109–110. *See also names of individual associations*
charity: anonymous, 109–110; changing understanding of, 62–64, 70–72, 89–90; educating public on, 70–72; *Gabbaé Sedaka* collections for, 69; in the Ottoman state, 62–63; Purim collections for, 50–54, 61, 69, 73, 178; rationalization of, 67–68, 73–75; on religious holidays, 61; taxonomy of poor, 64–67; in women's nature, 108–110. *See also* charitable associations; philanthropy; poverty
charity balls and soirées: in embourgeoisement, 98–102; free admission to women, 111; performances, 104; on Purim, 54–55, 97; social mobility and, 96–97
Chaves, Behor de, 164
chief rabbi (*haham bashi*) of Istanbul, 138, 140–141, 144, 152, 167
chief rabbi of Izmir: creation of office, 167–169; election of, 153, 163, 166; successor to (1899), 137–139; support for poor by, 172–174; as symbol of progress, 169–174. *See also names of chief rabbis*
children: apprenticeships and workshops, 5, 17, 76–77, 81, 82–84, 83*f*; as beggars, 43–44, 53; in bourgeois ideal of women, 96, 107–109; charity for needy, 63, 65–66, 72; Christian schools in upward mobility, 96; girl beggars, 47; orphanages, 28, 76–77; Russian refugees as beggars, 46–47, 51, 76–77; *Tanzimat* reforms and, 28; vocational training in *Alliance* schools, 17, 77, 81, 83–84, 83*f*, 154. *See also* vocational training
cholera outbreaks, 14, 39
circumcisions, payment for, 71
cizye (poll tax), 10, 124
class. *See* socioeconomic class
clothing, of women, 112–113, 119–120
Club des Chasseurs, 20
clubs and recreational associations, 19–20, 100–101, 101*f*, 104, 114–117
Cohen, Mark, 64
commercial education, 84–89
Communal Council: on 1884 proposed statutes, 155–160; on 1911 reforms, 163–165; appointed by chief rabbi (1901), 161; on *bedel* tax assessment, 147; disbanding in 1891, 157; electing members to (1896), 158–159; on financial state (1921), 149; on funding sources for *Ozer Dalim*, 71; *Gabbaé Sedaka* subsidy from, 44, 69; on *gabela* system, 125, 128–130, 134–137, 147, 149; on limiting number of collections, 73–74; members appointed by the chief rabbi, 161; in Palaccist vs. Kolelist split, 141; on public health measures, 40; on Purim carnivals and *kojitas*, 50, 54, 73; on rabbinical authority, 166, 168, 170–171, 173; on successor to Rabbi Abraham Palacci, 138–139, 160; on using *hahamhane* for soirées, 99
"conjunctural" poverty, 63–65
conversos, 23–24
Corpus Christi procession, 52
corruption: *Agada de la karne* and, 149; in the *gabela* system, 125, 127, 129, 135, 167; role of Ottoman sultan in, 145
Couriel, Rabeno, 134

dancing, women and, 111–112
Danon, Behor Yomtov, 44, 63
Danon, Chief Rabbi Nissim, 163–164, 171–172, 174
Dayan, Isaac, 67
Dayenu ("It Would Have Been Enough", poem), 148
defter de reklamos (claims repository), 64, 66
dengue fever, 14
derito komunal (direct tax), 129–130
Der Matossian, Bedross, 30, 192n132
djudería (Jewish quarter): clubs and recreational associations, 19–20, 100–101, 101*f*, 104, 114–117; kosher meat industry as destabilizing, 134–136, 140–141; public begging and public good, 42–46; unpaved streets in, 40–41, 41*f*. See also poverty
domestic economy, women and, 117–120

education of girls, 76, 83, 105, 107*f*
Efendi, Abdul Rahman, 51
Efendi, Haim, 95
El Comercial: on charitable events, 101–102; on economy in women, 117–118; in *gabela* conflict, 133, 135; on ladies' hats, 119–120; on new commercial ventures, 88–89; on new Ottoman parliament, 151; on role of women, 106–107; on Rothschild Hospital benefit, 58–59; on theater events, 111
Eldem, Edhem, 18–19
electric tramways, 197–198n141
Eli, Rabbi Joseph, 160–161
Eliezer, Mordechai, wife of, 67
El Komersio, 85–86
El Meseret: on begging as dishonoring community, 45; on class divisions (1899), 140, 142; on European-style dancing, 111–112; in *gabela* conflict, 133–134, 139–141; on Izmirli in global economy, 84–85; on *meclis umumi* delegates, 150; on outdoor outings, 117; on *Ozer Dalim* finances, 74; on a Purim soirée, 55; on unpaved streets, 40–41; on women's clothing, 113
El Novelista: advertisements for social events in, 104; on Chief of Police Mahzar Bey, 39; in *gabela* conflict, 133–136; on Karataş public elevator, 95; on leisure activities, 113–115; on *meclis umumi* delegates, 158, 159; on *Ozer Dalim*, 45, 74; on Purim plays, 56; reporting on society balls and events, 98, 100; on role of women, 107, 108; on the *Talmud Tora*, 76–77, 82
El Pregonero: on *gabela*, 128, 133–135; on giving to beggars, 71; on industriousness, 121; on Karataş, 96
el puevlo ("the people"): in 1884 statutes, 153–156; in conflict over *gabela* (1879), 132–133, 142–144; in the *meclis umumi*, 153–154, 156–157, 159, 162–165; role in the *kehillah* structure, 151–152; in "Simon" and "Reuben" debate, 3–5, 15; on Solomon Palacci as chief rabbi, 139; steady empowerment of, 156–157; taxation and, 154, 157–158; use of term in *Shavat Ani'im*, 132
El Soytari, 59, 75, 123–124
embourgeoisement, 91–122; aesthetic choices in, 92–93; charity balls and soirées in, 96–102; city-wide philanthropy in, 102–105; clubs and recreational associations, 19–20, 100–101, 101*f*, 104, 114–117; difficulty of, 91–92; European-style dancing and, 111–112; extravagance and frugality in, 32, 117–121; fashion in, 112–113, 119–120; gender role

reframing in, 105–113; Karataş and, 3, 94–95, 96; *Kordon* in, 20, 37, 46, 54, 103; leisure in, 19–20, 113–117; new relationship to surroundings in, 27; in other Mediterranean locales, 18; in Ottoman state, 18–19; Purim carnivals in, 50–52, 142; socialization across ethnic groups, 102–104; superficiality in, 121–122; theater in, 20, 37, 97, 100, 103–104, 113; of women, 92, 108–110, 111
Endelman, Todd, 105
Enlightenment, 16–17, 31, 76
epidemics, 14–15, 39–40, 102
Eskapa, Rabbi Joseph, 8
Eskola Nasional, benefit ball for, 96
esnafes (middling classes), 132, 147–148, 153
Esperanza, Saul, wife of, 64
Estrugo, Joseph, 162
European Jews, 6, 76, 116

Falkon, Abraham, 66
France: beggars' prisons in, 42; revolutionary-era Jews in, 23; vocational training in, 76, 85
Franco, Hiskia, 151
Franklin, Benjamin, 118
Franko, Yisrael, Alalud i Komp bank, 88
franko mahala (European quarter), 116
frankos, as power brokers, 131

Gabai, Jacob Ben, 58
Gabbaé Sedaka Society: classifications of poverty by, 64–66, 68; *defter de reklamos*, 64, 66; dissolution of, 69; financial instability of, 44–45, 69; formalized allowances by, 67; on *gabela* tax, 133, 136–137; loans by, 68; *mezadas* (monthly subscriptions) for, 44, 63, 68–69; rationalizing poverty, 31, 44, 63, 66–67; *regalos* by, 68; reorganization as *Ozer Dalim*,

70; Rothschild Hospital and, 57–58; *semanada* (weekly stipend), 67–68; on supporting the poor with honor, 43–44, 57. *See also Ozer Dalim*
gabela (sales tax on kosher meat): 1879 conflict over, 132–133; association changes and, 136–137; as catalyst for a public sphere, 137–142; changes in (1934), 149; under Chief Rabbi Solomon Palacci, 138–139; class conflict over (1899), 139–140; efforts to substitute other taxes, 124, 129–130, 134; excommunication over, 167; instability of, 127, 134; as main income for the community, 127–128; in other regions, 179–180; pressure to use for charity, 71; stakeholders and corruption in, 125–127, 126*f*; suspension and reinstatement of, 127, 157; uneven burden on poor by, 14, 124, 132
gabeleros (tax lessees), 125
Galante, Abraham, 43, 125
games and gambling, 114
Gemilut Hasadim Society, 64–65, 68, 81
girls, education of, 76, 83, 105, 107*f*. *See also* women
God's Will Society, 109, 110
Goffman, Daniel, 8
Göztepe, 93
Greeks, in Izmir: allegiances of, 45; on bourgeois simplicity, 119; boycott of Jewish peddlers by, 14; charity balls of, 97; Izmir as Greek homeland, 21; as merchants, 7, 9, 19–20, 84, 92; population of (1890), 10; public Orthodox celebrations of, 52; on the Purim carnival, 51–52; at upper class charity events, 100, 103–104

Habermas, Jürgen, 130
Habif, Jacob, 68
Habif, Nissim, 97, 115

INDEX

Habif, Senyor, 116
haham başı (chief rabbi of the Ottoman Empire), 138, 140–141, 144, 152, 167
haham başı of Izmir. *See* chief rabbi of Izmir
hahamhane (rabbinical complex): public reading of proposed statutes at, 155; Rothschild Hospital at, 56; as venue, 99
Hahamhane Nizamnamesi statutes, 152, 160
hai kevu'im (men studying on behalf of community), 166
Hakohen, Rabbi Elijah, 15
Halevi, Abraham, 68
Halevi, Chief Rabbi Moshe, 138–139, 141
Halevi, Menahem, 65
Halevi, Rabbi Elazar, 126f
hamal (stevedore), as image of a worker, 29
Harootunian, Harry, 27
Hart, Mitchell, 24
Haskalah, 22–23
hats, ladies', 119–120
Hatt-i Hümayun of 1856, 27
Hatt-i şerif of Gülhane of 1839 (Rose Chamber Edict), 27
Hazan, Aaron Joseph, 50, 134, 164
hekdeshim (trusts), 61
herem (excommunication), 149, 167
Hirsch, Baroness de, 118
household budgets, 118–119
Huli, Raphael, 64

iltizam (tax farming), 125
income tax, 124, 134
Irgat Bazar, 49, 51, 94, 109, 116
islahhanes (orphanages), 76, 83, 83f
Istanbul: *Alliance* apprenticeships in, 76; chief rabbi of, 138, 140–141, 144, 167; kosher meat industry in, 123, 129, 179–180
Istoria del Ospital Rothschild de Izmir, 57
Izmir: 1884 rationalizing reforms, 154–159; Armenian community, 7, 10, 20, 100, 103; begging in, 41–46; Catholics in, 23–24, 52, 102; in census of 1840s, 10–12, 11t; Corpus Christi procession in, 52; epidemics in, 14–15, 39–40, 102; fire in (1922), 21; Greeks in, 10, 14, 19–20, 52; housing for refugees, 47–48; *Kordon*, 20, 37, 46, 54, 103; Levantines in, 20; map of, 38f; neighborhoods within Jewish quarter, 38, 38f; origins of, 7–8; in Ottoman provincial administration, 36; police and public safety in, 39; poverty as damaging to "national" belonging, 45–46; prosperity of port, early modern period, 8, 9–10; public works by, 36–37; revised statutes of 1911, 162–163, 168; rules protecting public good, 35–36; Russian refugees in, 46–48, 51; satire on, 59; Western appearance of, 37–38. *See also* public health
"*Izmir ermozeado*" (*El Soytari*, 1910), 59
Izmirli (Jews of Izmir): anti-Jewish violence, 14; in census of 1840s, 10–12, 11t; class division among (1899), 139–142; commercial education for, 84–86; governing hierarchy (1860s), 152–153; historiographical silence about, 21–22; Jewish distinctiveness and, 6, 25–26, 105, 178–179; lack of artisanal tradition in, 84–85; modernity of, 22–23; origins of, 7–8; petition signing among, 141; plans for wide-ranging corporation, 87–88; population growth in, 9–10; prosperity of (early modern period), 8; social hierarchy reorganization (1884), 153

Jacob Ninyo and Company, 89
Jewish particularism, 6, 25–26, 105, 178–179

kabineto de lektura, 99
Kal Kadosh Bet Israel, 94
Kaplan, Marion, 105
Karaosmanoğlu family, 9
Karataş, 3, 48, 93–95, 94*f*, 96
karniseros/kasapes (kosher butchers), 125, 127, 134
kayafes, 127, 145
kazar ija (marrying off one's daughter), 68
kehillah (Jewish community structure): communal charity in, 72; historical changes in, 23; lay authority in, 152–155; proposed measures to manage poverty (1884), 154–155; reform measures (1884), 154–156; reform measures (1911), 162–164; reimagining of, 5; role of rabbinate in, 168–169. *See also* taxes
Klub de los Esnafes, 147
Kohen, Matitya, 115
kojitas (collections), 53–54, 61, 69, 72–74
Kolelistas, 139–142, 160
kolelut. See kehillah
Kordon, 20, 37, 46, 54, 103
kosher meat industry: *Agada de la karne* and, 123–124, 146–149; excommunication in not supporting, 167; illegal butchering and, 135; importance of *gabela* to community, 127–128; independent butchers, 137; in Istanbul, 123, 129, 179–180; *komision de karne*, 137; as mode of political expression, 140–141; outside of Izmir, 179–180; petitions against, 141; in "Simon" and "Reuben" debate, 3–5, 15; under Solomon Palacci, 138–139; taxing of slaughterers and butchers (1891), 157; threat from Ashkenazi *shohatim*, 128, 129. *See also gabela* (sales tax on kosher meat)
Kraemer Hotel and Palace, 20, 101–102
"*Kualo es la vera karidad?*" ("What is True Charity", *La Buena Esperanza*, 1902), 89
Kualo es una munisipalidad (pamphlet, 1910), 35.
kuchiyo ("knife", in *gabela* suspension), 127
kuchiyo libero (lifting of *gabela*), 147
kupa, 70
Kuri, Isaac, 58
Kuri, Nissim, 118–119, 165

La Boz de Izmir, 95, 133
La Boz del Puevlo, 133
La Buena Esperanza: on 1884 proposed statutes, 155–156; on 1899 Purim carnival, 142; on begging as humiliation, 43; on begging by Russian refugees, 46, 51; on commercial education, 85; educating public on modern charity, 70; on *Gabbaé Sedaka* Society, 67, 68; in *gabela* conflict, 133–134, 139–140, 145; on independent butcheries, 137; "*Kualo es la vera karidad?*", 89; on *meclis umumi* delegates, 157–158, 159; on modern clothing for women, 119; on *Ozer Dalim*, 70, 71; on philanthropic events, 102–104, 110–111; on police and public safety, 39; on rationalization of charities, 73–75; on raucous Purim beggars, 54; reporting on society balls, 97; on restricting Purim celebrations, 50–51; on *Talmud Tora*, 80; on women's charities, 109–110
La Buena Veluntad, 109
"Ladino", ix
Ladino press: as agent of social change, 58, 74, 133–137; on charity balls and special events, 96–98; expansion of, 133–135; on *gabela* conflict, 133–137;

on leisure activities, 114–117; on local business reinvigoration, 86–87; on *meclis umumi*, 159; on nominating Communal Council delegates, 158–159; on Purim carnivals, 50–51; on role of women, 92, 106–113; as source material, 30–31. *See also* names of individual publications
La Esperanza: advertising society balls, 97–98; on expulsion of foreign beggars, 39; on *Gabbaé Sedaka* Society, 43; on rationalizing reforms (1870s), 152; on role of bourgeois women, 108–019. *See also La Buena Esperanza*
La Verdad, 134
"Law on Vagabonds and Suspected Persons" (1909), 42
Lazareto shelter, 61
Le Courrier de Smyrne, 47
Lehmann, Matthias, 172
leisure activities, 113–117; clubs and recreational associations, 19–20, 100–101, 101f, 104, 114–115; games and gamblilng, 114; outdoor excursions, daylong, 116–117, 120; public lecture series, 115–116; socializing in cafés, 113–114
Le Journal de Smyrne, 47
"Let Us Respect Women" (*El Comercial*, 1907), 106–107
Levantines, in Izmir, 10, 20, 37
Levi, Haim, 162
Levi, Nissim, 94, 95
Liga de Pas i Solidaridad, 118–119
luxury, bourgeois self-restraint and, 117–120

Madrikhei Yosher ("Guardians of Ethics"), 137
Magen David society, 61
Mahmud II, Sultan, 62
Mahzikei Ani'im, 77, 79–81, 83, 99, 113

Malbish Arumin society, 61, 99
marranism, 24
maskilim, 17, 23, 76
mastur, 64
matchbook sellers, 47
mecelle, 27
meclis umumi: in choosing chief rabbi, 163–164; election of delegates, 153, 159, 162; formation of, 152, 161; proportional representation in, 161–162; public authority in, 158–159, 165; working class representation in, 152–154, 156–157
medeniyet (civilization), 16
Me'il Sedaka (Hakohen), 15
memune versus *delegado*, 159
men, economy and sobriety in, 120–121
Merchant Club (Greek Club; Hellenic Club), 19
mezadas for *Gabbaé Sedaka*, 44, 63, 68–69
Michels, Tony, 24
millets, 30, 144, 152–153, 166, 174
Mitchell, Timothy, 26
Mizrahi, Moses, 67
Mizrahi, Solomon, 121
modernity, 22–26; *conversos* and, 23–24; global capitalism in, 27; Jewish identity in, 24; in the Jewish world, 22–23; in Ottoman Izmir, 25–26; poverty and social stratification in, 26–27, 177–178; Russian Jews and, 23; as shared, global phenomenon, 26
Mohar u-Matan society, 61
Morati, David, 66
moutons de Panurge, 121–122
Munte, Suzanne, 100

Nabon, David, 162
naçao, 24
Nahum, Rabbi Haim, 171
Nashim Sadkaniot, 98, 101, 109
Niego, Raphael, 64

Oel Moed society, 61
orphanages (*islahhanes*), 28, 76–77
Ottoman state: bourgeois concept in, 18–19; capitalism and Westernization in, 25–26; centralization of *vakifs* in, 62–63; chief rabbi as representing *kehillah*, 167–169; first constitution (1876), 145; judicial system, 165–166; naming Rabbi Joseph Eli to chief rabbinate, 160–161; new parliament (1908), 151; preserving the *kehillah* structure, 174; strategies to eliminate poverty, 76; tolerance of diversity in, 6, 27; weakening religious authority in, 152, 166–168; Young Turk Revolution, 16–17, 19, 28–29, 161–162
Ottoman Water Company, 117
outdoor excursions, daylong, 116–117, 120
Ozer Dalim: annual Purim show by, 55–56, 97–98, 100; benefit social events for, 96–97, 98, 100–101, 104, 113; criticism of, 74–75; determination of need by, 68–69, 71; establishment of, 44, 68, 70, 157, 172; financial instability of, 71–72, 74; historical significance of, 72; on ladies' hats, 119; productivizing the poor, 89–90; Rabbi Palacci and, 172–173; ridding the community of beggars, 45, 52

Palacci, Chief Rabbi Abraham, 160*f*, 170*f*; choice of successor to, 137–139, 160–161; excommunication of journalist by, 135–138, 167; on *Ozer Dalim* refounding, 172–173; on rabbinic authority, 166, 168; on struggle against poverty, 172–173; support of *Alliance* by, 171–172; support of rationalizing statutes by, 169; on taxing slaughterers and butchers, 157

Palacci, Solomon: assuming chief rabbinate, 138–139, 160; *Palaccista* and *Kolelistas* division, 139–142, 173
Palaccistas, 139–142
Panionios sporting club, 19–20
Pariente, Semtob: banquet in honor of, 97; on begging as a trade, 43–44; on *Gabbaé Sedaka*, 57, 63; on *gabela*, 128–129, 133; *La Jeunesse Israélite* and, 115
Pasha, Halil Rifat, 93
Pasha, Hefzi, 39
Pasha, Kemal, 142, 161
Passover, charitable giving at, 61, 75
philanthropy: anonymous, 109–110; beginnings of modern Jewish philanthropy, 62; charity balls and soirées as, 96–98; clothing distribution, 108–109; community spaces for events in, 99–102; "Jewishness" in, 178; as moral benefit, 98; new socialization patterns in, 102–105; women in, 109–112. *See also* charity
philosophes, 17
Pinhas de Segura, Rabbi Raphael, 167, 168
plague outbreak in 1900, 14–15, 40
poetry recitation, at *Talmud Tora*, 79–80
Polako, Haim, 86–87, 97, 155, 169
Polako, Madame Dudu de, 102, 110
poorhouses, 63
"port Jews", 23–24
Portuguese Jews, 7
poverty: under Abdülhamid II, 63; begging networks and brokerages, 43–44; class consciousness and alienation, 132–133; commercial education and, 84–86; of foreigners, 65–66; *gabela* and, 71, 124, 132; increasing, 71–72; in Islamic tradition, 15; of Izmir's Jews in 1870s, 36; new attitudes to, 4–5, 15–16, 42–43, 62, 81–82, 84, 177; plans for wide-

ranging corporation, 87–88; plans to build housing for refugees, 47–48; representation of poor in general assembly, 154; Rothschild Hospital and, 56–59; strategies to eliminate, 75–77, 83–84; strategies to hide, 36, 57; *Talmud Tora* and, 76–82, 78*f*, 82*f*; in tax assessment of 1910, 12; taxonomies of, 63–67, 70; as threat to public order, 42–43, 54; Young Turks and, 28–29. *See also* beggars; charitable associations; charity; philanthropy; socioeconomic class
productivization, 17, 76, 82–84, 88, 92
public health: in 1884 statutes, 154; epidemics, 14–15, 39–40, 102; imperial government and, 39–40; local responsibility for, 35, 40; refugees and begging as threats to, 47
public lecture series, 115–116
Purim: beggars in respectable neighborhoods, 54; carnivals at, 49–51, 142; charitable events on, 54–55, 56, 97–98, 100–101; collections at, 54, 61, 69, 73; disapproval of spectacle at, 50–52; poverty revealed at, 50–54, 178; procession of beggars, 52–54; theater productions of Purim plays, 55–56, 98, 100–101

rabbinical courts, 165–166
rationalization: of charity in Izmir, 52, 63, 66–67, 72–75; of charity in Sephardi diaspora, 62–63; of *millet* structure, 152; of Ottoman provincial administration, 36–37; in reforms of 1884, 154–159; of taxation and conscription, 27–28
recreational associations and clubs, 19–20, 100–101, 101*f*, 104, 114–117
regalos (one-time gifts), 68
religious particularism/distinctiveness, 6, 25–26, 105, 178–179

Rofe Holim society, 61
Romano, Joseph, 109
Rothschild Hospital, 56–59, 94, 97, 161
Ruso, Behor, 65
Russian Pale of Settlement, 179
Russian refugees (1890s), 23, 46–48, 51

Sabbatianism, 21
Sala de Lektura, 116
Salonica: Jewish migrants from, 7, 18; Kosher meat industry in, 123; mediation offer from, 142; socialism and social class in, 180
"Salvation" (*Gabbaé Sedaka* pamphlet, 1879), 133
Sarfati, Isaac, 68
sedaka (charity), 69, 70–71
semanada (weekly stipend), 67–68
Shabbat Albasha, charitable giving during, 61
sharia courts, 165–166
shastre franko (Western tailor), 112
Shaul, Raphael, 68
Shavat Ani'im ("The Cry of the Poor", 1847), 131–132, 142–146
shohatim (ritual slaughterers), 126*f*; *Agada de la karne* and, 146, 148; Ashkenazi, 129; *gabela* and, 125, 127; *Madrikhei Yosher* independent butchery, 137; price ceiling complaints by, 165; in *sharia* court, 165; "Simon" and "Reuben" debate on, 3–5, 15; of Solomon Palacci, 138–139; threats of using foreign, 128; Young Turk inspired criticism of, 29. *See also gabela* (sales tax on kosher meat)
Shuhami, Benjamin, 65
Sidi, Alexander, 155, 169
Sidi, Jacques and wife, 96
Sidi, Madame de Leon, 108–109
"Simon" and "Reuben" debate, 3–5, 15
Smyrna: The Destruction of a Cosmopolitan Port, 1900–1922 (film), 22

Smyrne/Smyrna. *See* Izmir
social mobility: *Alliance* and, 91–92; Christian schools in, 96; Karataş as embodiment of, 93–96, 94f; proposed community corporation and, 88; in Russian Empire, 23. *See also* embourgeoisement
socioeconomic class: aesthetic choices and, 92–93; agents of change, 5–6; ascendency over religion and ethnicity, 92, 102–104; in census of 1840s, 10–12, 11f; citywide aristocracy development, 103–105; class conflict over *gabela*, 139–142; class consciousness among poor, 132–133; expansion of middle-class values, 17–20; failure of artisanal class, 84; Jewish mercantile class demise, 8, 9–10; modernity and, 26–27, 178; of Muslim neighbors, 180–181; negotiation of Jewish difference and, 179; *Tanzimat* in class conflict, 144–145; in tax assessment of 1910, 12; working class emergence, 147–148. *See also el puevlo* ("the people"); embourgeoisement; poverty; social mobility
soletreo, 30
Sosiedad Muzikal Israelit, 98
Sporting Club, 20, 100–101, 100f, 104
sporting events, 116
statutes of 1884, 154–159
statutes of 1911, 162–163, 168
"structural" poverty, 63–65

Talmud Tora, 78f, 82f; charity events, 98, 99, 101, 103–104; clothing donations to, 61, 108–109, 154; direct control by *Alliance*, 81; failure to foster upward social mobility, 178; financial crisis (1907), 161; on ladies' hats, 119; *Mahzikei Ani'im* reforms of, 80–82; musical performances by children, 117; party at, 79–80; poor conditions at, 76–77; in removing poverty, 80; vocational school at, 76–82, 154, 177; Women's Committee, 109
Tanzimat reforms: background of, 27–28; current scholarship on, 27–28; poverty and, 16, 27–28, 145; on public good, 27–28, 36; rabbinic authority and, 144–145, 166–168; structural changes, 27–28, 144, 152, 155; tax reform, 28, 145; urban space in, 16
Tarica, Albert, 85–86, 161–162
Tarica, Yisrael, Franko i Komp manufacturing house, 89
taxes: on alcoholic beverages, 158; *bedel-i askeri*, 12, 14, 69, 137, 147, 157–158, 168; census for, 129–130; direct (*derito komunal*), 129–130; income (*ariha*), 124, 134; other external taxes to Ottoman authorities, 6, 25–26, 105, 178–179; polarization from, 130–131; poll (*cizye*), 10, 124; *Shavat Ani'im* on, 145–146. *See also gabela*
theater: appropriate dress for, 112–113, 119; charity productions, 98, 100, 102, 104; in embourgeoisement, 20, 37, 97, 100, 103–104, 113; productions of Purim plays, 55–56, 98, 100–101; women performing in, 108, 111
tomar informasion, 66
truancy, 77
"truly poor", 63–64, 70. *See also* poverty
Turkish Republic, 149

Udon Bazar, 116
"*Una kesha*" ("A Complaint"; *El Novelista*), 134
upward mobility. *See* social mobility

vaccination program, 39
vagrancy, 16–17, 77

vakifs (pious endowments), 61–62, 94
ve-Aavtem et a-Ger Society, 65–66
vilayet system, 36
vocational training: in *Alliance* schools, 17, 77, 81, 83–84, 83*f*, 154; in France, 76, 85; for girls, 76, 83; *Talmud Tora*, 76–82, 154, 177

Watenpaugh, Keith, 26
water-powered public elevator, 95–96
Westernization, 25–26, 93, 105
women: appropriate dress for, 112–113, 119; charitable organizations of, 109–110; charitable works in nature of, 108–110; education of girls, 76, 83, 105, 107*f*; European-style dancing by, 111–112; habits of economy in, 117–119; ideal role of, 106–108, 109–110; simplicity in, 119–120; theater and, 108, 111
Workers Socialist Federation of Salonica, 180

Yehoshua, Rabbi Azariah, 8
Yisashar, Nissim, 89
Young Turk Revolution: empowerment of lower classes, 28–29; faith in reform from, 161–162; "Law on Vagabonds and Suspected Persons", 16–17; middle class and, 19

Stanford Studies in Jewish History and Culture
David Biale and Sarah Abrevaya Stein, Editors

This series features novel approaches to examining the Jewish past in the form of innovative work that brings the field into productive dialogue with the newest scholarly concepts and methods. Open to a range of disiplinary and interdisciplinary approaches from history to cultural studies, this series publishes exceptional scholarship balanced by an accessible tone that illustrates histories of difference and addresses issues of current urgency. Books in this list push the boundaries of Jewish Studies and speak compellingly to a wide audience of scholars and students.

For a complete listing of titles in this series, visit the Stanford University Press website, www.sup.org.

Omri Asscher, *Reading Israel, Reading America: The Politics of Translation Between Jews*
2020

Yael Zerubavel, *Desert in the Promised Land*
2018

Sunny S. Yudkoff, *Tubercular Capital: Illness and the Conditions of Modern Jewish Writing*
2018

Sarah Wobick-Segev, *Homes Away from Home: Jewish Belonging in Twentieth-Century Paris, Berlin, and St. Petersburg*
2018

Eddy Portnoy, *Bad Rabbi: And Other Strange but True Stories from the Yiddish Press*
2017

The authorized representative in the EU for product safety and compliance is:
Mare Nostrum Group
B.V Doelen 72
4831 GR Breda
The Netherlands